Canto is an imprint ⟨...
titles, classic and mo...
broad spectrum of s...
interests. History, lite...
archaeology, politics, religion, psychology,
philosophy and science are all represented
in Canto's specially selected list of titles,
which now offers some of the best and
most accessible of Cambridge publishing to
a wider readership.

THE MYTH OF THE MAGUS

THE
MYTH OF THE MAGUS

BY

E. M. BUTLER

*Formerly Schröder Professor of German in the
University of Cambridge*

CAMBRIDGE
UNIVERSITY PRESS

Published by the Press Syndicate of the University of Cambridge
The Pitt Building, Trumpington Street, Cambridge CB2 IRP
40 West 20th Street, New York, NY 10011–4211, USA
10 Stamford Road, Oakleigh, Victoria 3166, Australia

First published 1948
First paperback edition 1979
Canto edition 1993

Printed in Great Britain at the
University Press, Cambridge

*A catalogue record for this title is available
from the British Library*

*Library of Congress cataloguing information
data applied for*

ISBN 0 521 43777 6 paperback

To

R. G. B. and F. J. B.

Fain would I have known of any melodies of Orpheus, if any there are....
APOLLONIUS OF TYANA

CONTENTS

ILLUSTRATIONS

PREFACE

Qui s'excuse s'accuse; nevertheless I cannot refrain from a word of explanation on sending this vulnerable volume to press. It was originally designed as Part I of a book which has pulled apart into three, and this one falls between two stools, being too thorough perhaps as an exposition of the place of Faust in the history of magic, and certainly too sketchy as an outline of that vast magnetic field. The gaps in the bibliography have given me recurrent nightmares, though this has not forced me to fill them; for I was too fearful of falling into pits of learning, and floundering, and never scrambling out again to come to grips with Faust.

It is a relief to turn away from my own shortcomings and to pay tributes where they are due. First and foremost to the Syndics and officials of the Cambridge University Press for their unfailing courtesy, sympathy, patience and help. Then I owe so much to so many authors of so many books that it seems invidious to single any of them out. But Palmer and More must be mentioned and warmly thanked for *The Sources of the Faust Tradition*, a fascinating collection of magical and Faustian lore hitherto only referred to by the scholars and now presented to the general public in a stimulating, concrete and readable way, making dead knowledge live again. Nor shall I ever forget picking up *The Hero* by Lord Raglan on a station bookstall, and hardly noticing as I devoured it that the 'express' from Leeds to Manchester was running three hours late. If the gifted author should ever glance at the introduction to this book he will realize that his brilliant analysis of the hero in literature underlies my more heavy-footed approach.

A personal debt lies in the enduring memory of the vistas opened to me in the past by Jane Harrison, whose books are still here to keep her influence fresh; but I fear that she would shake her head rather sternly over the baldness and superficiality of the chapter called 'The Sages of Greece'; and but for the kindly advice of Mr Guthrie, author of *Orpheus and Greek Religion*, she would have had even more to condemn. The section on Zoroaster would also have been still less satisfactory than it is, were it not for some familiarity with Eastern thought, due to my friendship with the Secretary of the Pali Text Society, Miss Isaline Horner, who has generously spared the time from her multifarious duties to compile the index of this book, and to whose works and conversations about Buddhism I owe an incalculable intellectual debt.

There are others who might be mentioned; but it will be abundantly clear to my readers that, although this volume sprang from a Faustian impulse (the desire for more knowledge than I could attain to), I have not invoked the devil's aid and need tender no thanks to him.

E. M. BUTLER

CAMBRIDGE

INTRODUCTION

ORIGINS

(a) The Ritual Hero

The great gift made to the humanities in this super-scientific age is the flood-lighting of the twin-citadel religion and art by archaeological research and anthropological discoveries. The structural features of this towering edifice are at least dimly discernible now beneath the profusion of tangled customs and beliefs which all but obliterated them before; and certain traditional religious and aesthetic forms have assumed a more vital significance. Bewilderment is slowly yielding to comprehension of the origins and development of man's spiritual life. The keynote is certainly not simplicity, and yet uniformity is present. To survey the religions of the world is to wander through a vast banyan forest, whose mythological parent stem, rooted in ritual, will not easily be discovered in the prehistoric jungle whence it sprang—the breeding ground of all our riotous religious and poetical imaginings. The result is overwhelming in its complexity; roots, stems and branches are inextricably intertwined and indistinguishable from each other in their upwards and downwards, sideways, earthwards and skywards thrusts. But the process behind all this profuse and fantastic fertility remains essentially the same. The superabundant vitality, the incredible luxuriance, the infinite number of variations and aberrations from the norm, all spring, as in the banyan forest, from an unchanging and unending impulse, a rhythmical *perpetuum mobile*: rising and falling and rising again in nature through birth, life, death and resurrection; imitating this cycle in ritual and art.

The penetrating if flickering light shed upon this aspect of human behaviour by the pioneers of yesterday who have inspired the scholars of to-day now covers a field coterminous with the surface of the earth. And among other phenomena which such researches have rendered both more interesting and more comprehensible is that of magic, which a contemporary anthropologist has rightly declared to be 'the most powerful influence on human conduct the world has ever seen'.[1] This, rather than any hard-and-fast definitions, some of which would restrict it to 'pseudo-science' or 'pretended art' or 'debased religion', is the attitude I have found most fruitful to adopt in the following study. It was begun with the aim of placing the sixteenth-century Faust in the main stream of the magical tradition; and it has led me far afield. For I had not progressed beyond the fringes of the investigation before I realised that all Faust's predecessors and successors as well as Faust himself were essentially one and the same person under many different guises and bearing as many different names. Founders and teachers of religion; sacrificed saviour-gods; rebels and martyrs; sinners and saints; mystery-men and occultists; conjurers, charlatans and quacks; they all behaved in a similar manner and their lives went according to the same plan. It needed no Solomon in the post-Frazerian era to deduce a ritual origin in such circumstances; and the facts would seem to show that the legendary magician derives from that dim and distant hero, who, as king, god or priest, died to be reborn in kingship or seasonal rites; and that, although he gradually became a creature sealed and set apart in the magic circle, he was originally one of the countless dying gods whose distribution is world-wide. Indeed, an analysis of the magus-legend puts this beyond all reasonable doubt. In its most highly developed form it has ten stock features; and, although these are not all invariably present or equally important, all of them are interesting.

(1) *Supernatural or mysterious origin of the hero*. This might be divine, as with the half-gods or heroes of Greek mythology; or royal, which originally meant the same thing. It was sometimes represented as diabolic; often, too, as strange or mysterious.

(2) *Portents at birth*, vouching for the supernatural nature of the hero. A late instance of this is the legend of the happenings which occurred when Mahomet saw the light of day; heaven and earth were shaken, and (amongst many other marvels) all the idols of the world fell down.

(3) *Perils menacing his infancy*, from evil-wishers or the powers of evil. The story of Krishna's rescue from the wicked schemes of his maternal uncle Kansa is one instance amongst many of the dangers supposed to beset wonder-workers and sages at their birth.

These three features are epic in their nature rather than ritualistic. Their obvious purpose is to emphasise the divine nature of the hero, which the ritual assumed.

[1] Lord Raglan, *Jocasta's Crime*, Thinker's Library, London 1940, p. 73.

(4) *Some kind of initiation* is nearly always described. This may be into the mysteries of the cult about to be proclaimed, or into occult or diabolic wisdom. It is a period of preparation and is modelled upon initiation ceremonies. Austerities and often, too, temptations occur during this period which is either preceded, accompanied, or followed by

(5) *Far distant wanderings.* Sometimes to seek for wisdom; sometimes to spread it. The voyage may be supernatural and include a descent into the underworld and an ascent into heaven. This may occur either in the middle or at the end of the hero's life. It sometimes figures in both places. The legends of the Tartar shamans are full of accounts of these journeys into the heavens and into the underworld.

(6) *A magical contest.* This is an outstanding and constant feature in the lives of all magicians, whether legendary or real. Deriving from ritual, it is also rooted in reality, and is the confluent point where life and legend meet, mingle and enrich each other. Such contests are very common in Brahmanical writings. Indeed they are everywhere to be found. A telling instance of the ritual origin is the dramatic defeat of the prophets of Baal by Elisha.

(7) *A trial or persecution.* This may develop from the contest and reverse the position. The hero wins the magical contest, but is nearly always vanquished at the trial, which generally brings about his doom.

(8) *A last scene,* of a set nature, is frequently, though by no means invariably, present. It may be sacrificial or sacramental. It may embody a solemn and prophetic farewell. It may take the form of confession and repentance. It is feebly represented in antiquity; but came into prominence in medieval times in consequence of the Last Supper.

(9) *A violent or mysterious death.* The tearing to pieces of Orpheus is an instance of the first type which derives from the ritual of the dying god. What might be called the myth of the teaching god favoured a mysterious disappearance and conflicting accounts of the actual end, as in the legends about Empedocles. Very few outstanding magicians have died a natural death in legend or in life. Their departure may be followed by the descent into Hades mentioned under (5); and is almost invariably succeeded by

(10) *A resurrection and/or ascension.* The latter, rather rarer, is represented by the ascension of Elijah in Hebrew literature and of Oedipus in Greek drama. Both have survived in a modified form into our own times.

Such, in skeleton form, is the myth of the magus. It will be seen that it is an elaboration of the kingship ritual, the basis of which, according to Hocart, is the death of the hero and his rebirth as a god. It also runs parallel to the stock features discerned by Gilbert Murray in Greek tragedy; the *pathos* of the year-daimon, which comprised an *agon* or contest, a *pathos* or violent sacrificial death, and a *theophany*, resurrection or apotheosis. Much the same course was run in kingship rites in Egypt, Mesopotamia and Palestine, according to Hooke:

This pattern consisted of a dramatic ritual representing the death and resurrection of the king, who was also the god, performed by priests and members of the royal family. It comprised a sacred combat, in which was enacted the victory of the god over his enemies, a triumphant procession in which the neighbouring gods took part, an enthronement, a ceremony by which the destinies of the state for the coming year were determined, and a sacred marriage.[1]

Hocart also mentions the sacred marriage in coronation ceremonies; but this feature has left only faint and sporadic traces on the myth of the magus, which is a specialised version of the heroic myth deriving from royal ritual. Women are not totally absent from the legendary tales about magicians; but in general they play a small and atrophied part. The Eastern magi were supposed to be celibates, which may have affected the tradition; yet Zoroaster himself was married three times; Solomon had seven hundred wives; Simon Magus cohabited with Helena, and so did Johannes Faust. On the whole, however, love-interest plays no great part in the lives of magicians, who had more urgent things on their minds. However much embroidery of an epic and aesthetic nature was superimposed on the original pattern; whatever strange flights of fancy were undertaken, and whatever liberties of a romantic nature, love did not, except in one or two instances, make the magician's world go round.

(b) The Professional Practitioner

If the lifeline of the legendary magician followed ritual precedent, the feats he was said to perform derived from the functions of the medicine-man, witch-doctor or wizard, whose daily round and common task it was to perform for the benefit of the tribe or community by means of charms, spells, incantations and various other acts of sympathetic, imitative, propitiatory or coercive magic, those vital and seemingly miraculous operations whose life-giving power was symbolised and concentrated in the great periodic, seasonal and other rites. His office often entailed the performance of such ceremonies either in the character of hero or priest; but it also

[1] *The Labyrinth*, ed. Hooke, London 1935, p. v.

embraced other activities; and where great communal rites were absent, consisted in semi-public or private performances. The feats attributed to his legendary successors fall into two categories. In the one group are to be found a series of marvels for which no practical origin suggests itself, being mere manifestations of power. Such are the levitation and flying feats, the assumption of animal forms or the bewitching of others into such shapes; and the cloak of invisibility. They all probably hail from ritual. Levitation and flying are often faded reminiscences of the ascension or apotheosis. Many initiation ceremonies symbolise the passing from one state to another by the assumption of animal masks or skins, especially where the totem system prevails; and according to Jane Harrison the same is true of invisibility:

Disappearance and reappearance is as common a rite in initiation as simulated killing and resurrection....Both are rites of transition, of passing from one state to another.[1]

These ritualistic marvels, amongst the most sensational on the magician's list, have therefore been severed from the lifeline and used for purposes of display. But the majority of the miracles derive from the practical functions of the medicine-man or wizard, whose paramount duty has always consisted in ensuring the prosperity of the tribe, clan or society to which he belonged, or of the patrons to whom he was attached.

In order to fulfil such an onerous task successfully, a professional magician must first and foremost, as a basic requisite, possess no small degree of power over the minds of his fellow men. One would expect, and indeed one finds among the shamans of Siberia and the witch-doctors of Africa, a recognised superiority in such practitioners, whether intellectual, spiritual or personal. To use the term which has lately become fashionable, they have more *mana* than the general run of humanity. This innate power is much increased by widespread belief in its reality; but it can make itself felt by the incredulous, and sometimes commands belief by extraordinary manifestations. Granted this essential gift, the next one can hardly fail to be present. The medical powers of magicians are symbolised in the names of witch-doctor and medicine-man. These gifts of healing and hurting, the latter especially often from a distance, are implemented by

[1] Jane Harrison, *Ancient Art and Ritual*, London 1918, p. 111.

ceremonies aimed at the mind of the patient. These are sometimes, but not always, reinforced by specifics and antidotes in which sympathetic magic and medically effective drugs may be used separately and also combined. Remarkable cures and remarkable ills still result from such methods, especially when both doctor and patient or victim are firmly persuaded of their efficacy. The extension of the power of hurting to the power to kill by poisoning the mind or the body, or by a mixture of the two, is too obvious and too easy a development to call for comment. But the claim to be able to restore the dead to life will not be allowed so readily. It has, however, been repeatedly reported. Elijah raised the widow's son; Empedocles emphatically stated that he had this power; it was libellously said of Cagliostro that he attempted it in Russia, failed and fraudulently substituted a living for a dead child. So that the possibility of such a miracle was still credited in the eighteenth century; and present-day shamans and shamankas are believed to perform it frequently. The hardy tradition may be a reminiscence of the ritual resurrection of the hero-king; but whatever its origin, it is often to be met with among the feats performed by the legendary magician.

To wield power over life and death would ensure respect; but the control of nature was even more vital to the community as a whole. Joshua arresting the course of the sun and moon, and the witches declaring that they can raise the wind, reflect the primitive notion that the main function of the king, priest or magician was to ensure the food supply of the tribe by promoting fertility in man, beasts and crops. This was the chief aim of seasonal, kingship and creation rites. But it devolved upon the professional magician, especially in times of stress, to make the appropriate magic for the conditions desired. The dangers inherent in this office are vividly illustrated by the tragic end of the prophets of Baal after their signal failure in rain-making. How many other luckless kings and priests, one wonders, went the same way? Yet belief in the magic control of the weather has never quite died out. By the law of averages a fair percentage of successful ceremonies is ensured. Failure can also be attributed to the anger of the god, or blamed on the wickedness of the people, or explained by some error in the performance of the rite. Moreover, accumulated observation, handed down in the shape of traditional lore, could at least help the practitioner in determining the most likely times for floods and rains and the best times for sowing and reaping. One can hardly help supposing that his powers of observing natural phenomena must have been sharpened by the office he was called upon to fill.

Whether a more general awareness of external conditions and interrelations came to his aid when exercising his mantic powers and quickened his inspiration is problematical. But at least it seems likely that the gift of prophecy was developed at a less primitive level of society than that of rain-making. Once acquired, however, it became of paramount importance. Knowledge of future or distant events is undeniably useful. If I know that I am to die to-morrow, I can set my house in order. If I know that an enemy is marching against me, I can arm myself to withstand him. It is a short step from taking such precautionary measures to fulfilling a prophecy oneself, as can be seen in *Macbeth*. Belief that foreknowledge of the future includes the power to control it follows inevitably. For all these reasons and others of a less definable and more spiritual kind, the mantic art has undergone a process of development which, for variety, complexity, elaboration and often abstruseness, has not its equal among magical practices, and can hardly be paralleled in any other field of spiritual endeavour. It is beyond the scope of this study to enumerate, let alone describe, its manifold and perplexing branches; but, whatever method was and is employed, preliminary religious rites are rarely absent, ranging from full-dress ceremonials to professional patter. Even when the seer works by inspiration and not interpretation, formalism plays a part. From the priest at the altar scrutinising the entrails of the sacrificial victim, through modern interpreters of dreams and down to the fortune-teller at a village fair; from the most sublime of prophets to the most squalid of quacks, no one possessing or claiming the gift of divination will ever lack a following of some sort. Oneiromancy and astrology still flourish to-day, and they figure prominently in legend, too. Whilst necromancy, depending on the fifth main function of the magician, spirit control, is a constantly recurring feature.

The control of spirits probably arose in the first instance from attempts to communicate with the spirits of the dead, one of the forms of ancestor worship. This was linked with the ever-present desire for tribal prosperity. It was hoped to avert evil or to ensure benefits from the departed spirits by magical means; good harvests, fortune in war, the prevention of plagues and other disasters, and also to acquire knowledge of future or distant events. This latter reason was the main purpose of necromancy proper, divining by means of the dead the most sombre and sinister of magical rites, ominous in its very nature, as when the Witch of Endor summoned Samuel to foretell the issue of the impending battle to Saul. The method, whether propitiatory or minatory, was implemented by solemn and often terrifying ceremonies, still practised, though not very impressively, by spiritualists to-day. It seems more than likely that spirit control in the narrow sense, communication with super-natural beings, derived from necromancy; but, be that as it may, magicians who have practised this esoteric art have been innumer-able; and, where contact has been claimed, they have generally ascribed their wonders and miracles and their divinatory powers to the spirits guiding them or at their command. These beings, like the shades of the dead, are invoked by means of sacrificial or other rites and propitiated by prayers. In black magic, the rites are for the most part of a threatening nature, generally preceded in the Christian variety by propitiatory prayers and ceremonies addressed to the Trinity in order to enlist divine aid before summoning elemental or evil spirits.

In the second group, the myths of Prometheus and of Deucalion and Pyrrha indicate another power, demonstrated in creation rites. This was possessed by some of the great gods and heroes, and there-fore by magicians too. It did not bulk large in the equipment of the ancients; but it was one of the supreme ambitions of medieval sorcerers. This brings the functions of the practising magicians, on which the feats of their legendary representatives are based, to a close; for the procuring of treasure, like the bringing of victory in battle, falls under the general heading of the prosperity of the tribe.

It will readily be allowed that a real magician who could perform all these functions, or persuade the community that he was per-forming them, would play an outstanding part in any society: healing the sick, raising the dead, ensuring the food supply, promoting fertility in general, procuring success in hunting, fishing and wars; establishing smooth and profitable relations with the spirits of the dead, demons and deities, whose power was darkly felt; and, in addition, forecasting future events. The Hebrew priests and prophets can be observed fulfilling these various duties zestfully in the Old Testament; and Empedocles, in one of his *Fragments*, gave a comprehensive, if concentrated, account of the powers attributed to a wonder-working sage in his day:

By my instructions you shall learn medicines that are powerful to cure diseases, and re-animate old age; you shall be able to calm the savage winds which lay waste the labours of the husbandman, and when you will, send forth the tempest again; you shall cause the skies to be fair and serene, or once more shall draw down refreshing showers, re-animating the fruits of the earth; nay, you shall recall the strength of the dead man, when he has already become the victim of Pluto....I am revered by both men and women, enquiring the road to boundless wealth, seeking the gift of prophecy....[1]

Empedocles did not mention contact with or control over the spirit world. Believing himself to be one of the immortals, he probably took it for granted. Otherwise he covered the ground which the practising magician occupied. This passage contains a fairly broad hint that the magician who can bless crops can also blight them, and bring foul weather as well as fair. The danger emanating from these functionaries has always been recognised; the danger they are in themselves from vengeance, human, diabolic or divine, is illustrated again and yet again in history and in legend. If the hero of many a rite had to die for the sake of society, the flesh and blood magician was often put to death for a similar reason; and, unlike the sacrificed god, because he was thought to be guilty of a social crime or a spiritual sin. Evil intentions and magic practised for personal and private profit altered the hue of the practitioner; but they did not lessen his presumptive powers or the dread with which he was regarded. It is evident too that the white magician of one tribe would be the black magician of the next, supposing them to be hostile. Common sense also whispers in one's ear that absolute powers, such as they were thought to wield, must corrupt them; whilst any fraudulent pretence to possess these gifts would inevitably degrade them.

The extremely practical functions which the tribal magician was called upon to perform, generally with an eye on the food supply, are found scattered profusely through the legends, where they figure as miraculous feats or supernatural phenomena, often entirely

[1] Quoted in the *Encyclopaedia of Religion and Ethics* in the article 'Empedocles'.

disconnected from their utilitarian origins. The aesthetic impulse is at work in such cases, describing marvels for their own sake, ignorant or forgetful of the prosaic basis on which it built, or merely indifferent to it. Other miracles were lavishly added, *disjecta membra* of the rites, torn from their original context; or, though much more rarely, flights of inventive fancy. The social importance of the professional practitioner began to be lost from view beneath a spate of sensational feats which were an object and an end in themselves. What is more, these feats assumed such dominance in the legends that they blurred the ritual design beneath them. Moreover, when myth began to mould the lives of great religious sages, their legendary deeds sprang up like tares among their sayings and deflected attention from morals to marvels. And yet, behind all the historical and mythical heroes of magic is the ghost of an actor-victim, performing or suffering a sacrificial act, and the shade of a real medicine-man calling down the rain.

The rise of this composite being to great heights and his subsequent downfall into degradation, followed by his later partial recovery; his always ambiguous position in society and the aura of strangeness, radiant and murky by turns, which puzzles the mind, is the theme illustrated by the lives and legends, or legendary lives of the twenty odd heroes of this book. In this slight and superficial contribution to the history of ideas, I have kept as far as possible on the legendary level, reproducing widespread conceptions and beliefs rather than historical data. I have not plumbed the depths of scholarship, nor scaled the heights of philosophy and religion. I have reserved for a future study the course of the mythopoeic process in literature, although literature has naturally been used for its evidential value in the present one. In view of this selectiveness and my own limitations and shortcomings, *The Myth of the Magus* is bound to appear shallow and crude to all the specialists in the various fields on which I have touched so lightly. I am not an orientalist, nor a Hebrew scholar; I am not a Classical scholar, nor yet a medievalist; I am not an archaeologist nor an anthropologist; neither a theologian nor a historian. I am not even a magician. Moreover, there is so much more to all the individual magi and magic-mongers than I have been able to indicate in considering the legends about them. Libraries have been written about some, volumes about others and books about nearly all. This at least goes to show that the conception of magic has been traditionally attached to some very famous people; and it is the vicissitudes of the tradition before and after Faust which I have attempted to trace, observing, as it were, the foam on the crest of the waves rather than the breakers themselves, let alone the depths of the sea.

It has sometimes proved impossible not to be drawn into speculations on the possible basis of objective reality underlying the supernatural claims made by or for various magicians; but I have avoided doing so as much as I could. For the nature of the evidence, when there is any evidence to scrutinise, is generally valueless from the critical point of view. The hostile and friendly witnesses are equally biased; and few indeed and far to seek are the dispassionate observers. Lecky very truly said that where supernatural phenomena are concerned humanity believes in the teeth of the evidence, or disbelieves in spite of the evidence, but never because of the evidence. An open mind, although it has proved no open sesame to the magic cave, is the attitude I have tried to adopt to each individual magician; but my main concern has been to assess his part in the development of the tradition. For the only solid ground beneath one's feet when investigating witchcraft or magic or their rich relation, religion, is their tenacious and ineradicable existence in the minds of men. It is there that they have proved their undeniable power. And this is the criterion on which I have based my personal selection among the hosts of Magic. Many have been excluded for lack of space. But those considered have all wielded either over their contemporaries or over posterity, whether in life, legend or literature, that mysterious fascination which is their prerogative-in-chief.

PART I. THE GOLDEN AGE

Chapter I. THE WISE MEN OF THE EAST
(a) The Magi
(b) Zoroaster

II. HEBREW HOLY MEN
(a) Moses
(b) Solomon

III. THE SAGES OF GREECE
(a) Pythagoras
(b) Apollonius of Tyana

IV. THE DOWNFALL OF THE MAGUS
(a) Christ
(b) Simon Magus

THE WISE MEN OF THE EAST

(a) The Magi

According to some authorities the Median mages were known long before the days of Zoroaster as a magico-priestly caste, one of the six tribes of the Medes enumerated by Herodotus (484–406 B.C.). It is from this race of men that the word 'magic' is derived, although its etymology is disputed and obscure. Used by the Greeks, however, *magia* signified originally the religion, learning and occult practices of the Eastern magi; and our chief source of knowledge about these mysterious men is the prince of all historians, Herodotus himself. The facts which he recounts are scanty, but singularly revealing, since they occur in situations and are connected with ideas with the lustre of the golden age of magic upon them. It was the age of symbolic prophetic dreams; and when Astyages, doomed to be the last king of the Medians, dreamt of danger to himself in connection with his daughter Mandanē, he made haste to consult the magians. They confirmed him in his apprehensions that the dream denoted a threat to his kingship; which he attempted to avert by marrying Mandanē to a quiet and insignificant though well-born Persian called Cambyses, who ranked well below a middle-class Median in his estimation. The doom however crept closer; and an even more ominous dream about the forthcoming fruit of Mandanē's womb was brought to the magi to interpret. They confirmed the king's own apprehensions: the unborn child was destined to reign in his stead. A Sophoclean series of events was then enacted. The child, Cyrus, instead of being put to death, as Astyages had ordered, was smuggled out of the way and brought up secretly by a herdsman in a distant district. But blood will tell. The little boy was elected to the office of king among his village playmates, and in this capacity was brought to the notice of Astyages, who immediately recognised him for what he was. He took an appalling revenge on the disobedient servant; but it was with a strange mingling of compunction and pride in his grandson that he sent for the magi again and told them what had happened:

The Magians said: 'If the child is still alive and became king without any arrangement, be thou confident concerning him and have good courage, for he shall not be ruler again the second time; since some even of our oracles have had but small results, and that at least which has to do with dreams comes often in the end to a feeble accomplishment.' Astyages made answer in these words: 'I myself also, O Magians, am most disposed to believe that it is so, namely that since the boy was named king the dream has had its fulfilment and that this boy is no longer a source of danger to me. Nevertheless give counsel to me, having well considered what is likely to be most safe both for my house and for you.' Replying to this the Magians said: 'To us also, O King, it is of great consequence that thy rule should stand firm; for in the other case it is transferred to strangers, coming round to this boy who is a Persian, and we being Medes are made slaves and become of no account in the eyes of the Persians, seeing that we are of different race; but while thou art established as our king, who art one of our own nation, we both have our share of rule and receive great honours from thee. Thus then we must by all means have a care of thee and of thy rule. And now, if we saw in this anything to cause fear, we would declare all to thee beforehand; but as the dream has had its issue in a trifling matter, both ourselves are of good cheer and we exhort thee to be so likewise; and as for this boy, send him away from before thine eyes to the Persians and to his parents.'[1]

Unhappily for them, this humane interpretation proved false. Cyrus rose up against his grandfather and overcame him in 550 B.C. Astyages impaled those magians who had persuaded or rather agreed with him to let Cyrus live; and the latter founded the Persian Empire and held the Medes in subjection. During the reign of his son Cambyses (529–522 B.C.), however, the magi made a bold and guileful bid to seize the power again. One of their number, Patizeithes, had been appointed governor during Cambyses' absence in Egypt, which suggests that the caste still retained much of its former prestige. This vice-regent was in the secret of the assassination of the king's brother Smerdis by royal command, and he also knew that this unnatural deed, prompted by fear of usurpation, was being hushed up. He conceived the daring scheme of proclaiming a magian Gaumata, who resembled the dead man, to be Smerdis, the brother of Cambyses, and seated him on the throne. The plot was successful for a time, as many precautions were taken to keep Gaumata in the background. When Cambyses heard what had happened, he first believed that Smerdis had not been slain; but on being reassured by the assassin, he tumbled to the imposture and was setting out to unmask the false Smerdis when he met with a fatal accident and died, having first made known the facts to some of the Persian nobles and charged them to re-establish their dominion over the Medes. Great confusion was, however, caused in the minds of all by the declaration of the assassin after Cambyses' death that he had not killed Smerdis, a deed which he now feared to acknowledge; and Gaumata enjoyed an undisturbed rule of seven months:

...and during them he performed acts of great benefit to all his subjects, so that after his death all those in Asia except the Persians themselves mourned for his loss: for the Magian sent messengers abroad to every nation over which he ruled, and proclaimed freedom from military service and from tribute for three years.[1]

Granted that there was a large admixture of policy in such measures, they show wisdom and a sense of those benefits which make for peace and prosperity; for even the more reprehensible magicians have generally shown a truer understanding of what constitutes human happiness than most rulers and conquerors. It is also true, however, that fraud all too often debases their instincts: fraud and the lust for power. The false Smerdis was discovered, and the shameful secret, that Cyrus had branded him for some offence by cutting off his ears, was also disclosed. Once certainty about his identity was established, Darius, the son of Hystaspes, entered the palace with six other Persian nobles, determined to make an end of the impostor. They came in an evil hour for the magians. The assassin of the real Smerdis, whom they were attempting to bind irrevocably to their interests, had publicly confessed to the whole truth of the situation and committed suicide before them all. The palace was still in an uproar when the conspirators forced an entrance into the private chambers of the magians, killed Patizeithes and Gaumata and then undertook a general slaughter of all the magians they could seize. Darius commemorated this insurrection by the famous inscription in which he spoke of the usurpation of Gaumata the magus, his own successful plot against him and the restoration of the

[1] Herodotus III, 67, tr. Macaulay.

Achaemenian dynasty. The Persians for their part kept the memory of this victory alive by an annual festival, the *magophonia*:

> This day the Persians celebrate in common more than all other days, and upon it they keep a great festival which is called by the Persians the festival of the slaughter of the Magians, on which no Magian is permitted to appear abroad, but the Magians keep themselves within their houses throughout that day.[1]

It is strange to think of these public rejoicings persisting side by side with the continued ascendancy of the Magians. For what the latter had lost in political importance after the restoration of the Achaemenians they seem to have gained in an even more powerful spiritual control than before. This empire over men's minds had already marked them out among the Medes; it now earned for them the distinction of officiating as the recognised priests of the Persians. No religious rite could be celebrated without them:

> ...a Magian man stands by them and chants over them a theogony... seeing that without a Magian it is not lawful for them to make sacrifices.[2]

What such an office meant in days when rites and sacrifices were indispensable to all undertakings and of almost daily occurrence can be at least partially understood to-day; although we may no longer be able to recapture the particular shade of religious awe with which such priests were regarded, and which did not hinder the rejoicings during the *magophonia* nor yet insure the Magians against the fate which Astyages meted out to those whose gifts had been found wanting. Precarious indeed, if not downright dangerous, was the lot of these men who were forever being called upon to utter short-term prophecies on the subject of national victories or disasters. When forced into this position, they seem on the whole to have prophesied smooth things, as when they interpreted the rather ominous vision of Xerxes before the expedition against Athens as having reference to his dominion of the whole earth; or again when they insisted that a solar eclipse boded disaster to the Athenians. They may have known better in both cases, and feared to say so. One thing is certain: however often and however signally their individual predictions were falsified, the caste as such never lost prophetic prestige. Immediately preceding Xerxes on that same

---

[1] Herodotus III, 79, tr. Macaulay. [2] Ibid. I, 132.

fateful expedition, in the sacred chariot drawn by eight white horses, they were as vital to the undertaking as the army itself, pouring libations in honour of the heroes who fell at Troy, sacrificing white horses for good omens by the river Strymon, allaying the storm raging round Cape Sepias by the sacrifice of victims and the chanting of incantations. Thus these members of a subject race imposed themselves upon their conquerors.

They were distinguished in many ways from other men, said Herodotus; and if this were the case in Asia, how much more impressive they must have seemed to the Greeks by their strangeness, thus adding to their power. For the Magi penetrated into Greece, India and some say even into China; and throughout the ancient world their power was recognised. It transcended religious differences, for there has always been something universal and international in the nature of magic; and however strange their rites might appear to Herodotus and later to Plutarch, this did not subtract from their value as the great magicians of antiquity, the professional readers of dreams and diviners by the stars.

As far as one can tell by the descriptions of Herodotus and Plutarch the Magian religion was either a primitive or a debased form of Zoroastrianism; and it seems on the whole more likely that magianism (to coin that word) preceded Zoroastrianism and was reformed by it, the magians themselves later belonging in their official capacity to the higher form, whilst privately practising the older rites. Too little however is really known about this subject to dogmatise; but, as regards their divinatory powers, an interesting feature emerges from the tales Herodotus tells. The dreams told to the magians are always highly symbolical dreams, whose interpretation seems perfectly obvious. Thus when Astyages saw a vine growing from the womb of his daughter overspreading the whole of Asia, it hardly needed a prophet to tell him what that meant. And yet he consulted the magians. It seems possible at least that this was a polite fiction; a roundabout way of saying that he was uneasy about the Persians, who might regard Mandanē's offspring as a pretext to dethrone him and bring the Persians to power. If this were so, he was in fact consulting the magians as politicians rather than as priests, using perhaps the recognised language of such oriental despots when they wished for religious (or moral) support for one of their contemplated political crimes. When

Astyages' feelings changed, so too did the advice of the Magians, who appear more subtle than psychic in this particular tale; but at least, as was also the case with Gaumata, not unduly anxious for bloodshed—pacifiers rather than inciters to violence.

The history of this strange caste, pieced together from Herodotus, is almost like a brief symbolical abstract of the myth of the magus as it will appear in this book. A period of undisputed sway; loss of power when the race from which they sprang went under; the assumption of a false identity; the discovery of the fraud by means of a mark which branded the usurper as a criminal; and withal a continued and even increasing spiritual ascendancy after a fearful revenge had been exacted. All this is strangely prophetic of the days to come. Meanwhile the Greeks had given to the intransitive verb μαγεύειν 'to be a magus', the transitive sense: 'to enchant, to bewitch, to charm'. Even in the darkest days, that power would never quite desert their spiritual descendants; not even though the magi themselves came out of the East to proclaim and worship the newborn Christ, and then, returning to their own homes, were heard of no more.

(b) Zoroaster

> I saw a book in Khúsrau's royal hall,
> Writ in the Pahlaví, for so they call
> That ancient tongue—the great arch-priest of fire,
> Had placed it there—chief of the learned choir.
> Within the book in varied tale were told
> The deeds of ancient kings and heroes old.
> There too the Zandavastá's sacred line,
> Was traced, holy Zartusht's book divine;
> And there the story of his wondrous birth,
> And all that marked the sage's stay on earth.
> Time-worn the volume and the mystic page,
> Was veiled in doubt, and dim with mists of age.[1]

So wrote Zartusht-Běhrám in the thirteenth century: and in spite of the wealth of scholarship and learning lavished on Zoroastrianism, notably in the *Sacred Books of the East*, the position of the founder remains substantially the same to-day. For mythology surged

[1] Cf. John Wilson, *The Pársí Religion*, Bombay 1843, pp. 447f.; E. B. Eastwick's translation of the *Zartusht-Namah*.

round him like a tide running in, submerged him, and then retreating, left on the shore of life fragments strewn hither and thither, the flotsam and jetsam of a great wreckage, which included the religion he had taught:

As the Parsis are the ruins of a people, so are their sacred books the ruins of a religion. There has been no other great belief in the world that ever left such poor and meagre monuments of its past splendour.[1]

Taking the *Gâthas* to be documents of this religion in its earliest and purest form, it would seem that the process it underwent was roughly the same which is observable in the development of Buddhism, that is to say the victory of magical ritual and magical legend over doctrine. What marks Zoroastrianism out is the completeness of the conquest, which has made of Zoroaster, who probably lived in the seventh century before Christ, an almost purely mythical figure, whom Williams Jackson vainly attempted to humanise; and of whom even the High Priest of the Parsis in Karachi confessed in 1938:

We know everything of the life of Mohammed; we know something of the lives of Buddha and Jesus; we know practically nothing of the life of Zoroaster.[2]

By the Greeks he was regarded as the Magian *par excellence*; and from my point of view, he is the most perfect example of the obliteration of life by legend. This being so, and the actual Avestan and Pahlavi texts having survived in so fragmentary a state, I have not scrupled to use certain features in the late *Zartusht-Namah* which, though only suggested in the Zoroastrian scriptures as we have them now, were probably traditional, but may also have suffered contamination from Hebrew, Greek and Christian sources. According to the scholars who have worked over the texts, the *Gâthas* may have been composed at any period between 1500 and 900 B.C.; the oldest portions of the later *Avesta* a short time before Darius (521–485 B.C.); the latest parts of the *Avesta* in the third and fourth centuries B.C.; and the Pahlavi texts, written about A.D. 900, were probably composed during the Sassanian Age (A.D. 211–640).

[1] *S.B.E.* IV, p. xiv; Darmesteter's Introduction to the *Vendîdâd*.
[2] M. N. Dhalla, *History of Zoroastrianism*, New York 1938, p. 310.

Prophecies preceded the birth of the future lawgiver of Iran; and the Glory of Ahura Mazda entered the womb of the mother of the girl who was to give birth to Zoroaster:

Thereupon, when Aûharmazd had produced the material of Zaratûst, the glory then, in the presence of Aûharmazd, fled on *towards* the material of Zaratûst on to that germ; from that germ it fled on, on *to the light which is endless*; from the light which is endless it fled on, on to that of the sun; from that of the sun it fled on, on *to* the moon; from that moon it fled on, on to those stars; from those stars it fled on, on to the fire which *was* in the house of Zôis; *and* from that fire it fled on, on to the wife of Frâhîmrvaña-zôis, when she brought forth that girl who became the mother of Zaratûst.[1]

After receiving both the guardian spirit and the material body of the God as well as the Glory, the girl gave virgin birth to the prophet, who was also said to have descended from the sky through the flames of the ether, probably another way of describing the coming down of the Glory. A still more attractive version made of Zoroaster the descendant from emigrants of a great transatlantic continent reaching our earth after a prodigious expedition. Here again, the underlying idea of the coming down of the god is essentially the same. Miraculous portents naturally accompanied the birth of such a child. Besides the mother's dream recounted in the *Zartusht-Namah*, is the striking incident that the prophet laughed aloud when he saw the light of day, whereas 'save this child, every infant born into the world has wept'.[2] No writer on the prophet of Iran has ever omitted that laughter, which enlightened the whole house; and Pliny, who duly mentioned it, also said that his brain palpitated so violently as to repel any hand laid upon his head. Meanwhile that Glory with which Zoroaster will be forever surrounded in men's minds irradiated the house and village of his nativity; all nature rejoiced, and a thrill of great gladness ran through Ahura Mazda's creation. Deadly fear and rage on the other hand had convulsed Ahriman and his creatures ever since the coming of the prophet had been announced. Even before his nativity, the cohorts of evil had attempted to destroy him; and now, in panic and anger, the arch-fiend and his servants tried by every means in their power to rid themselves of this menace to their effectiveness. And the world seemed overfull at the time of wicked priests or black magicians; the

[1] *S.B.E.* XLVII, pp. 17f.; Pahlavi *Dînkard*, Book VII.
[2] *Zartusht-Namah*, ed. cit. p. 483.

Karaps and the Kigs, in other words the supporters of the old
religion which Zoroaster had come either to reform or to replace.
They may in fact be the Pahlavi designation for the Median Magi.
But whoever they were, they represented the adherents of Ahriman,
the spirit of evil, perpetually warring against Ahura Mazda, and
they did their utmost to kill his envoy in infancy. In vain: the hand
raised to stab him was withered; beasts would not harm and fire
would not burn him. He was destined to grow to manhood and to
attain to a greatness thus strikingly described:

...*there* is manifested in him a mind which is more capacious than the whole
world, *and* more exalted than every worldly possession, with an understanding whose strength is perfectly selected, an intellect of all-acquiring
power, and a sagacity of all-deciding ability; also with the much heedfulness
of the kingly glory, and the full desire for righteousness, the efficacious
diligence and authority, and even the superiority in mightiness and grandeur
of strength which are in the character *of* these four classes of his, which are
priesthood, warriorship, husbandry, and artisanship; *besides* a perfect
friendship for the sacred beings *and* the good, *and* an awful enmity for the
demons *and* the vile.[1]

This 'awful enmity' was the *leitmotiv* of his life; and, as we have
seen, it was mutual. At a very early age, Zoroaster began to arm
himself spiritually to withstand evil and also to prepare himself for
his sacred mission. According to some he began to observe a strict
silence at the age of seven; and a long solitary period of initiation was
subsequently spent in the wilderness, where he lived in a mountain
cave on a snowclad peak, subsisting solely on curds and milk. It is
traditionally reckoned that he was thirty years of age when the first
revelation of Ahura Mazda was granted him. This was followed at
various intervals by seven other visions; six conferences with the
Amsháspands or archangels and another colloquy with Ahura Mazda.
The angelic conferences were of an eminently practical nature,
tending to promote the prosperity of the people, which from time
immemorial has been the gospel of the medicine-man:

And freedom of assault, exemption from persecution, and proper
maintenance of the five species of animals, *were* prescribed...to Zaratûst
with seemingly very awful admonition.... Care for the proper maintenance
of the Varahran fire, and the propitiation of all fires, is explained to him...
and he was fully admonished about various proper preservations of the

[1] *S.B.E.* XLVII, pp. 46f.; Pahlavi *Dînkard*, Book VII.

metals, *and as to* not producing warlike accoutrements of gold.... *And Zaratûst was* also thus admonished...about the care and propitiation of the earth...and he *was* told about the care and propitiation of water...and he *was* informed about the care *and* propitiation of plants.[1]

Much stranger and more impressive is the Avestan account of the assault and temptation by Ahriman and his attendant demon:

From the region of the north, from the regions of the north, forth rushed Angra Mainyu, the deadly, the Daêva of the Daêvas. And thus spake the evil-doer Angra Mainyu, the deadly: 'Drug, rush down and kill him.' O holy Zarathustra! The Drug came rushing along, the demon Bûiti, who is deceiving, unseen death.

Zarathustra chanted aloud the Ahuna-Vairya: 'The will of the Lord is the law of righteousness. The gifts of Vohumanô to the deeds done in this world for Mazda. He who relieves the poor makes Ahura king.'

He offered the sacrifices to the good waters of the good Dâitya! He recited the profession of the worshippers of Mazda!

The Drug dismayed, rushed away, the demon Bûiti, who is deceiving, unseen death.

And the Drug said to Angra Mainyu: 'Thou, tormenter, Angra Mainyu! I see no way to kill Spitama Zarathustra, so great is the glory of the holy Zarathustra.'

Zarathustra saw (all this) within his soul: 'The wicked, the evil-doing Daêvas (thought he) take counsel together for my death.'

Up started Zarathustra, forward went Zarathustra, unabated by Akemmanô, by the hardness of his malignant riddles; he went swinging stones in his hand, stones as big as a house, which he obtained from the maker, Ahura Mazda, he the holy Zarathustra. 'Whereat on this wide, round earth, whose ends lie afar, whereat dost thou swing (those stones), thou *that* standest by the upper bank of the river Darega, in the mansion of Pourusaspa?'

Thus Zarathustra answered Angra Mainyu: 'O evil-doer, Angra Mainyu! I will smite the creation of the Daêva; I will smite the Nasu, a creature of the Daêva; I will smite the Pairika Knathaiti, till the victorious Saoshyant come up to life out of the lake Kasava, from the region of the dawn, from the regions of the dawn.'

Again to him said the Maker of the evil world, Angra Mainyu: 'Do not destroy my creatures, O holy Zarathustra! Thou art the son of Pourusaspa; by thy mother I was invoked. Renounce the good Religion of the worshippers of Mazda, and thou shalt gain such a boon as Vadhaghna gained, the ruler of the nations.'

Spitama Zarathustra said in answer: 'No! never will I renounce the good

[1] *S.B.E.* XLVII, pp. 161 f.; Pahlavi *Zâd-Sparam*, Chapter XXII.

Religion of the worshippers of Mazda, either for body or life, though they should tear away the breath.'

Zarathustra chanted aloud the Ahuna-Vairya. The holy Zarathustra said aloud: 'This I ask thee: teach me the truth, O Lord....'[1]

This tremendous temptation scene, which reads as if it had taken place at the very dawn of time, has much of the magical contest about it; and in the *Dînkard* version another fiend disguised as a beautiful courtesan was also put to flight by the prophet. But Zoroaster's victory on this occasion was the prelude to a life of struggle and conflict which ended only with his death. Ten years of wandering, some say as far as China, in the attempt to gain converts to Ahura Mazda, earned him a series of rebuffs and failures which was not relieved till he gained a solitary disciple, one of his own cousins. This, however, proved to be the turning-point of his career, preceding as it did the conversion of King Vishtaspa, who was to become the champion of the new faith. A bitter conflict engaged in at the royal court finally brought about the triumph of Zoroastrianism. The king seemed to be on the point of accepting it after a great session with the priests of the older faith, the Kigs and Karaps, represented as black magicians. This controversy lasted three days, during which Zoroaster answered thirty-three questions propounded to him by his adversaries, and answered them so convincingly that Vishtaspa was won over to his faith. The priests thereupon poisoned the king's mind against the prophet, so that he was condemned to death, preceded by 'awful imprisonment and punishment'. Thus far the *Dînkard*. The *Zartusht-Namah* elaborates the means by which this change of heart was effected, and though they smack of medieval rather than ancient times, they bring into prominence an accusation perpetually levelled against religious innovators, the charge of black magic:

The wise men made secret search for all that is most impure in the world, such as blood and filth and things impure, and the divided heads of a cat and a dog, also the bones of carrion, and much they were, at that moment, able to find. They carried these things to the house of Zartusht....[2]

The 'discovery' of this damaging paraphernalia was duly reported to Vishtaspa, and a fearful doom upon the prophet was uttered. He

---

[1] *S.B.E.* IV, pp. 209 ff.; *Vendîdâd*, Fargard XIX. Vadhaghna was said to have ruled the world for a thousand years.

[2] *Zartusht-Namah*, ed. cit. p. 503.

was thrown into prison and left to starve. The divine intervention of Ahura Mazda saved him. Vague references in the Zoroastrian scriptures to a triumph gained by the cure of a black horse were elaborated in the *Zartusht-Namah* into a fantastic tale, which may have been traditional. The king's favourite courser was smitten by a strange and horrible catastrophe: its legs were drawn up one after another into its belly, and no power on earth, it seemed, could make it whole again. The news reached Zoroaster in prison, and he charged himself with the cure of the beast, provided that one boon were granted for each leg that reappeared. This was agreed to; and on the condition that the king should accept the faith, that his son should fight for it, that the queen should adopt it, and that the 'wise men' should be punished by death, the fourfold miracle was accomplished. The king then craved four boons, one of which was finally conferred upon him and the three others severally on members of his household. Three archangels appeared upon horseback clad in green and in all the panoply of war, glorious and terrible; and after stern admonitions to the king to hold fast to the faith, coupled with promises if he complied, he was granted the power to foresee his own future; the gift of immortality until the resurrection was conferred on one of his sons, that of invulnerability on another; and his grand vizier was fittingly endowed with universal knowledge. As for Zoroaster, who also asked for immortality, he was granted a vision of the whole earth, of paradise and hell and of the future course of the religion. These various gifts were bestowed by means of magic draughts, magic incense, a magic pomegranate, and, in Zoroaster's case, by one drop of 'something that resembled honey'.

This long and fantastic trial episode was the last event to receive sustained attention in the extant scriptures or by later legend makers. For the spread of Zoroastrianism by the Holy Wars now monopolised their attention; and oddly enough the prophet himself was given no outstanding part in them. The variant versions of his death, said to have occurred at the age of seventy-seven, add to the abiding impression of a glory that is gone which surrounds this mythical figure from first to last. Iranian sources state that he was killed by an infidel Turkish wizard; or more impressively that he was slain during the Holy Wars with eighty other priests in the great Temple of the Fire of Balkh; or again, that he was torn to pieces by wolves, the servants of the evil Ahriman. Greek and Latin patristic writers circulated the story that he perished by fire as a punishment for practising astrology, that diabolic and forbidden art; for (like the wise men at King Vishtaspa's court) they regarded him as a black magician; although a more kindly view, which made of him one of the Magi, a forerunner and prophet of Christ, also prevailed. But the last words about Zoroaster's end on earth are best spoken by a poet:

> The host reached Balkh, the world was wrecked with sack,
> And slaughter. Making for the Fane of Fire,
> For hall and palace decked with gold, they gave
> Them and the Zandavasta to the flames.
> The fane had eighty priests, God's worshippers,
> And all before the Fire the Turkmans slew,
> And swept that cult away. The Fire, that erst
> Zarduhsht had litten, of their blood did die;
> Who slew that priest himself I know not I.[1]

The obscurity or the mystery which surrounds Zoroaster's death would favour the conviction of his eventual resurrection. This notion was metaphysically and symbolically expressed. His seed was said to have been deposited at the bottom of a lake. In this lake three young girls will conceive when bathing and bring forth at intervals of a thousand years a hero to renew the world. The last of these, the final incarnation of Zoroaster, will be the saviour Saoshyant ('from the regions of the dawn'), who will bring about the complete destruction of evil, of Ahriman and his hosts, found truth and justice upon earth and resurrect the dead.

As early as the *Avesta* the miraculous birth, the portents and perils, the initiation and temptation, the distant wandering, the contest, the trial and persecution, the violent death and the resurrection are all indicated. The hero of ritual looms large behind this legend; and the primitive medicine-man is almost equally in evidence, the magician of the simple folk:

One *marvel* is the disclosure by Zaratust, in complete beneficence, medical knowledge, acquaintance with character, and other professional retentiveness, secretly *and* completely, of *what* is necessary for legal knowledge and spiritual perception; also the indication, by revelation, of the rites for driving out pestilence, overpowering the demon, and witch, and disabling sorcery and witchcraft. The curing *of* disease, the counteraction of

---

[1] Firdausí, *Sháhnáma*, tr. Warner, London 1910, v, p. 92.

wolves *and* noxious creatures, the liberating of rain, *and* the confining of hail, spiders, locusts, and other terrors of corn *and* plants and adversaries of animals, by the marvellous rites.... And the disclosure to mankind *of* many running waters from marvellous streams, and remedies for sickness which *are* mixed by well-considering physicians...and the worldly advantage of others.... [1]

Such were some of the revelations of the prophet who was sent by God with this message to mankind:

Inform the people of the world, that so they may see things both hidden and revealed. Whatever is bright and full of light, let them know that that is the brightness of my glory. They will not err in their worship of me, if they turn their faces to that which is bright. If they observe my commandments, Ahriman shall fly from them; nothing in the world is better than light, both among small and great. Of light we created angels and paradise, afterwards hell was formed from darkness. Wherever you may be in the two worlds you will find no place void of my light. [2]

[1] *S.B.E.* XLVII, pp. 75 f.; Pahlavi *Dînkard*, Book VII.
[2] *Zartusht-Namah,* ed. cit. p. 495.

PLATE I

Idealized portrait from a sculpture supposed to
represent Zoroaster

CHAPTER II

HEBREW HOLY MEN

(a) Moses

Although the real Moses probably lived long before the real Zoroaster, assuming that both are historical persons, the Hebrew lawgiver seems closer in time to us, because the real or fictitious hero of Exodus has never been completely rapt away into mythological clouds. Yet Moses the magician as he appears in the Bible only needed some slight manipulation in the Talmud, in the Jewish apocalypses, and by Josephus and 'Philo' to be assimilated into the magus-myth.

Divine paternity was never claimed for the prophet of Jahweh, for this notion would have been too repugnant to Jewish conceptions of monotheism; but 'Philo' tried to insinuate the possibility of a dual nature, of an immaterial Moses existing before the historical one. It never took on, however. The legend of the child born into slavery, adopted by Pharaoh's daughter and later chosen to be the mouth-piece of the Lord, was too strong. The perils surrounding his infancy and his whole race, on the other hand, were an outstanding and integral feature of the story of his life. Talmudic legends added portents in the shape of dreams; both Pharaoh and the mother of Moses saw visions of his future greatness which would outweigh all the splendour and power of Egypt. Moreover, the infant cleansed the daughter of Pharaoh of leprosy when she lifted him out of the water; and later, with a prophetic gesture, he took the crown from the king's head and placed it upon his own.

The period of initiation as described in the Bible was inaugurated by the encounter with the angel of the Lord in the burning bush on Mount Sinai (Horeb), and was completed during the forty days and nights on the same mountain, face to face with Jahweh. It was preceded and followed by those years of wandering in the wilderness which differ in kind from the distant journeys taken by other magicians in their search for wisdom or their efforts to disseminate it. For Moses was accompanied by his people and was seeking for the promised land. From this point of view it was more like an odyssey than a pilgrimage. Material advantage was in the forefront of the minds of the people themselves; and their leader was hard put to it at times to sustain the part of medicine-man successfully. Yet the search for wisdom was not neglected, since the central feature of the story was the communication of the Torah by Jahweh to Moses, and by the prophet to his people. The Apocalypse of Baruch elaborated the occasion by inventing a series of visions or spiritual journeys undertaken by Moses from Mount Sinai, when the Lord showed him the depths of the abyss, the greatness of Paradise, the mouth of Gehenna, the place of renunciation, the region of faith and the land of hope.

After the tragic last scene on the final ascent up Mount Sinai, when Moses saw the promised land and learnt that he was never to enter it, he died in the land of Moab

...according to the word of the Lord. And he buried him in a valley in the land of Moab, over against Beth-peor: but no man knoweth of his sepulchre unto this day.[1]

...and his likeness was changed gloriously: and he died in glory according *to the mouth of the Lord and he buried him* as he had promised him, and the angels lamented at his death, and lightnings and torches and arrows went before him with one accord...for he loved him greatly; and he buried him with his own hands on a high place of the earth, and in the light of the whole world.[2]

...and as he was going to embrace Eleazar and Joshua, and was still discoursing with them, a cloud stood over him on the sudden, and he disappeared in a certain valley, although he wrote in the holy books that he died, which was done out of fear lest they should venture to say, that because of his extraordinary virtue he went to God.[3]

From this account to the Assumption of Moses (surviving as such only in the title to a Testament of Moses) is a very short step forward, which was further vouched for by the appearance of Moses at Christ's transfiguration in the Scriptures. But this resurrection had evidently been preceded by a descent into Hades, according to Jude's reference to the combat between Michael and the devil for

[1] Deuteronomy xxxiv. 5, 6.
[2] [Philo] *Biblical Antiquities*, tr. James, London 1917, p. 132.
[3] Flavius Josephus, *The Antiquities of the Jews*, tr. Whiston, London 1906, p. 113. Both '*Antiquities*' are of the first century A.D. as is also the Apocalypse of Baruch.

the body of the prophet. There was also another tradition which developed from the mystery surrounding his place of burial. This was to the effect that he had been slain by his people. His previous relations with them, and the language of the prophets, particularly Hosea, lend colour to such a view (latterly upheld by Freud). This ending harmonises not only with the *pathos* in ritual and ritual-drama, but also with the frequent catastrophes unpopular magicians meet with in real life. Portents and perils at birth, initiation, long and distant wandering, a mysterious and possibly violent end, an assumption, a descent into Hades, and a resurrection, they are all there.

But it is the magical contest which bulks largest in the story of Moses the magician. It is the most signal and arresting of all the innumerable life-and-death encounters between rival practitioners of which the history of magic is so full. And it transcends them all, because the fate of nations hung upon the issue. The greatness of its proportions and the religious sanction under which the hero was supposedly acting have blinded many to the actual nature of the contest described, which consisted entirely of works of evil and destruction, the hall-mark of black magic all the world over. On a very grand scale and for very high motives Moses anticipated the worst atrocities attributed to African witch-doctors and the inhuman methods of gangster leadership in order to free his people from an intolerable slavery, a slavery at least intolerable to him. This is the background to one of the most grandiose and sombre as well as the grimmest of the stories of the world.

The situation described between the Israelites and the Egyptians was that of an immigrant minority, constituting a potential menace, and suffering tyranny and oppression in consequence. It was full of possibilities for an agitator; but unlikely to develop dangerously unless an agitator arose. To judge by the account in Exodus, the Israelites as a whole were sunk in a state of mental and moral apathy, and were both nursing their grievances and hugging their chains. Although Pharaoh's policy was their gradual extermination by the elimination of the male issue, his effort to counteract the rising birth-rate was thwarted more often than not; they still increased and multiplied. Food they seem to have had in abundance, they were permitted to own flocks and herds; and their grievously heavy labours were sometimes at least supervised by men of their own race.

As might have been expected in such circumstances, the initiative to throw off their bondage did not come from them; they were too far gone in the sickness of slave mentality.

But there was a man in their midst, born into their own race, who had been brought up among their oppressors and had imbibed from them an entirely different attitude towards life. The wrongs of the down-trodden Israelites weighed upon his mind and became an obsession with him; for they were his own people, the heirs of a greater and happier past. Wrath seized him violently when he saw an Egyptian maltreating an Israelite, and he slew the offender. The deed was discovered and reported to Pharaoh; and Moses was forced to flee to the peninsula of Sinai as a poverty-stricken exile.

Among the hills which crown the high plateau there is one which at that time was called the Mount of God. It was holy ground to the Egyptians, and also to the Arabs, who ascended it as pilgrims and drew off their sandals when they reached the top. Nor is it strange that Sinai should have excited reverence and dread; it is indeed a weird and awful land. Vast and stern stand the mountains, with their five granite peaks pointing to the sky; avalanches like those of the Alps, but of sand, not of snow, rush down their naked sides with a clear and tinkling sound resembling convent bells; a peculiar property resides in the air; the human voice can be heard at a surprising distance, and swells out into a reverberating roar; and sometimes there rises from among the hills a dull booming sound like the distant firing of heavy guns.... As he wandered on the mountain heights he looked to the west and he saw a desert; beyond it lay Egypt, the house of captivity, the land of bondage. He looked to the east and he saw a desert; beyond it lay Canaan, the home of his ancestors, a land of peace and soon to be a land of hope. For now new ideas rose tumultuously within him. He began to see visions and to dream dreams. He heard voices and beheld no form; he saw trees which blazed with fire and yet were not consumed. He became a prophet; he entered the ecstatic state.[1]

In these surroundings and in that state, the ominous and ambiguous hour approached which heralded a revelation. It came in the guise of possession or control by a fierce, volcanic god, breathing fire and slaughter, anathema and revenge, the *alter ego* of the man who was determined to be the saviour and leader of his people and to proclaim the worship of one god, the God of Abraham, of Isaac and of Jacob. From this moment onwards, Moses suffered the awful fate of a man

[1] Winwood Reade, *The Martyrdom of Man*, Thinker's Library, London n.d. pp. 148, 150.

ground between the upper and the nether millstones: between something fierce, inexorable and daemonic driving him on, and a wayward, rebellious people obstructing him; not to mention the fearful hardships besetting his path and the inimical races determined to repel the meditated intrusion into their territory. Well might he continually remind the Israelites of the miracles he had accomplished in Egypt.

These, as I have said, were of a sinister nature. The magic Moses had probably learnt in Egypt, and in which Jahweh also instructed him, proved more potent than that of the wise men, the sorcerers and the magicians of Pharaoh; although it would seem that Aaron was really more proficient than Moses, or at least equally necessary for the success of the performances. But, whoever may have been the agent, the contest ended in victory and glory to the power of the control which it was explicitly undertaken to prove. Again and again Jahweh declared that he had hardened the heart of Pharaoh the better to destroy him and establish his own power. Malignantly inspiring the rejection of one ultimatum after another by the blinded adversary, Jahweh rained plagues, pestilences and slaughter down upon thousands and finally exterminated them in the passage of the Red Sea. Power over natural phenomena was in terrifying evidence throughout, used in the service of destruction. These miracles are the works of a cruel mind intent only on despotic control. One hardly knows whom to pity most in the reign of terror Jahweh is reputed to have set up in Egypt in order to establish monolatry: Pharaoh, blinded by the god who was determined on his destruction; the Egyptians suffering vicariously for Pharaoh's sins; the Israelites who at the outset had implored their leader to let them alone so that they might serve the Egyptians, and were now led or driven out into the wilderness; or Moses himself in the clutches of a fierce, driving and irresistible force.

The expedition which followed the fearsome events in Egypt is one of the most painful in story. Longing for the land of flesh-pots, the mirage of another country flowing with milk and honey perpetually sickening their hearts with hope deferred, the wretched Israelites cannot be said to have borne their sufferings with fortitude; whereas the indomitable courage of Moses and his iron determination not to allow them to revert to slavery or polytheism stands out in stark and tragic contrast. Amongst all his other difficulties, he was suffering under that fearful disability which always lies in wait for religious founders who establish their doctrine by miracles and are then expected to continue as they have begun. Moreover, these miracles were vitally necessary to the survival of the race who had followed him out into the wilderness, and were in fact those benefits in the shape of food and water which medicine-men are always called upon to supply. Manna appeared as if by magic during one crisis, and water miraculously gushed from the rock at another. But the quails sent down in answer to urgent prayers for meat poisoned those who ate them, which was interpreted as due to the wrath of Jahweh for their impious desires. With so stubborn, so rebellious and so murmuring a people, it was not surprising that many of the wonders worked were of a menacing description. When massacres and fearful threats of Jahweh's wrath failed, mysterious plagues appeared; whilst terrifying trumpetings and fiery manifestations became the order of the day once the magician's familiar spirit was announced to have taken up his residence in the tabernacle.

Taking it all in all, therefore, the magic performed by Moses or through Moses was dark of hue; that is to say that whoever wrote or edited the epic of Exodus was on the wrong side of the magical fence. That nevertheless the total impression is far indeed from being a chronicle of evil, and on the contrary diffuses a feeling of awe and at times of great holiness, is due to the religious conviction and fervour of the writer. The gradual uphill struggle from monolatry to monotheism, the giving of the ten commandments, the vastness of the design, the sombre splendour of the setting are all on a scale which somehow counteracts the vengefulness and the malignancy. There is something so awe-inspiring about the terrible god, something so tragic and sublime about his harried prophet, that both transcend good and evil, and magic, black or white. It is doubtful whether any divinity before or since has ever attained to the stature of Jahweh. It is therefore only natural that the magical contest presided over by him should be the greatest and the most famous in the history of the world; whereas Zoroaster's temptation by Ahriman, the Spirit of Evil itself, stands out vividly amongst all others which have ever been described.

(b) Solomon

The story of Moses as told in the Bible, although it has all the outstanding features of the magus-myth, is nevertheless by no means so stereotyped as the legend of Zoroaster, and gives the impression of a quasi-historical account of an actual series of events. It is highly individual, even allowing for later legendary accretions, and is presented in a manner which renders it unique, and has left little or nothing for subsequent ages to do. Crystallised in its scriptural form, this wonderful epic of a migration could hardly be (and certainly never has been) improved upon. And the hero, Moses himself, lives a life of such intense reality as to throw Zoroaster quite into the shade. Moreover, both have come down to posterity as law-givers rather than magicians, however much the medicine-man and the ritual hero of magic have contributed to their existence. As far as Moses is concerned, the reiterated insistence that all his miracles were the work of Jahweh himself has fostered the prophetic as against the thaumaturgic aspect. Grim, awful, tragic and sublime, he still seems eternally to proclaim in our ears: 'Hearken, Israel, the Lord thy God, the Lord is one.'

The legend of Solomon developed along very different lines. Mythopoeic imagination swooped down upon the figure of the wise king, seized upon him avidly, and has never let him go. Yet the future arch-magician of legend was not represented in the earliest extant account of his life (Kings and Chronicles) as practising magic at all, although something mysterious undoubtedly surrounded him.

A younger son of David by Bathsheba, he was singled out by his father to succeed him (for 'the Lord loved him').[1] Having put down the rebellion of his older brother Adonijah, who aimed at usurping the throne, and having been proclaimed and anointed king by his dying father, Solomon did in fact become ruler over Israel, and secured an alliance with Egypt by marrying Pharaoh's daughter. It is then recounted that the Lord appeared to him in a dream and said: 'Ask what I shall give thee.' Solomon asked for an understanding heart in order to be able to judge the people. He was granted 'a wise and an understanding heart; so that there was none like thee before thee, neither after thee shall any arise like unto thee'. And because he had not desired riches or honour, these were added

[1] 2 Samuel xii. 24.

as a reward: 'so that there shall not be any among the kings like unto thee all thy days'; or more emphatically still: 'such as none of the kings have had that have been before thee, neither shall there any after thee have the like'.[1]

This momentous scene was immediately followed by the famous judgement between the two harlots who were both laying claim to the same infant child; and further testimony to Solomon's wisdom and knowledge was added shortly afterwards:

And God gave Solomon wisdom and understanding exceeding much, and largeness of heart, even as the sand that is on the sea shore. And Solomon's wisdom excelled the wisdom of all the children of the east country, and all the wisdom of Egypt...and his fame was in all nations round about. And he spake three thousand proverbs: and his songs were a thousand and five. And he spake of trees, from the cedar tree that is in Lebanon even unto the hyssop that springeth out of the wall: he spake also of beasts, and of fowl, and of creeping things, and of fishes. And there came of all people to hear the wisdom of Solomon, from all kings of the earth, which had heard of his wisdom.[2]

If this tribute to Solomon's wisdom is striking, the impression of his riches and glory produced by the account of the building of the Temple is indelible. With the aid of Hiram of Tyre, the materials, the workmen and the treasurers were assembled; and after seven years the labour was completed in all its magnificence, the ark of the covenant was installed, and the Temple dedicated to the Lord. A second vision was granted to Solomon when the ceremony was over, in which a covenant of future glory for himself and his people was accompanied by solemn warnings against worshipping other gods. This scene resembles that between King Vishtaspa and the archangels, but was to have a different sequel. And perhaps a hint that Solomon was declining from worship to worldliness accompanies the long-drawn-out descriptions of the ensuing building of his own marvellous palaces and the peerless and wonderful throne. The visit of the Queen of Sheba to prove the king 'by hard questions' added the testimony of an alien world to his reputation for wisdom, glory, riches and might, and shows the still wise and virtuous king at the very zenith of his power. The author of Chronicles left the matter there with some additional embellishments such as that silver was as

[1] Cf. 1 Kings iii. 5 ff. and 2 Chronicles i. 7 ff.
[2] 1 Kings iv. 29–34.

common as stone in Solomon's day; but Kings had a sad story to tell of his declining years. Amongst the seven hundred wives who, with three hundred concubines, formed the king's harem, there were many 'strange women', who worshipped alien gods, and finally turned his heart away from the sole worship of the Lord; so that he went after Ashtoreth, the goddess of the Zidonians, Milcom (or Moloch), the abomination of the Ammonites, and Chemosh, the abomination of Moab, built altars to them on high places, and burnt incense and sacrificed to them and others. The Lord rebuked him sternly for this, prophesied retribution to his successors, and stirred up adversaries against him. Solomon seems to have lost the empire over Edom as a result before he died and 'slept with his fathers'.

This picture of a king supremely wise, powerful and rich, who wrote the Proverbs, the Song of Songs, Ecclesiastes and the Book of Wisdom, but succumbed to idolatry towards the end of his life and died under a cloud, made a very strong appeal to widely differing types of imaginations. No more telling instance could be found for the processes of legend than the course this story ran; and in particular it illuminates the vicissitudes of the myth of the magus; its unpredictable choice of heroes, its mysterious period of incubation; its oral peregrinations; its almost simultaneous emergence in the literature of widely separated peoples; its stereotyped features presented with infinite variations; its inexhaustible vitality. There are few figures in the history of the world which have been so persistently and so unwaveringly dogged by the limelight of legend as that of Solomon both in the East and the West. He is one of the most brilliant of the fixed stars in the magical firmament. As long as the word magic lasts, his name will endure; and as long as the practice persists, his authority will be invoked in all civilised lands. It would probably be a life's work to make a descriptive catalogue of all the sources where tales about him are to be found, ranging as they do from the Near East to India, the Malay Peninsula, the Slavonic countries, and as far west as Ireland. The Bible, the Talmud, the Koran, the *Arabian Nights*, a wealth of Persian and Turkish poetry; the Greek *Testament of Solomon*, the *Gesta Romanorum*, Old French, German and English legends; the medieval *Claviculae Salomonis* translated into all European tongues, and still circulating for practical purposes to-day; all these contributions and hundreds more have kept, are keeping, and will keep his name vividly in the forefront of the minds of those who approach or enter the field of magic for whatever reason. And, as if all this were not enough, Masonic tradition, harking back to the building of the Temple, has given to Solomon a new occult significance in modern times. The luxuriance of fancy displayed on the subject of the wise king, and the overpowering radiance with which he has been surrounded, produce much the same effect on the present-day reader as Solomon in all his glory is said to have made on the Queen of Sheba thousands of years ago. Only magic could account for this bewildering profusion.

Looking back at the story told in Kings and Chronicles one can see how inevitably the notion of magic would arise from such a method of presentation, even if it did not originally underlie it, as seems probable. Solomon's wisdom and riches were stated to be divine gifts in a special sense, in fact of supernatural origin. The forever celebrated judgement about the child has all the effect of an inspiration, of preternatural wisdom in the garb of mother-wit. It struck a chord in the East which still vibrates to-day; and legion are the judgements of Solomon to which it gave rise, all on the same pattern; for the East loves wisdom, and the Near East loves it best in a pithy parable form. The passages quoted above from Kings, the Proverbs and the Book of Wisdom (though the attribution of the latter to Solomon is certainly erroneous) helped to confirm his reputation for more than mortal knowledge, such as no other man had possessed. As for the divinely granted riches and honour, no one who reads steadily through the description of the Temple, the palaces and the throne in Kings and Chronicles can resist the cumulative impression of a greatness and glory transcending human endeavour. Hiram of Tyre fades into the background and an army of spirits (whom one soon begins to think of as jinn) replace him and his workmen, spontaneously engendered by an atmosphere of oriental splendour and luxury which anticipate the *Arabian Nights*. We are already in a legendary world; and the Queen of Sheba, with her 'hard questions' and her acknowledgement of spiritual defeat, can be recognised now as a rival magician worsted in the contest with the hero. That she should have been a woman may have been meant symbolically; it certainly points forward to Solomon's subsequent downfall, owing to the strange women with whom he fell so desperately in love, as Josephus was later to put it. The tone of the Song of Solomon would certainly contribute to the picture of a monarch swayed by that passion which many waters cannot quench. Whilst the tragic implications of his fall from grace re-echo in the piercing laments of the Preacher who once 'was king over Israel in Jerusalem'. This phrase in the context in which it occurs may have arisen from a tradition of Solomon in exile; it undoubtedly disseminated that notion. And altogether one gets the impression, from what the Bible recounts, that a good deal was deliberately omitted.

Although the attempt to arrange the stories about Solomon in a logical order results naturally in a coherent life-history on recognisably mythical lines, nevertheless throughout the ages it has been the stories and not the legendary career which have fascinated the world; and although Hammer-Purgstall consulted the *Suleimannáma* of the Turkish poet Firdusi (not to be confused with the Persian Firdausí) in seventy folio volumes, still (to judge by his extracts and his complaints) even this monumental work is a collection of tales and episodes rather than an epic. Fleg has made an artistic whole of the wealth of material, and St John Seymour's collection of legends about Solomon gives the events I am about to summarise in much the same order.

The royal child, whose name meant peaceable, was provided with an annunciation in the familiar style, a thwarted attempt on his life in infancy by Beelzebub, and supernatural wisdom manifested in an extraordinary judgement at the age of three, and continuing in the form of asking and answering questions of his elders during his boyhood and adolescence. The initiation, combined with a temptation or a test, was of course the occasion when the Lord appeared to Solomon in a dream asking him to choose a gift. Legend added the magic ring whose four stones gave the wise king power over the winds and forces of nature, over the birds and beasts, over men and over all the spirits, whether celestial, terrestrial or infernal. He was thus transformed overnight into the most potent wizard the world has ever known, representing as it were the wish-dream of the primitive medicine-man. The unequal conflict between wisdom and power was engaged. The magic ring made everything miraculously easy. The wicked spirits who were trying to hinder the building of the Temple were enslaved by its means and forced to labour in its erection. Even their chief Asmodeus, Solomon's great adversary, was subdued by the power of the ring and obeyed the king's commands. Thus the Temple was reared at last, the palaces too, the peerless and dazzling throne with its magical approaches, engineered and controlled by the jinn; all testified to a power and a splendour without parallel in the world.

Yet all was not well. Unknown to Solomon, the demons had secretly buried books of magic beneath the throne and were later to spread the rumour that by these means he had subjected the spirits to his will. In other words they were preparing an accusation of black magic against him, much as the Kigs and Karaps had done in the contest with Zoroaster, and were already planting those proofs which still survive to-day. Ignorant of these machinations, Solomon was nevertheless not a happy man. Surrounded by almost blinding glory, wielding supernatural power, and the world at peace around him, the mood to which Ecclesiastes bears tragic testimony often clouded his soul. Wisdom he had in superabundance, but absolute knowledge he had not; and several stories witness to the limitations of his power. Love and death proved to be beyond his control. He could not arrest the course of fate and was ignorant of its established decrees. More humiliating still, he had not the wherewithal to satisfy the hunger of a single whale, let alone its seventy thousand kin. And sometimes even his judgement failed him. It is with a certain sense of shock that we learn from Josephus how in a riddling contest with Hiram, Solomon could not solve all the riddles proposed and lost a great deal of money by his failure. The West, less enamoured of wisdom than the East, and considerably more suspicious of it, was inclined at one period to view Solomon with the same sensations which inspired such hostility to Aristides the Just. The medieval legends of Solomon and Saturn, and Solomon and Marcolf (or Morolf), took a fiendish delight in displaying the wise king of tradition defeated at every turn by the native wit of a cunning rogue. But whether to his ignominy or his glory, the contest for wit and wisdom, concentrated in the greatly expanded encounter with the Queen of Sheba, runs parallel with the Asmodean conflict, and derives ultimately from the same source in ritual.

The far-distant journeys which rarely fail to enliven the legendary lives of magicians occupy a central position for Solomon, who was borne by the wind or on his magic carpet over the whole of his dominions, and also visited the heavens, and went down to the utter-

most depths of the sea. Descriptions of the magic carpet almost
outrival the descriptions of the throne; and the royal progress
through the air was conducted with such pomp and ceremony, and
accompanied by so many marvels and wonders, that imagination
to-day flags in pursuit, returning with relief to the disillusionment
of Ecclesiastes. It all ended with the world-weary recognition that
there is nothing new under the sun, that all is vanity, and that all the
glories of the world must turn to dust again. Our great wisdom is
but folly, and pleasure of the senses is the only positive gain a man
can expect from life.

'He grew mad in his love of women, and laid no restraint on
himself in his lust';[1] and it was in order to please his many alien wives
that his debauchery led to idolatry and delivered him up into the
power of Asmodeus, the fiend he had once controlled absolutely.
In a moment of folly, he allowed him to seize his ring, and his power
went with it, down to the bottom of the sea, whither Asmodeus cast
it. The latter now assumed the form of Solomon and sent the king
into exile whilst he reigned in his stead. According to the Talmudic
legends, the fallen monarch, reduced to beggary, recognised his
errors and repented of them. His rebirth in virtue obtained him
divine forgiveness, shown by the miraculous recovery of the ring
from the belly of a fish. Solomon, once more in power, imprisoned
Asmodeus and all the other demons in a jar, sealed it with the magic
ring and lowered it into the depths of the sea. Its subsequent
fortunes do not concern the hero of this tale, since it remained
undiscovered during his lifetime; and he died in the odour of
sanctity, uttering prophecies about the destruction of the Temple
and its final invisible rebuilding. Or so Hebrew tradition reported;
whilst Christian legend insisted that he died in his sins, as indeed
would seem also to have been the view of the author of Kings; and
a medieval Scottish story maintained that he was condemned to be
eaten daily by ten thousand ravens until the end of the world. These
conflicting opinions reflect religious prejudices; but the account
adopted by the Koran has proved to be the favourite. When his
death approached, Solomon begged the Lord that it might be
concealed from the jinn, so that they would continue their work on
the Temple. This wish was granted. Solomon died upright leaning
on his staff. It was not until a year later, when a worm succeeded in

---

[1] Josephus, *The Antiquities of the Jews*, p. 232.

gnawing through this support, that the body fell to the ground and the jinn became aware of the deception. They stopped work immediately; but the Temple was complete, or so said some: others maintained that it was unfinished.

There remained his books to be reckoned with. The spurious books of magic, according to some, were now 'discovered' by the demons beneath his throne, and have circulated ever since under Solomon's name. According to others, Solomon himself burned his magical books before his death, and indeed committed all his writings to the flames, which, however, refused to consume Proverbs, Ecclesiastes and the Song of Songs. Of the three books on magic, said to be burnt, two survive until to-day; or at least are claimed to survive:

And this *Key of Solomon* opened all the treasures of magic arts. And this *Ring of Solomon* contained all the gestures by which spirits may be tamed. And *The Testament of Solomon* named all demons by name, and recited all spells and incantations that rout them or draw them hither, expel them or provoke their malice.[1]

According to Josephus, Solomon simply left his magical lore behind him, and it was practised in his day:

God also enabled him to learn that skill which expels demons, which is a science useful and sanative to men. He composed such incantations also by which distempers are alleviated. And he left behind him the manner of using exorcisms, by which they drive away demons, so that they never return; and this method of cure is of great force unto this day; for I have seen a certain man of my own country, whose name was Eleazar, releasing people that were demoniacal in the presence of Vespasian, and his sons, and his captains, and the whole multitude of his soldiers.[2]

The legend of Solomon, like the legend of Moses, has an individual stamp which is lacking in the legend of Zoroaster. The fierce Hebrew prophet, who performed in the name of Jahweh deeds of magic much more ghastly than Solomon was ever rumoured to have committed, has escaped that moral condemnation which fastened on Solomon with all the tenacity of the Jewish sense of sin, because of his idolatry. The fearful spiritual danger latent in all magic, the following after false gods, or devil-worship, is the shadow which the Scriptures cast over Solomon. This shadow, becoming luminous,

[1] E. Fleg, *The Life of Solomon*, tr. Garvin, London 1929, pp. 225f.
[2] Josephus, op. cit. pp. 218f.

enveloped him in the radiant mists of magic for the generations that were to come.

Solomon was of royal descent, the son of David, but not the son of God. No Hebrew could be that. There is hardly a trace of the descent into hell; and although he reigned for a year after his death this is at best an atrophied form of resurrection, if certainly a mysterious one. Legend loved Solomon; but in spite of all it has done for him, he bears less resemblance to the divine victim of ritual origin than to the fallible human practitioner, tempted at every stage of his career to misuse his miraculous power.

CHAPTER III

THE SAGES OF GREECE

(a) Pythagoras

The legendary lives of Zoroaster and Moses finally went according to plan; but the descent into Hades (in both cases described as a vision) was a late addition, as was also the assumption of Moses; whereas Zoroaster's future rebirth as the saviour Saoshyant, deriving from the same ritual notions of resurrection, was an integral part of his story, and his death also conformed to tradition in being a violent one. Furthermore, the supernatural origin of the prophet of Iran differentiates him from his Hebrew compeers. It would, therefore, seem that the pattern superimposed on the life of Moses as told in the Bible had certain features which were not originally Semitic: the divine origin, the descent into hell, and the violent or mysterious death. For, though the assumption was also a mythological after-thought, it figured in the story of Elijah, and was hinted at least about Enoch. The other three elements, everywhere latent or assumed in primitive ritual, and probably highly developed in Egypt, came to their clearest expression in Greek mythology, where gods descended amongst mortals and ascended again to heaven; and where the great heroes were half-gods who often went down into the shades to rescue some beloved mortal. The tales told of Apollo, Dionysos, Orpheus, Theseus and Heracles, of Demeter and Persephone are impregnated with these ideas, and indeed radiant with them in a strange and fascinating way.

Before proceeding to consider two Greek sages whose legendary lives reproduced many features of the great gods and heroes of Greece, I should like to pause for a moment over Euripides' *Bacchae* in which history and ritual have been fused in art, and in which a magical operation is performed on the stage during the contest between 'Dionysos' and Pentheus. In the Dionysiac rites, it was the god himself who was torn to pieces, either in bestial or in human form, or represented as torn. In Greek drama, the tragic hero often suffered a similar fate, either actually or spiritually. The *agon* of the rites developed into the dramatic conflict as we know it to-day against an adversary whose original ritual significance is now forgotten. In the *Bacchae* it still haunts the action, and notably in the ambivalence between the antagonists: the slain and the slaying daimon of the rites. Pentheus suffers the fate of the victim-god. And this makes him the hero of the drama from the aesthetic point of view, since it is he who arouses the tragic emotions of pity and fear. The contest between the two adversaries develops into a magical experiment, in which the magic is all on one side; this is part of the tragic situation, and an intensification of the orthodox trial by magical skill, in which the rival's magic is weaker. Pentheus has none, and is therefore doomed from the outset. 'Dionysos', on the other hand, represents the most striking exponent of the art to be found in the poetry of the world.

This strange and ultimately tragic race of men who work on humanity by magic has not changed very much since the fifth century B.C., and magicians still provoke or suffer the same kind of catastrophe which overtook Pentheus and Agave in this play. The new god, in his own person or in that of his representative, vanquished and destroyed most horribly the adherent of the old religion, after a contest whose sinister and uncanny nature makes one's blood run cold. For here, spell-bound with horror, we see the bewitching and beglamouring by magical means of the rival in the contest; we see the victim hideously transformed from a hot-headed, youthful, vigorous opponent into a slobbering slave, and led off to an ignominious doom, to an almost unthinkable end. We do not know, we shall never know, whether the mind of Pentheus was destroyed by the power of suggestion, or (as Verrall believed) by drugs; or whether it was a 'psychic invasion', 'the entry of the god into his victim';[1] that is to say, a case of magical obsession as distinguished from mystical communion with the god, which the chorus represents. Obsession or possession by a spirit is in general on the 'black' side of magic, and certainly seems to be so here, to judge by the degradation of character which it effects in Pentheus, whereas the chorus, however ecstatic their tone, are reverent religious worshippers. This same ambiguity between good and evil, complicated by the melting and merging of religion, mysticism and magic, prevails throughout. It is possible after all that the palace miracle only occurred in the

[1] Euripides, *The Bacchae*, ed. Dodds, Oxford 1944, p. 163.

minds of some of the Maenads; it is equally possible that it was a supernatural manifestation; or, as Professor Dodds puts it, that the god was represented in this episode as 'the whimsical magician, the weaver of fantasies'.[1] We may, and in fact we must, draw our own conclusions as to whether the Lydian was 'Dionysos' in disguise or merely a fanatical priest, possibly self-deceived. There is no final answer to any of these questions. The very nature of magic is ambiguity, but it is none the less potent for that. And in this case a religion of indescribable beauty, rapture, holiness and joy prevailed over an uninspiring official cult by inhuman, indeed devilish, means.

The character of the 'mysterious, smiling, heartless Stranger'[2] who came out of the East disquiets the mind with its irreconcilable qualities of spirituality and gentleness, treachery and fierceness, beauty and guile. His power is equally ambiguous; it seems to be divine in some of its manifestations, fiendishly malignant in others, and the shadow of imposture falls upon some. Pentheus called him 'a foreign wizard skilled in spells'; he may have been nothing more than that; but he controlled the Bacchants absolutely, he sent all the women of Thebes to rave and dance upon the hills, he debauched the mind of Pentheus; and he had the still more perilous gift of mystical self-intoxication. He transcends our comprehension in this work or art much as all his kith and kin elude complete understanding in life. The judgements of the critics about 'Dionysos' in the *Bacchae* have a strong family resemblance to the judgements made about magicians by their contemporaries. Some, seeing imposture somewhere, set about detecting it everywhere and go to the utmost extremes of sophistry in order to account 'naturally' for unaccountable happenings. Others shut their eyes to the trail of evil 'Dionysos' leaves behind him, and appeal to 'blind natural forces' in order to rhyme holiness and godhead with petty spite and malignancy of an all too human pattern. It is the tragic dualism at the heart of all great magicians which confronts and confounds us here in the person of this baffling, beautiful and yet baneful being.

The same contradictory emotions are aroused by the character of Pentheus. Moral condemnation alternates with exaggerated approval or a Freudian interpretation of the hero-victim's sex-ridden mind.

[1] Euripides, op. cit. ed. cit. p. 144.
[2] G. Norwood, *The Riddle of the Bacchae*, Manchester 1908, p. 66.

Perhaps Verrall (so much out of favour to-day) has given the most objective description: '...Pentheus is in the wrong, and, as tragedy demands, provokes, without deserving, his fate.'[1]

But however strong the feelings of pity, fear, admiration or disgust induced by the antagonist, the revelation of the nature of magic is the bewildering experience, 'the added dimension of emotion'[2] which the *Bacchae* provides, holding the balance true between the glamour, the glory, the exultant beauty, the purity, holiness and calm conveyed in the choric odes, and the savagery, the subtlety, the malignancy and the inhuman misuse of power depicted in the action. The Mosaic contest has greater proportions, but it is one-sided as far as the author's sympathies go, reflecting a relatively simple-minded and unquestioning belief. The encounter between 'Dionysos' and Pentheus is emotionally much more disturbing to witness than that between Moses and Pharaoh. Two short, pregnant, increasingly uncanny scenes cry out to be interpreted and elude interpretation. We have seen a magician at work; we have witnessed the results; what happened within the palace we do not know, because we cannot know, any more than we shall ever know what was in the smiling Stranger's mind. But the revelation of what magical power can do and of the effect a magician can have has been made to us once and for all. It could only thus have been made in the golden age of magic. Think of Goethe's Faust, think even of Marlowe's Faustus, and the distance between the practitioners of the art in antiquity and modern times becomes visible.

So extreme an expression of what Nietzsche would call Dionysiac magic must have startled the spectators by its grim realism and possibly dismayed the Hellenic world. Conscious or unconscious revulsion against such appalling practices may therefore have helped to fashion the legend of Pythagoras along recognisably 'Apolline' lines. For though it has come down to us in shreds and patches, the patience and ingenuity of scholars (culminating in the monographs of Isidore Lévy) have pieced the tatters together and presented us with a coherent and plausible reconstruction of the legends current about Pythagoras in the fourth century B.C., of which Iamblichus and Porphyry in the third century A.D. have given only disconnected fragments. The degree of probability underlying the various hypo-

[1] A. W. Verrall, *The Bacchants of Euripides*, Cambridge 1910, p. 56.
[2] Euripides, op. cit. ed. cit. p. xliii, quoting James Adam.

theses adopted or made by Lévy must remain conjectural; and the revolutionary conclusions he draws from them need not be accepted; but in his view the lost legend of Pythagoras was the prototype of all those which came after it; and therefore the story told in the Gospels and the doctrine to be found there derive ultimately from Pythagoras with a lesser admixture of Jewish elements; or, to use his phraseology, the Pythagoras of legend conquered the East, and by that means the whole world in the person and teaching of Christ.

The question of priority in this excessively complicated case is only another instance of my main thesis; the common origin in ritual of all these magus-myths, which made it almost inevitable that they should contaminate, sophisticate and modify each other. To survey them is not unlike standing on the bridge of Passau and watching the waters of the Inn, the Isar and the Danube swirling into each other. A hundred yards below the confluent point they are completely indistinguishable. Nevertheless, if Lévy is right in one of his main hypotheses, if in fact Philostratus' *Life of Apollonius of Tyana* is a close imitation of Apollonius' *Life of Pythagoras* (now lost), then it must also be allowed that the legend of the latter had a far-reaching influence on the myth of the magus as it developed in the Near East and the West.

The sources for this story are scattered references to the hero in Greek works from the fifth century B.C. onwards, the biographical notices of Iamblichus and Porphyry; and hints to be gleaned from the highly interesting Egyptian legend of Siosiris, in which the Mosaic conflict and details from the life of Pythagoras seem to have been fused into one fantastic whole. Moreover, Philostratus' *Life of Apollonius of Tyana* can be used with due caution to fill in some of the gaps. From these many and various references and compilations we learn that the philosopher who lived in the sixth century B.C. was the subject of a Pythian prophecy made to his father Mnesarchus. The latter was oracularly informed that the child with whom his wife was then pregnant would surpass in beauty and wisdom all who had ever lived. From that moment the mother Parthenais was called Pythais, and the notion of immortal parentage followed inevitably:

> Pythais, fairest of the Samian tribe,
> Bore from th'embraces of the God of Day
> Renown'd Pythagoras, the friend of Jove.[1]

[1] Iamblichus, *Life of Pythagoras*, tr. Taylor (1818), London 1926, p. 2.

The beautiful child, the son of Apollo, was promoted in the natural course of myth to be the god Apollo himself, some said the Pythian, some the Hyperborean Apollo; others maintained that he was Paeon, or one of the daemons who inhabit the moon, or an unnamed Olympian god. But the identification with Apollo prevailed on the whole over the other versions, and gave rise to the story of how Abaris, priest to the Hyperborean Apollo, recognised the godhead in Pythagoras, whereupon the latter confessed it to him privately, showing him his golden thigh in confirmation and acknowledging a divine mission to humanity. It was also said of him that 'rising up in the Olympic games, he showed his golden thigh';[1] and the Pythagoreans themselves were so much convinced of his divinity that they avoided using his name, referring to him by designations such as 'himself' or 'the divine one'.

Great beauty and precocious wisdom marked out the 'long-haired Samian' in his childhood. The aged philosopher Thales professed that he could teach him nothing he did not already know, and sent him to Egypt to acquire the ancient mystery-wisdom of that land. Recognised as one of the immortals by the sailors on the ship which brought him over, Pythagoras was received and instructed by the priests of Egypt; made captive by Cambyses, he was carried to Babylon, where he was initiated into the mysteries of the Chaldaeans and the Magi, and learnt the most perfect worship of the gods. According to Diogenes Laertius (second–third century A.D.), he was a disciple here of Zaratas or Zoroaster, an interesting juxtaposition of names which shows that the Greeks believed the prophet of Iran to be the older of the two and in some way responsible for the Pythagorean doctrine. Having been instructed and purified by this sage, Pythagoras at length returned to Greece from which he had been absent, it was said, for forty years, an unusually long period of initiation, but exactly answering to the length of time the Israelites spent wandering in the wilderness. His ministry began in Samos, but was not successful in his native land, and he departed thence to Croton in Italy. According to Porphyry, it was during this journey that he descended into the cave of Ida on the Island of Crete. Lévy is almost certainly right in interpreting this as a faded reminiscence of the *katabasis* or descent into Hades, which (when it figures in the myth of the magus in the middle of the hero's life) is always regarded

[1] Ibid. p. 75.

as part of his initiation into hidden knowledge, including instruction about the rewards and punishments in the after-life as described by Virgil in the *Aeneid*. Pythagoras underwent purifying rites before descending into the cave, spending a morning by the sea and a night by the river, wrapped in a black fleece. He then went down and remained away for twenty-seven days, executing rites in honour of Zeus and witnessing the annual ceremony of the throne raised to that deity. Diogenes Laertius was emphatic about the non-marvellous nature of this descent; saying that Pythagoras had claimed to have gone down to Hades, to have spent a year in the nether regions, and to have witnessed many marvels there; whereas in reality he had remained during the whole period in a cave, secretly supplied with news and necessaries by his mother. Echoes of this sceptical attitude are heard in Iamblichus' *Life*, when a hostile interlocutor taunted Pythagoras with making such claims; and proposed that, as he was about to descend into Hades, he should be the bearer of a letter to the speaker's dead father, from whom he would expect a reply. As this man had just been guilty of putting many people to death, Pythagoras retorted that he was not about to descend into the abode of the impious where he well knew that murderers were punished. All of which seems to show that Lévy is right in believing that the *katabasis* was a central feature of the original legend.

Continuing on his way after the episode on Mount Ida, Pythagoras miraculously foretold the exact number of a great draught of fishes brought to land, demanding for recompense that they should be put back into the sea, and compensating the fishermen for doing so. He then arrived in Croton where he held a series of public sermons which converted the inhabitants of the city to the doctrines he preached and the precepts he advocated. The transmigration of souls, pure sacrifices to the gods, a chaste life and ascetic practices were the most outstanding beliefs and virtues he advocated. So enthusiastic were the young men in particular that under his leadership they entered a secret society, in which all goods were held in common. The doctrines he inculcated in his disciples were esoteric, and the society itself was organised after the fashion followed by the secret societies of to-day. It is in fact the first of its kind of which detailed knowledge has been preserved. The postulants were put through severe tests of obedience, endurance and abstinence, closely watched by Pythagoras the while. If admitted probationers, they underwent a period of five years' silence, during which time they listened to the instructions of Pythagoras 'behind the veil', but were not allowed to see him. They then went through a further period of three years as 'esoterics' and were admitted into his presence. Should they be expelled from the society for any offence against it (the gravest of all was the communication of the secret doctrine to the profane), property twice the value of what they had brought into the society was given to them, and a tomb was erected to them in the society's precincts; for they were regarded as dead and were therefore not recognised by any of the members if met with in the world outside. A monastic, pious and frugal mode of life was observed by the community; and their arcane doctrines were kept

...with the greatest silence from being divulged to strangers, committing them unwritten to the memory, and transmitting them orally to their successors, as if they were the mysteries of the Gods.[1]

Moreover, a story told by Iamblichus of a dying Pythagorean shows that they recognised each other by secret signs and symbols and were in duty bound to come to each other's aid when such symbols were displayed.

The secrecy with which the doctrines were preserved is probably accountable for the fact that Pythagoreanism seems to have been a profound subterranean influence rather than a cult or a creed. The gospel traditionally attributed to him is one of great spirituality and purity; the immortality of the soul; rewards and punishments after death; the doctrine of transmigration; the emphasis on chastity; the adoring at altars undefiled by blood; the substitution of sacrificial victims by millet, cakes, honey and incense; the avoidance of all foods foreign to the gods 'because it withdraws us from familiarity with the gods';[2] the dislike of killing animals for food (for slaughtering leads to war and 'war is the leader and legislator of slaughter'[3]); the divination, not by the entrails of beasts, but by numbers; the contempt for worldly renown and wealth; the advocacy of gentleness and the condemnation of any kind of violence and excess; these are some of the tenets of a religion, which, assimilated into Orphism, profoundly affected Plato and also Christianity.

The teaching man-god Pythagoras, with whom this religion is associated, was said to have been involved in a life-and-death conflict

[1] Iamblichus, op. cit. p. 116.　　　　　　[2] Ibid. p. 57.
[3] Ibid. p. 98.

with a wicked opponent, the cruel tyrant Phalaris. When and how
Pythagoras fell into the power of Phalaris is not reported; but the
divine hero was captured, flung into prison and threatened with
death. The charge against him was that of wizardry, and although
Abaris appeared to defend him, things at one time looked so black
that both of them were in danger of their lives from the incensed
tyrant. But Pythagoras had divine foreknowledge that he was not to
die at the hands of Phalaris. Like 'Dionysos' in the *Bacchae* he
showed no fear; he spoke up bravely against tyranny, denied that
the gods were the cause of evil, blaming our misfortunes on human
intemperance, and philosophised firmly 'in the midst of dreadful
circumstances'.[1]

He performed however what is still more generous than this, by effecting
the dissolution of tyranny, restraining the tyrant when he was about to
bring the most deplorable calamities on mankind, and liberating Sicily from
the most cruel and imperious power....For on the very same day in
which Phalaris put Pythagoras and Abaris in danger of death he himself
was slain by stratagem.[2]

Although these two sentences are separated in the text, they seem to
be saying that Pythagoras was responsible for the stratagem that
liberated Sicily from the tyranny of Phalaris, as 'Dionysos' had
liberated Thebes from the tyranny of Pentheus. And indeed it is
impossible to read the mangled and muddled account of the conflict
described by Iamblichus without a vivid remembrance of the ghastly
events in the *Bacchae*. But Pythagoras, in line with the bias given
to his nature throughout, was not explicitly connected with the
assassination.

The victory over the man who called him a wizard was followed, as
so frequently happens in the lives of the magi, by catastrophe and
defeat. A wealthy and powerful Crotonian called Cylus, who had
not been admitted to the society, revenged himself upon the sect by
setting fire to the house of Milon where the Pythagoreans were
assembled, thus encompassing the death of the leader and forty
disciples. This second *magophonia* in story probably represents some
uprising against the sect accompanied by persecution, and figures in
all the Pythagorean legends; but the death of the leader in the
burning building was not generally accepted. The attack was said by

[1] Iamblichus, op. cit. p. 113.　　　　　　　[2] Ibid. p. 114.

many to have occurred during the absence of Pythagoras, who had left Croton for Metapontum in Sicily on account of the hostility of Cylus and was thought to have died there. Thus Iamblichus, with curious vagueness, finished the story of his hero's life. He probably hardly knew what to make of the conflicting accounts. Diogenes Laertius asserted that the hostility which had broken out in Croton followed Pythagoras to Metapontum. The philosopher took refuge in the Temple of the Muses; but he was besieged there, and died of hunger after forty days' starvation. Another version described him in full flight before his enemies, arriving at the margin of a flowering bean-field and refusing to cross it, because he would have crushed the souls it contained; whereupon he was done to death. There are also traces of a tradition by which he disappeared mysteriously in a narrow defile, was thought to have ascended to heaven and to have been seen again upon earth.

The complete version of the legend of Pythagoras includes a prenatal prophecy, divine origin, distant journeys, initiation, a *katabasis*, a victorious conflict, persecution and a violent or mysterious ending, to which an ascension and resurrection were probably added, to judge by the *Life of Apollonius of Tyana*. In fact the only features totally absent from the complete scheme of the myth of the magus are the perils during infancy and a last recorded scene. His doctrine of reincarnation vouches for some kind of reappearance; and the resemblance between his conflict with Phalaris and that in the *Bacchae* brings the ritual element in this legend very clearly before one's mind.

What is more, the miracles attributed to Pythagoras are in many cases gentler versions of the marvels reported of the Maenads in Euripides' drama, and they also resemble those of Orpheus. Pythagoras tamed a savage Daunian bear by whispering in its ear, compelling it to take an oath never to touch a living thing again; he charmed a white eagle soaring over Mount Olympus to come and perch on his hand, the while he gently stroked it; he caught and dismissed unharmed venomous and deadly serpents; he persuaded an ox to refrain from eating beans (symbols of the soul in transmigration); and he saved the fishes from dying on dry land whilst they were being counted, so that not a single one of them perished. These various anecdotes show a power over the brute creation, which, like the Dionysiac miracles, derived from sympathy; but which, unlike those marvels, had no fierce and ravening side. Nature acclaimed him in the person of the river Nessus who hailed him by name; and amongst his other powers were

> ...infallible predictions of earthquakes, rapid expulsions of pestilence and violent winds, instantaneous cessations of the effusion of hail, and a tranquillization of the waves of the rivers and seas, in order that his disciples might pass over them.[1]

The power over natural phenomena, claimed by the medicine-man, is here indicated; and Pythagoras' power over the minds of men was proved by the electrifying and enduring effects of his sermons at Croton. He also possessed the art of healing, using melodies and incantations against the passions of the soul and the sickness of the body; and he gave many proofs of his power to predict events. But the most signal of all his supernatural gifts was his knowledge of the lives of the soul. He remembered his own previous existence and those of others; he mentioned that he was Euphorbus who slew Patroclus, and that Myllias of Croton was King Midas; he recognised, or so a mocker said, a former friend incarnate in a dog. This startling, indeed, sensational, faculty had a long oriental history behind it; it was destined to survive throughout the ages down to our own times. And the theory of reincarnation on which it was based, and which was traditionally attributed to Pythagoras, not only seized upon contemporary imaginations, but has never been forgotten and is very much to the fore in the West again to-day. It has always been a tenet of the East; and from Eastern sources Pythagoras undoubtedly learnt it, if it is true that he was the first of the sages of Greece who proclaimed it in set terms. Herodotus recounts an interesting offshoot from it. He claimed that some of the strangest legends he had heard derived from a weird 'spectre-man' called Aristeas, who was said by others to be a Pythagorean. This man declared that his soul would leave his body whenever he wished and return to it when summoned back. His corpse was said to have vanished on one occasion after his death. He reappeared seven years later, wrote a poem, and then disappeared again. He was next seen two hundred and forty years afterwards in Metapontum. He also enjoyed the reputation of being a great traveller and a great healer. He left an indelible impression behind him and was resurrected under another

---

[1] Iamblichus, op. cit. p. 72.

name in modern times, which have also seen the revival of secret societies along Pythagorean lines.

It seems clear therefore that Pythagoras must be given a central position in any history, however sketchy, of the myth of the magus as it developed in the West. And indeed, since Greek thought has been the predominant influence in modern Europe, it can cause no surprise to anyone to find that a Greek model suggests itself in many cases of latter-day magicians' lives.

(b) Apollonius of Tyana

In Philostratus' *Life of Apollonius of Tyana*, the sinister elements of magic, so conspicuous in the *Bacchae*, have also been eliminated; and once more Apollo, and not Dionysos, controls the magical scene. The unruffled serenity of the man of Tyana is far removed from the mystic glory of Zoroaster, the spiritual intensity of Moses, the dazzling splendour of Solomon, and the dangerous power of 'Dionysos' In fact he represents in the history of magicians a striking example of something they rarely attained to: sophrosyne, or calmness of the soul, an Apolline victory over a Dionysiac force. It is for this reason, because he incorporates the Pythagorean traditions, that I place him before Christ, although Philostratus' biography is a work of the early third century A.D., and the hero lived in the first century of our era, if we are to allow (and it seems unnecessarily sceptical not to do so) that he ever lived at all. A figure combining holiness with civilised behaviour, humour with wisdom, fortitude with urbanity and humaneness under extreme provocation is not to be met with every day, and among magicians appears as fabulous as the unicorn. But such was Apollonius, a devout Pythagorean, preaching purity, asceticism, the barbarousness of blood sacrifices and the transmigration of souls in the Socratic manner, and exemplifying them by his mode of life; for he was indeed no ordinary mortal.

He was divinely begotten by Proteus, who announced his approaching nativity to the mother, telling her that she was about to bring Proteus himself to birth; and his actual coming was preceded by a dream, urging her to go out into a meadow and pick flowers. Here, surrounded by a circle of singing swans, she ushered the infant into the world; and a hovering thunderbolt was interpreted, not as a menace, but as an indication that the child would transcend

55

earthly things and approach the gods. Certainly no other perils, either secular or infernal, clouded the infancy of the sage. His initiation into the mysteries of Pythagoras began by a self-imposed silence lasting five years and was completed when he visited the Indian Brahmans and was made privy to their occult wisdom and magical lore. This is the farthest point eastwards to which the magi of antiquity were yet known for certain to have penetrated in search of knowledge, and the wisdom of Egypt is represented as definitely inferior to that of India in this biography, which adorns the tales of Apollonius' wanderings with those fantastic mythological details of a geographical kind in which the Greeks delighted, and of which Aeschylus gave such a wonderful example in *Prometheus*. Apollonius was a great wanderer; seeking and then spreading truth, he journeyed through Babylonia, India, Egypt, Greece, Sicily and Italy. Like Pythagoras before him, he descended into a cave whose other name was Hades. Going down into the abode of the god Trophonius in Lebadea 'in the interest of philosophy' (although the priests, who regarded him as a wizard, attempted to hinder him), he wrapped himself in his philosophical mantle and disappeared with the question on his lips: 'What, O Trophonius, do you consider the most complete and purest philosophy?'[1] He emerged miraculously at Aulis seven days later, bearing the answer of the god, a volume of the tenets of Pythagoras.

His death was highly mysterious. According to one account, he entered the temple of Athene at Lindus and was never seen again. A more circumstantial version represented him as vanishing from Dictynna in Crete at dead of night. He had been denied entry to the temple by the priests, and had even been thrown into bonds; for they believed that he was a robber with designs on the treasure, and also a wizard, because the fierce watch-dogs of the precincts fawned upon him. But Apollonius loosened his bonds, and calling out to his gaolers, he ran to the temple doors, which opened to receive him and closed again behind him. A chorus of girls' voices was heard singing: 'Hasten thou from earth, hasten thou to heaven, hasten.'[2] Some time after this translation, he reappeared upon earth to preach the doctrine of the immortality of the soul to a doubting

---

[1] Philostratus, *Life of Apollonius of Tyana*, tr. Conybeare, Loeb Classics, London 1917, II, p. 383.
[2] Ibid. II, p. 401.

PLATE II

Apollonius of Tyana

youth and completely converted him. Vopiscus, in his *Life of Aurelian*, also relates that this emperor was dissuaded from razing the city of Tyana to the ground by the appearance of Apollonius, whom he recognised from his statues, and who charged him to abstain from shedding the blood of the innocent.

The *agon* or contest is a twofold one in Apollonius' life, as it was in the life of Solomon. To begin with there is an almost continuous series of arguments, ending in the victory of Apollonius, or rather of the doctrines of Pythagoras. For this purpose the sage had his disciple and supposed first biographer Damis always at hand; and this possibly fictitious adherent was used along with other characters in the book as antagonists in the arguments, which came to a head in the full-dress dispute between Apollonius and the gymnosophists of Egypt, who were worsted by Brahmanical doctrines. The Socratic method is particularly in evidence in the conversations with Damis, who is often trapped into making foolish remarks in order that his preceptor may preach the Pythagorean creed. Philostratus, although an agreeable and at times a skilful narrator, was no Plato; and it does not do to remember the *Dialogues* when listening to Apollonius' discourses on the art of painting or flute-playing, the behaviour of elephants and kindred topics. But when serious ethical questions were broached, his nobility of mind became manifest.

As he approached the image of the Colossus, Damis asked him if he thought anything could be greater than that; and he replied: 'Yes, a man who loves wisdom in a sound and innocent spirit.'[1]

'Look not on that which is laid by as wealth—for how is it better than so much sand drifted no matter from whence...for gold lacks lustre and is mere dross, if it be wrung from men's tears....'[2]

'For I have studied profoundly the problem of the rise of the art (philosophy) and whence it draws its first principles; and I have realised that it belongs to men of transcendent religious gifts, who have thoroughly investigated the nature of the soul, the well-springs of whose existence lie back in the immortal and in the unbegotten.'[3]

'In all my actions I have had at heart the salvation of mankind.'[4].

The culminating debate or argument was the contention between Egyptian wisdom, represented by the gymnosophists, and the Brahmanical lore into which Apollonius had been initiated, another

[1] Ibid. I, p. 509.
[2] Ibid. I, p. 553.
[3] Ibid. II, p. 43.
[4] Ibid. II, p. 325.

form of the conquest of a new kind of religion over an old, for Indian thought was less familiar to the Greeks than Egyptian wisdom at that time. It was, however, skilfully interwoven with the main conflict, to which it was incidental. This was with a malignant professional rival called Euphrates, who envied the man of Tyana and resolved to destroy him after being worsted by Apollonius in an attempt to gain the favour of Vespasian. A resourceful intriguer, he went about blackening the philosopher's reputation, and he it was who embroiled him with the powerful gymnosophists. However, Apollonius succeeded in establishing tolerable relations with them after the contest, something in the nature of an armed neutrality. A much worse ordeal was now in store for him. He had already in the past undergone a trial at Rome at the hands of Tigellinus on a charge of impiety against Nero, but had inspired such terror in Tigellinus, who recognised him for a god, that he had been released. But the accusation now brought against the sage by Euphrates was a much graver one. He lodged information to the effect that Apollonius had conspired with Nerva against the Emperor Domitian, and had mutilated an Arcadian boy in order to divine the date of Nerva's accession to the throne by an examination of the victim's entrails. This gravest of charges, high treason reinforced by black magic, was tantamount to the death sentence; and Apollonius was warned by his friend Democritus to keep away from Rome at all costs. But this seemed unworthy to the philosopher, who preferred to stand his trial and prove his innocence. Thrown into prison and evilly treated, he was finally brought before Domitian in a threatening and ominous manner; but his personality had something of the same effect on the emperor which it had had on Tigellinus, and shows affinity too with the change wrought in Pentheus by 'Dionysos'.

And when he came to the fourth question which related to Nerva and his friends, instead of hurrying straight on to it, he allowed a certain interval to elapse, and after long reflection, and with the air of one who felt dizzy, he put his question in a way which surprised them all; for...he beat about the bush....[1]

Apollonius answered resolutely, calling for trustworthy witnesses to the charge, aroused loud applause in court, and was acquitted by the emperor, who feebly added that he must remain in Rome for a private interview with him.

[1] Philostratus, op. cit. II, p. 281.

Thereat Apollonius was much encouraged and said: 'I thank you indeed, my sovereign, but I would fain tell you that by reason of these miscreants your cities are in ruin, and the islands full of exiles, and the mainland of lamentations, and your armies of cowardice, and the senate of suspicion. Accord me also, if you will, opportunity to speak; but if not, then send someone to take my body, for my soul you cannot take. Nay, you cannot take even my body, "For thou shalt not slay me, since I tell thee I am not mortal."' And with these words he vanished from the court....[1]

And not only did he quit the court 'in a manner so godlike and inexplicable'[2] as to astound that assembly, but, leaving it before midday, he appeared miraculously at dusk to Demetrius and Damis at Dicaearchia, where he had a hard task in persuading them that he was not a ghost.

Spectacular though this triumph was, it seems less remarkable to-day than the written defence which Apollonius had prepared, but was not called upon to give. This contains some eloquent passages, imbued at times with pathos, particularly at the point when he proved his innocence of the charge of black magic by establishing an alibi.

I never sacrificed blood, I do not sacrifice it now, I never touch it, not even if it be shed upon the altar....What then...was I really doing on that night?...Philiscus of Melos, who was my fellow-pupil in philosophy for four years, was ill at the time; and I was sleeping out at his house, because he was suffering so terribly that he died of his disease. Ah, many are the charms I would have prayed to obtain, if they could have saved his life. Fain would I have known of any melodies of Orpheus, if any there are, to bring back the dead to us. Nay I verily think I would have made a pilgrimage even to the nether world for his sake, if such things were feasible.... With how little regard then for the truth this accusation has been drawn up, is clearly proved by the testimony of these gentlemen; for it appears that it was not in the suburbs, but in the city, not outside the wall, but inside a house, not with Nerva, but with Philiscus, not slaying another, but praying for a man's life, not thinking of matters of State, but of philosophy, not choosing a revolutionist to supplant yourself, but trying to save a man like myself.[3]

Throughout this defence, Apollonius claimed that he was inspired and assisted by the gods, and finally declared that he was not mortal; but the passage I have just quoted seems to deny the possibility of a descent into the nether world, and also the resurrection of the dead,

---

[1] Ibid. II, p. 283 (the quotation is from the *Iliad*, XXII, 13).
[2] Ibid. II, p. 357. [3] Ibid. II, pp. 317 ff.

both of which feats were reported of him in other parts of the biography. This very lengthy document may therefore belong to an earlier period than the *Life*, and may possibly be genuine. The accusation of black magic, which dogged Apollonius throughout his life and beyond, is a stock charge against all wonder-workers; few of them escape it wholly; and the avowed aim of Philostratus' biography was to clear his hero's name on this score; yet to a modern mind it seems strange that the most high-minded and humane of the whole tribe should have been specially singled out for such condemnation, whereas Moses never had to face it at all. The contamination of the water supply, the blighting of crops, the murrain on the cattle, the boils and blains on the Egyptians, storms and hails, and the slaughter of the first-born; these miracles directed against the bitter enemies of the Israelites might pardonably strike the latter as white magic; but Apollonius, on a higher level of civilisation, would never have subscribed to that view, as is evident in that portion of his defence in which he dealt with the plague he had averted in Ephesus.

Let us suppose that among the Scythians or Celts, who live along the rivers Ister and Rhine, a city has been founded every whit as important as Ephesus in Ionia. Here you have a sally-port of barbarians, who refuse to be subject to yourself; let us then suppose that it was about to be destroyed by a pestilence, and that Apollonius found a remedy and averted it. I imagine that a wise man would be able to defend himself even against such a charge as that, unless indeed the sovereign desires to get rid of his adversaries, not by the use of arms, but by plague; for I pray, my prince, that no city may ever be wholly wiped out, either to please yourself or to please me, nor may I ever behold in temples a disease to which those who lie sick should succumb in them.[1]

This is the *leitmotiv* of all the miracles he is said to have performed; they were markedly philanthropic. He was no longer in that intimate connection with crops and herds manifest in the legends of Zoroaster, Moses and Dionysos. The magical banquets of the Brahmans and their magical cups and automatic cup-bearers already show (as do similar tales told of Solomon) the transformation from reality to romance which the primitive sorcerer's supposed effect on the food supply underwent as human prosperity came to be measured in terms of gold instead of the fruits of the earth. Already Empedocles

[1] Philostratus, op. cit. II, pp. 317 ff.

boasted of the boundless wealth his magic arts could procure; and Solomon outdid all other magicians in this respect. The man of Tyana (like Pythagoras) despised riches; but he knew where they were to be found. Medicine-man and gold-diviner melt together in the following tale. Touched to the heart by the sad plight of a father who had four daughters to endow, he persuaded him to sink his modest capital in the purchase of a little olive grove with a garden and beehives attached to it. The olive trees repaid the venture by yielding an unusually large crop, though they failed signally elsewhere that particular season. So far the medicine-man; but a hidden treasure was also discovered in the ground, so that the father had it both ways, owing to the ineradicable benevolence of Apollonius.

This second Pythagoras, or teaching man-god, was a very remarkable healer and exorcist. The detection and averting of the plague of Ephesus (attributed by his enemies to sorcery) naturally caused a sensation; for the sage, recognising the demon of the pestilence under the disguise of a blind old beggar, persuaded the inhabitants to stone him to death, and by these drastic means rid the city of an ugly visitation. Ritual stonings and scourgings to avert disease derive from the practice of witch-doctors; whereas his raising of the dead points back to Elijah, Elisha and Empedocles. The tale is told with caution, perhaps in order to harmonise it with Apollonius' attitude in his defence. The girl he brought back to life had died in the very hour of her marriage. Philostratus suggests that perhaps she was in a trance, and that Apollonius, detecting this, revived her by the touch of his hand and the sound of his voice. It was, however, a seemingly miraculous cure. In the company of the Brahmans he healed a demoniac boy by means of a letter addressed to the spirit in possession, containing threats of an alarming nature (obviously a written charm); he also cured a lame man, a blind man, a paralytic, and a woman suffering in labour. This last miracle was effected by a species of imitative magic redolent of the age.

> He bade the man, whenever his wife should be about to bring forth her next child, to enter her chamber carrying in his bosom a live hare; then he was to walk once round her and at the same moment to release the hare....[1]

He healed a youth bitten by a mad dog and cast a demon out of a young man who had an evil reputation for licentiousness, but who

[1] Ibid. I, p. 319.

was not suspected of possession until Apollonius detected the presence of the evil spirit.

Now when Apollonius gazed on him, the ghost in him began to utter cries of fear and rage, such as one hears from people who are being branded or racked; and the ghost swore that he would leave the young man alone and never take possession of any man again. But Apollonius addressed him with anger, as a master might a shifty, rascally and shameless slave and so on, and he ordered him to quit the young man and show by a visible sign that he had done so. 'I will throw down yonder statue', said the devil, and pointed to one of the images which were in the king's portico, for there it was that the scene took place. But when the statue began by moving gently, and then fell down, it would defy anyone to describe the hubbub which arose thereat and the way they clapped their hands with wonder. But the young man rubbed his eyes as if he had just woke up, and he... modelled his life in future upon that of Apollonius.[1]

He routed a hobgoblin, tamed a mischievous satyr, exposed and defeated a beautiful vampire preying upon his disciple Menippus; so that his control of the spirits was marked. He also summoned up Achilles from the shades in order to converse with him about the Trojan War. Disdaining earlier methods, he dug no trench in which to collect the blood of a sacrifice shed in order to attract the departed shade. He merely offered up a prayer to Achilles after the fashion taught him by the Brahmans, and the great hero came.

He had also the gift of prevision, foreseeing many things that were to come to pass, and actually visualising the assassination of Domitian at the moment when it was taking place many leagues beyond the sea. Here again the charge that his mantic powers were due to sorcery had to be answered by Philostratus:

Wizards, whom for my part I reckon to be the most unfortunate of mankind, claim to alter the course of destiny by having recourse either to the torture of phantoms or to barbaric sacrifices, or to certain incantations or anointings....But Apollonius submitted himself to the decrees of the Fates, and only foretold that things must come to pass; and his foreknowledge was gained not by wizardry, but from what the gods revealed to him.[2]

Apollonius himself spoke in this way about prophecy:

For the gods perceive what lies in the future, and men what is going on before them, and wise men what is approaching.[3]

[1] Philostratus, op. cit. I, pp. 391 ff.
[2] Ibid. I, p. 489. Conybeare translates εἴδωλον by 'lost spirit', which seems to me unnecessary.   [3] Ibid. II, p. 323.

He remembered in great detail his former existence as the pilot of an Egyptian ship and recognised Amasis King of Egypt in a tame lion, led about like a dog, and urged that suitable honour should be shown to him.

Only the perils at infancy are absent from the legend of Apollonius of Tyana. Otherwise it is complete. He had also all the gifts of the practical magicians; power over the minds and bodies of men, the control of nature, although very slightly marked; mantic gifts of a high degree; spirit control, including the power to summon up the shades of the dead. He aimed, as he stated, at the welfare, not of any single tribe, community or country, but at the spiritual regeneration of mankind; and the strong ethical bias of Philostratus' biography never lets the reader lose sight of the main issue, however many marvels occur incidentally. It is small wonder, therefore, that he lived on in men's minds as a great example and was worshipped as a god, and natural enough that Hierocles in the early fourth century A.D. should have used him for anti-Christian polemics; declaring Christ to be at least no greater a sage, no more remarkable a worker of miracles and no more potent an exorcist than the man of Tyana. Philostratus himself had obviously had no such purpose in writing the *Life*, and indeed gives the impression that he was entirely ignorant of the Gospels. His purpose was to defend his hero against the charge of wizardry. On that charge the Christian apologist Eusebius now seized in his answer to Hierocles; and (a second Euphrates) began to blacken the sage's character, as well as making savage fun of him. He treated him as a mixture of charlatan and wizard in league with an evil spirit who acted as his familiar, and by whose diabolic agency he exorcised demons. He could do no less as a champion of Christianity in the last and bitterest stages of its struggle against paganism, whereas at least one earlier writer of the Christian persuasion betrayed a more open mind:

If God is the creator, and lord of created things, how is it that the talismans of Apollonius have power over parts of creation? For they restrain, as we see, the violence of the sea and the force of the winds and the attacks of vermin and wild beasts.[1]

[1] Pseudo-Justin, *Questions and Answers for the Orthodox*, alleged to have been written A.D. 150, but probably later. This is question 24, quoted by R. Gleadow, *Magic and Divination*, London 1941, p. 72.

Eusebius, infuriated by the comparison with Christ, had no difficulty in answering this question. It was all due to the blackest of black magic. Yet the reputation of Apollonius survived this onslaught; and the Greek wonder-worker was still a thorn in the flesh of the Catholics in 1625 when Naudé wrote his defence of all great men falsely accused of magic. Far from clearing Apollonius of this charge, as he did for all the other characters in his book, he concentrated his efforts on making a fool of him, threw doubt on his existence and treated him harshly as a mere second-rate imitation of Christ. In the course of this philippic, he enumerated all the parallels he found in the two stories, thereby making some resemblances much more striking than they actually are, but keeping silent on the subject of divine origin. He instanced as proofs of slavish imitation:

1. The annunciation.
2. The singing swans and the herald angels.
3. The thunderbolt and the star of Bethlehem.
4. Royal letters of homage to Apollonius and the adoration of the magi.
5. Apollonius' youthful discourse in the Temple of Aesculapius and Christ in the Temple.
6. The questions put to Apollonius by Damis and other disciples and those Christ's disciples put to him.
7. The intervention made by Apollonius on behalf of an unhappy eunuch, and the woman taken in adultery.
8. A phantom seen by Apollonius on Mount Caucasus and the Temptation.
9. The incredulity of the Ephesians and that of the Jews.
10. The casting out of demons.
11. The girl resurrected by Apollonius and Jairus' daughter.
12. Apollonius' unexpected appearance to Damis and Demetrius after the trial and Christ at Emmaus.
13. The ascension of Apollonius and that of Elijah and Enoch.

Like the omission of the divine origin, the ascension of Christ was probably not mentioned because the juxtaposition of ideas seemed too blasphemous to Naudé; but it is odd that the trial scenes should also have been left out in favour of some very far-fetched parallels. This misleading list would certainly convince anyone who did not know the book that Philostratus had plagiarised from the Gospels. As it is, the only episode that might give that impression to an unbiased mind is the conversation between Apollonius and Demetrius and Damis, when these friends believed him to be a phantom on his miraculous reappearance after the trial.

Whereupon Apollonius stretched out his hand and said: 'Take hold of me, and if I evade you, then I am indeed a ghost come to you from the realm of Persephone, such as the gods of the underworld reveal to those who are dejected with much mourning. But if I resist your touch, then you shall persuade Damis also that I am both alive and that I have not abandoned my body.' They were no longer able to disbelieve, but rose up and threw themselves on his neck and kissed him, and asked him about his defence.[1]

But otherwise the undoubted parallels between the two stories are more satisfactorily explained by their origin in a common tradition about all religious wonder-workers, the kind of miracles they performed and the events which befell them. Apollonius was certainly modelled on Pythagoras and Socrates; but Philostratus' debt to the Gospels seems altogether illusory. Only analysis reveals the resemblance; and analysis lays bare the essential similarity between all the tales of magicians, whenever, wherever and however told.

[1] Philostratus, op. cit. II, p. 261.

CHAPTER IV

THE DOWNFALL OF THE MAGUS

(a) Christ

The downfall of the magus when antiquity waned was directly due to the appearance of Christ. When the old gods fell, they dragged their mortal or half-mortal representatives, the prophets, priests and magicians down with them into obscurity and exile. Apart from the religious reasons for this collapse, it would also seem that the story of the Gospels was too well told not to discourage, or at least outshine, any subsequent imitations. Both as god-man and as the hero of a mystery tale, Christ represented a limit beyond which human imagination could not go in developing the magus-legend. The mould was shattered by the content and only fragments remained. Very slowly too, but none the less surely, the welter of mystery religions and individual cults was absorbed into the dominant one or went underground. The religious scene from the death of Christ to the dawn of the Middle Ages in Europe is not unlike the Punjab, the 'land of five rivers': all rising in the same way, all following a natural course, one flowing into the other, and the other into the next, until all at last unite to form that mighty stream of many waters which bears the name of Indus.

Although the life of Christ as recounted in the Gospels is too familiar to need detailed repetition, it is convenient to enumerate the stock legendary features which it contains: the divine origin and miraculous birth; the annunciation and nativity portents; the menace to the hero during his infancy; the initiation by John the Baptist, in which traces of an *agon* may linger, since the Baptist acknowledged Christ to be greater than he, in much the same way as Abaris made obeisance to Pythagoras. But the real contest was with Satan, in which the old god-magician was worsted in a trial of spiritual strength. This, like Zoroaster's, took the form of a temptation, the bait being worldly might and power. It was triumphantly withstood, and had been preceded, again like Zoroaster's, by a prolonged and solitary fast. The interesting and seemingly symbolical feature of this temptation was Christ's refusal to perform works of magic in order to prove his divinity. It was almost like a prophecy that there was to be no more magic allowed, and certainly a statement that magic was devilish. And yet Christ practised it, for his miracles do not differ from the similar and sometimes identical feats of his predecessors and successors. The last supper or sacrament is a wonderful sublimation of the sacrificial feasts, in which the saviour-god was eaten, or represented as eaten, by his worshippers; and the trial and crucifixion, with the ritual mockery, buffetings and scourgings, derive from similar practices. The disappearance of the body from the tomb was a feature of the legends about Aristeas; the descent into hell (first mentioned in Ephesians), the resurrection and ascension also followed ritual precedent. In fact the canonical life of Christ seems to be blending history and ritual in somewhat the same way as Euripides' *Bacchae*, and reads almost like a mystery drama transposed into epic form; whereas the life of Apollonius of Tyana is more like a historical novel. It is also the fullest extant ritual life we possess. The distant journey is represented by the flight to Egypt and also by the wanderings in Palestine during the period of the ministry.

Apart from the doctrine preached, the story thus simply and shatteringly told, with nothing wild, fantastic or incredible in its method of presentation, was destined to have the lasting effect which it produced, because of its emphasis on the tragic and terrible end. Mysterious and violent deaths had been a constant feature of magical legend; but here the actual tragedy of the dying god is depicted in a sober, telling and unforgettable way; and Christ is represented throughout as 'a man of sorrows and acquainted with grief'; this humanising of what in the legends of Osiris and Dionysos had been divine mysteries made a reality of the sacrifice which staggered the whole world. Moreover, the actual hero of what was to become a great mythological religion seems to have been a most extraordinary and compelling person:

The Prophet of Nazareth did not differ in temperament and character from the noble prophets of the ancient period. He preached, as they did, the religion of the heart; he attacked, as they did, the ceremonial laws; he offered, as they did, consolation to the poor; he poured forth, as they did, invectives against the rulers and the rich....If we regard Jesus only in his relations with those whose brief and bitter lives he purified from evil and illumined with ideal joys, we might believe him to have been the perfect type of a meek and suffering saint. But his character had two sides, and we must look at both.... Jesus was not able to display the spirit of a persecutor in his deeds, but he displayed it in his words. Believing that it was in his power to condemn his fellow-creatures to eternal torture, he did so condemn by anticipation all the rich and almost all the learned men among the Jews.[1]

This dualism in the great prophet seems to have coloured the later accounts of his infancy; and altogether the apocryphal writings about Christ are extremely instructive, since they show the mythopoeic process, begun in the Gospels, continuing under its own steam. In the Book of James or Protevangelium, the miraculous birth of the Virgin Mary and her early life in the temple push the supernatural origin of the coming god farther back, as was also done for Zoroaster. Her miraculous conception, the doubts of Joseph, the annunciation by Gabriel and the miracles accompanying Christ's birth are then recounted, and several new features added to those already circulated by the Gospels. All creation paused during the moment when the child was ushered into the world

...and behold a bright cloud overshadowing the cave.... And immediately the cloud withdrew itself out of the cave, and a great light appeared in the cave so that our eyes could not endure it. And by little and little that light withdrew itself until the young child appeared: and it went and took the breast of its mother Mary.[2]

The similarity with the Glory of Zoroaster is striking; and the miracle of healing produced by the touch of the newborn child was also reported of Moses; but the author of the Gospel of Thomas, who elaborated the childhood of Christ into a heroic saga, gave a rather unexpected turn to the developing legend. It has many details in common with tales about other godlings, but it outshines them all, because the writer seems to have known a good deal about children, and also to have observed certain characteristics in the adult hero of the Gospels. The obstreperous child depicted by 'Thomas' behaves exactly as any high-spirited and abnormally gifted little boy would behave; but, as the bystanders noted with horror and learnt to their dismay, his words became deeds, and all those died who moved him to wrath. The turbulence of the infants Krishna, Heracles, and

[1] Winwood Reade, *The Martyrdom of Man*, pp. 176ff.
[2] *The Apocryphal New Testament*, tr. James, Oxford 1926, p. 46.

Siegfried was nothing to this; and he has earned the opprobrious title of 'supernatural little bully'. Supernatural powers and a child's mentality would however result in just such conduct, as the tales told of that infant prodigy and *enfant terrible*, Helena Petrovna Blavatsky, go far to prove.

There is a mixture of childish make-believe and magical lore in the games he was said to play: making sparrows out of clay and giving them the power of flight; irrigating the land by causing streams to run into pools, probably with serious intent, for when a playmate tried to interfere, Jesus withered him. And well he might, since the land would suffer sadly if wizards did not act upon the water supply; but where most children would have to be content with a withering look, this child could kill outright. He made a terrifying ringleader too, sliding along a sunbeam as if it were the easiest thing in the world. Following in his wake, the other children all fell down and hurt themselves, though he kindly made them whole again. Not so the pitchers which they hung on sunbeams in imitation of his; those were smashed beyond repair. His was not; and even if it had been, it would have earned him no rebukes at home; for when he once broke a jar on his way to the well, he carried the water back in his cloak instead, much the same miracle as Rama's mother Renuka performed daily, according to Hindu legend. Utterly different from his associates, he naturally would stand no nonsense from them, killing without scruple any of his comrades who attacked him, and blinding those adult fools who thereupon accused him of murder; but he was perfectly ready to restore their sight as soon as they repented. With such formidable powers as these, he acquired an evil reputation, and sometimes was blamed for disasters in which he had had no hand. On one occasion a child was pushed or fell from the roof of a two-storeyed house and was killed on the spot. Jesus was erroneously accused of being responsible for the catastrophe. The godling, full of injured innocence, jumped down from the roof and set about resuscitating the victim, so that he might testify in his favour. He made the lives of his pastors and masters a misery to them, because he was so much cleverer than they were, and took full advantage of it; but he was an invaluable member of the family, performing prodigies of reaping and sowing, a gift which the Russian hero Ilya of Murom inherited. A baby Samson or an infant Heracles for strength, he could pull a wooden beam to the length required by his father Joseph; and he cured his brother James of the snake bite, a miracle also performed by Krishna in his childhood. It was chiefly when he was with the other children that his high spirits got the better of him. They seem to have lived under a reign of terror, and fled from him once to hide in a cave or cellar. The women sitting outside tried to prevent Christ from finding them, by declaring that only goats had gone in; whereupon on Christ's command, a flock of goats came leaping out. At the entreaty of the terrified women, he changed them back again into human form 'and from that day the children were not able to flee from Jesus'.[1]

It hardly seems fair, but then magic is the very reverse of justice; and it was lucky for all concerned that, although quick to wrath and to smite, there was no abiding vindictiveness in the child. He was always healing and restoring to life those whom he had injured and slain, as well as the victims of accidents; and when he had inadvertently ruined the garments sent to a dyer by plunging them all into a black vat, it only needed his mother's intercession to make him undo the mischief and bring them out of the inky solution one by one whatever hue the dyer named. This last tale illustrates the essentially childish nature of all his pranks, however mischievous. The miracles of killing and resurrecting represent a child's dream of omnipotence. Anything done could be undone in a trice if the spirit so moved him. This infantile notion of the immunity of the immortals is in the nursery tradition, and the saga of the apocryphal Christ-child has the fascination of psychological consistency. Even so would a baby demi-god behave at the dictates of his untutored whims, if a god could in fact ever be a baby. Moreover 'Thomas', whether consciously or not, was showing the child as father to the man who now and again is glimpsed in the Gospels. Impatience of maternal control; irrational fury with a fig-tree for not bearing fruit out of season, finding vent in a withering curse; bitter abuse of his enemies who were all to be damned in hell; the outburst of rage and physical violence against the money-lenders in the temple; they all remind one of that unregenerate child who could not bear to be thwarted. But the radiance of the godling sliding down a sunbeam has waned.

The ministry of Christ received few additions in the Apocrypha. But a Coptic fragment expanded by a significant item the tale

[1] *The Apocryphal New Testament*, p. 68.

of the conflict between the hero and Satan. The devil challenged his rival by casting nets and hooks in the wilderness, boasting the while:

> It is not a wonder to catch fish in the waters; the wonder is in this desert, to catch fish there.[1]

Although successful at first, this effort of the rival magician to outdo Christ's miraculous draught of fishes (and his haul of souls) ended in disaster for the adversary. When commanded to repeat the performance, he agreed, and was thereupon surrounded by a great cloud of smoke and his power disappeared.

The story of the passion inevitably attracted the mythologists who were embellishing the Gospel narratives; and the trial scenes in particular were greatly expanded. In the Acts of Pilate the trial was given pride of place over the crucifixion, was adorned with many attendant miracles and imbued with a strongly anti-Semitic character, naturally resulting in a tendency to whitewash Pontius Pilate. The chief charges brought by the Jews against the Messiah included the profanation of the sabbath, the claim to be the Son of God, the accusation that he was born of fornication, and that he was a sorcerer to whom all the devils were subject, so that he cast out demons by Beelzebub, their chief. This stock charge of black magic against wonder-workers had been reported in the Gospels, although not at the trial; it could hardly fail to make its appearance in a full-length dramatic scene, written to inspire hatred against Christ's accusers and also to repel hostile rumours and put the divinity of the hero beyond the shadow of a doubt. This latter aim also informs the detailed description of the resurrection by so-called eye-witnesses, who testify to attempts made by the Jews to prove that the body had been merely smuggled away. The efforts to counter sceptical and rationalistic explanations of the miracle, already apparent in the Gospels, were energetically redoubled in the apocryphal passion tales. They are not particularly convincing.

Conviction on the subject of the crucifixion of Christ is a much easier matter; for the bitter cry in the Gospel of Peter: 'My power, *my* power, thou hast forsaken me'[2] sounds like a great wave breaking from the sea of legend on to the shore of life. It is even more charged with emotional truth than the heart-broken canonical lament, and

[1] Ibid. p. 149.   [2] Ibid. p. 91.

someone surely must have uttered it; for no writer, even if a writer of genius, could ever have invented that.

A totally different impression is received from the Acts of Pilate and the Gospel of Bartholomew which describe the descent into hell. Here literature has clearly taken a hand in shaping legend. It is an extremely exciting and stirring episode with its dramatic movement: the rejoicings of the prophets as they become aware of the approach of the redeemer; the terror of hell and Satan, their panic-stricken conference, their futile efforts to resist; the glorious shout ringing out after all those ages from the Psalms of David:

And again there was a cry without: Lift up, ye princes, your gates, and be ye lift up, ye everlasting doors, and the King of glory shall come in. And again at that clear voice Hell and Satan inquired, saying: Who is this King of glory? and it was said unto them by that marvellous voice: The Lord of hosts, he is the King of glory. And lo, suddenly Hell did quake....[1]

It was no mean poet who imagined that scene, and distributed David's verses between Christ and the infernal powers; no ordinary mind which described the entry into paradise of the thief with his cross. But it was a poet, and not a chronicler of events, who saw and emphasised the symbolical significance of the tree of the cross vanquishing Satan's tree of transgression and knowledge. This is the most memorable metamorphosis undergone by the vegetation spirit descending and returning again. The legend of Orpheus and Eurydice is more beautiful; but the *katabasis* of Christ is unparalleled for grandeur.

The temptation of Zoroaster; the contests between Moses and Pharaoh and 'Dionysos' and Pentheus; the splendour of Solomon; the purity of Pythagoras, the defence of Apollonius, the crucifixion and the *katabasis* of Christ; these outstanding features of ancient legends justify the title given to this part of the book: 'The Golden Age of Magic'; and may reconcile those who feel offended at finding Christ among the magians of old. For magic in those days partook of the nature of the divine. All the great gods were magicians; and all the great magicians were believed to be divinely inspired. The Christ of the Apocrypha and of the Gospels was no exception to this rule.

The apocryphal feats of sowing and reaping, the canonical miracles of the loaves and fishes, the supernormal draught of fishes,

[1] *The Apocryphal New Testament*, pp. 133 ff.; *Acts of Pilate*.

the incident of the fig-tree and the transformation of water into wine show the same relationship to the food supply of the tribe which obtained among primitive peoples and haunted the legends of magicians, lawgivers and gods. In close connection with this is the power over the elements, described by Empedocles as part of the influence over the crops; but shrunk to mere miracles of display in the Christ-child's Promethean might over fire, and the later quelling of the winds and the waves and passing over the waters. The connection with the medicine-man of old is even closer. As a child he blinded, withered and slew all those who annoyed him; but was equally quick to restore them to health and life again if properly appealed to. As a man he cured lunatics, paralytics, lepers, the dumb, the blind, the withered, the woman with the issue of blood and those afflicted with demoniacal possession. His method varied between exorcism proper and faith healing; and the raising of the dead, done both in youth and manhood, followed well-established Hebrew precedents. The coin found by his direction in the fish's mouth, like the hidden treasure divined by Apollonius, is an indication that in the future gold rather than plentiful crops would be demanded of magicians. He saw his own end approaching; but he was finally proved to be wrong on the larger question of the end of the world. Necromancy proper, or divining by means of the dead, is the only function of the normal magician's stock-in-trade which he did not exercise. But in raising Moses and Elijah at his transfiguration, he used the actual gifts for purposes of magical display; and the liberation of the shades of the righteous from Hades blends necromancy with Orphic legend and apocalyptic dreams. His power over the minds of men is signal indeed, since it has lasted two thousand years and is not broken yet. And one of the instances of that power is the decline of the conception of many roads to truth, and of many gods and magi as signposts along the roads.

(b) Simon Magus

The story of Simon Magus is the first fully developed legend of the fortunes and fate of the black magician, that is to say of the adversary of the conquering daimon of the rites, who now enters the scene as the hero-villain of the action. Both Moses and 'Dionysos', as we have seen, practised a sinister form of magic; but both of them were on the winning side, justified and triumphant. Not so the unfortunate Simon, round whose legendary figure all the darker notions about magic are concentrated and luridly illuminated by the vivid imaginations of early Christian heresiologists. Reputed to be the founder of Gnosticism, he was mythologised into the first and arch-heretic, guilty therefore of the spiritual sin against the Holy Ghost for which there is no forgiveness. He was violently attacked in much the same way as Apollonius of Tyana. That is to say he was abused for being both a charlatan and a diabolist. The inconsistency in this double accusation is only apparent. For the Father of Lies was thought to work very largely through delusions, and indeed to be capable of little else in the shape of miracles. Although none of the feats claimed by Simon could be mentioned in the same breath for frightfulness with those of Moses, his crime, like that of Solomon, inspired superstitious horror; and his name became anathema because he set himself up against Christ.

Divine origin, shading off into divinity, had been claimed or implied for most of the great magicians of the past. Simon lagged not at all behind his predecessors, asserting that he was the transcendent god of the Gnostic cosmos, or at other times the redeemer. For Gnosticism, like Zoroastrianism, from which it derived, was founded on the principle of dualism.

It followed from that hypothesis (1) that matter was intrinsically evil— a lower world standing over against that higher one into which the soul sought to escape; (2) that the soul was native to the higher world, and had fallen from it, previously to its conscious existence, as the result of some cosmical disaster; (3) that the soul could be restored only by a Divine intervention, since its progress was hopelessly barred by its imprisonment in matter. The ideas which thus presented themselves to Gnostic speculation were set forth and elaborated in terms of mythus. It was assumed that man's spiritual nature was derived from a Divine being, who had fallen out of the world of light into the world of darkness. The process of deliverance involved, in the first place, the restoration of this fallen being, and the restoration could not be effected except by the voluntary descent of another Divine being, equal or superior in rank. Around these two beings—the fallen Divinity and the Redeemer—the Gnostic mythus in all its variations may be said to turn...the commingling of the higher principle with the lower evolves a cosmos out of chaos. As the agent of creation, Gnosticism assumes a *Demiourgos*, who...governs the world created by him in the belief that he himself is the Supreme God....A singular feature of

Gnosticism is the identification of this inferior God with the God of the Old Testament. . . . He was not . . . identified with Satan, but he was clothed with inferior attributes and limited to the one task of blind creation.[1]

The main symbolism, which the evolvers of the Simon-legend parodied into the myth of Simon and Helen, appears to have been sidereal; thus the Logos and his Thought, the World-soul, were symbolized as the Sun (Simon) and Moon (Selene, Helen); so with the microcosm, Helen was the human soul fallen into matter and Simon the mind which brings about her redemption.[2]

This is the mythical background against which Simon Magus was made to play his legendary and lamentable part. His claim to be the redeemer laid him open of course to the charge of blasphemy; and since this man of straw was contending with an all-powerful adversary (as history has proved), it was inevitable that his lifeline, drawn on the traditional pattern, should be the negative of the positive picture, white being shown as black, and black appearing as white.

Simon Magus is reported to have learnt magic in Egypt, and to have been initiated into the sect of Dositheus, which comprised twenty-nine male disciples and the woman Helena. Dositheus, it was said, claimed to be a manifestation of the Standing One or supreme principle of pre-Simonian and Simonian Gnosis. Simon entered into a magical contest for leadership with Dositheus and won it. When the latter attempted to smite the rebel with his rod, it passed through his body as if it had been smoke. Whereupon Dositheus acknowledged Simon to be the Standing One, resigned the leadership to him and shortly after died. But the real conflict was still to be engaged. According to the story told in Acts, Simon the Sorcerer was worshipped as a god in Samaria, but found his miracles outshone by those of Philip. This so much impressed the native magician that he believed and was baptised. He was then still further amazed when he witnessed how the Holy Ghost was given to the people by the laying on of hands. Very foolishly he offered money in order to purchase this power. He was righteously rebuked by Peter, swallowed the rebuff and appeared repentant for his sin. But the

---

[1] Hastings, *Encyclopaedia of Religion and Ethics*, VI, article 'Gnosticism', pp. 236–7.

[2] G. R. S. Mead, *Fragments of a Faith Forgotten*, London 1900, p. 168. Another name for the fallen Aeon or Power was Sophia.

heresy hunters could not be satisfied with so tame an ending for the supposed founder of Gnosticism whose dangerous tenets had been partially adopted by Saint Paul; indeed Baur and his followers, struck by the remarkable similarity between the doctrinal aspects of the Petro-Simonian and Petro-Pauline controversies, regard Simon Magus as a mere legendary symbol for Paul. But if this is true of the origin of the story, the symbol came to life; and, fictitious as Simon Magus almost certainly is, he lives intensely in his legend. His was a nature, as described in the Apocrypha and by pseudo-Clement, too vainglorious to be content with playing second fiddle to any man alive in matters of magic. The tension and tautness of a spirit frenziedly striving above and beyond itself vibrate discordantly in the hostile accounts of his doings and sayings, producing a poignant kind of pity, the reverse of the effect intended. Gradually one begins to side with the sorcerer whose fame was transformed into infamy whenever he came up against Peter, for the latter was always at his heels convicting him to the beholders. It was a long and wearing struggle, full of vicissitudes of an increasingly disastrous nature. Simon's nerve began to fail him; and well it might, when even his own dog testified against him, and a seven months' babe was endowed with a man's voice for the same purpose. In a panic, he threw his magical books into the sea, lest Peter should get hold of them and convict him of sorcery, and betook himself hot-foot to Rome, whose emperor and citizens still believed in his divinity, and would surely protect him against his implacable adversary.

Peter was behind him, accompanied by his one-time enemy and present friend Paul; and the luckless Simon was now called upon to undergo publicly the nerve-racking business of upholding his prestige before Nero, who sent for the two rivals to have it out before him. Peter proposed a very simple test, that Simon Magus should read his thoughts and tell him what he had just said to Nero and what had been done as the result.

Nero said: Do you mean me to believe that Simon does not know these things, who both raised a dead man, and presented himself on the third day after he had been beheaded, and who has done whatever he said he would do? Peter said: But he did not do it before me.[1]

This was the crux of the matter, and inevitably recalls the diagnosis

[1] P. M. Palmer and R. P. More, *Sources of the Faust Tradition*, New York 1936, pp. 30 ff.; quoting from the *Acts of the Holy Apostles Peter and Paul*.

made by the soothsayer in respect of the relationship between
Antony and Caesar:

> Thy demon, that's thy spirit which keeps thee, is
> Noble, courageous, high, unmatchable,
> Where Caesar's is not; but, near him, thy angel
> Becomes a fear, as being o'erpower'd: therefore
> Make space enough between you.[1]

It was this intimate knowledge that his power evaporated in Peter's
presence which made Simon hedge now, and fling the challenge
back, thus contributing to yet another of his rival's triumphs. It was
a cheap triumph; for, as Simon had just threatened to send his angels
to avenge himself on Peter, the latter knew what to expect, and had
prepared himself for the emergency. Beside himself with rage,
Simon cried out:

Let great dogs come forth and eat him up before Caesar. And suddenly
there appeared great dogs, and rushed at Peter. But Peter, stretching forth
his hands to pray, showed to the dogs the loaf which he had blessed; which
the dogs seeing, no longer appeared. Then Peter said to Nero: Behold, I
have shown thee that I knew what Simon was thinking of, not by words,
but by deeds; for he, having promised that he would bring angels against
me, has brought dogs, in order that he might show that he had not god like
but dog-like angels.[2]

In this parlous situation, Simon staked his all on a power or a trick
which had already made him famous. He stated that on the next day
he would ascend into heaven; and he evidently hoped to fly away
and disappear as he had done more than once in the past. Nero,
nothing loth, ordered a lofty tower to be raised in the Campus
Martius and all the people and dignitaries to be present at the
spectacle:

Then Simon went up upon the tower in the face of all, and crowned with
laurels, he stretched forth his hands, and began to fly. And when Nero saw
him flying, he said to Peter: This Simon is true; but thou and Paul are
deceivers. To whom Peter said: Immediately shalt thou know that we are
true disciples of Christ; but that he is not Christ, but a magician, and a
malefactor. Nero said: Do you still persist? Behold, you see him going up
into heaven...and Peter, looking stedfastly against Simon, said: I adjure
you, ye angels of Satan, who are carrying him into the air, to deceive the
hearts of the unbelievers, by the God that created all things, and by Jesus

---

[1] Shakespeare, *Antony and Cleopatra*, Act II, Scene iii.
[2] Palmer and More, op. cit. p. 31; quoting from the same source.

Christ, whom on the third day He raised from the dead, no longer from this hour to keep him up, but to let him go. And immediately, being let go, he fell into a place called Sacra Via, that is, Holy Way, and was divided into four parts, having perished by an evil fate.[1]

The thwarted ascension of this Icarian-minded magician is a transparent piece of propaganda against magic as distinct from miracles. Philostratus tried to draw a dividing line between them, but the early Christian fathers had an infallible test: marvels produced in the name of Christ were divine, any others diabolic; the first were called miracles, the second magic. Christ refused to perform magic when tempted to do so by the devil: Simon Magus constantly asserted that he was not a magician, but the Son of God. His downfall symbolises the fall from eminence of a whole caste. The act of ascension or apotheosis ceased from then onwards to play an integral part in the lives of magicians. It lost its ritual significance and its dramatic function as the climax of an action, and dwindled into one of the many feats sorcerers were expected to perform. Solomon's magic carpet was the medieval substitute for the ancient theophany. Magic steeds, magic cloaks, witches' broomsticks, pantomime fairies are all faded reminiscences of the days when heroes, demi-gods and prophets were caught up to heaven, and when sages vanished away in temples or from lofty mountain heights. The great classical age of magic was rung to its grave when Simon Magus fell into the Holy Way and perished there.

The abortive ascension had been preceded by a faked resurrection, brought about by a magical trick. Simon bewitched a ram to assume his countenance until it had been beheaded 'in a dark place'; the executioner then became aware of the imposture, but dared not report it to Nero, who was naturally astounded when Simon reappeared after three days, having, it would seem, made good his claim to be no magician, but the Son of God. The substitution of the ram may have been suggested by the story of Abraham and Isaac, which has been plausibly interpreted as a symbol for the change from human to animal sacrifice. Simon's seemingly miraculous feat was to have endless repercussions. It would be in the highest degree unwise to state of any legendary or traditional anecdote that it occurs

---

[1] Palmer and More, op. cit. pp. 33 ff. In the *Acts of Peter* Simon is represented as breaking his leg in three places, and dying later; cf. *The Apocryphal New Testament*, pp. 331 ff.

PLATE III

The Death of Simon Magus. By Benozzo Gozzoli

anywhere for the first time; and spurious deaths, amongst which decapitation may well have figured, were a constant feature of ritual. But this is the earliest instance I know of in which a magician appears to die by decapitation and is then made whole again. A passage in Philostratus' *Life of Apollonius of Tyana* seems to be referring to such a phenomenon, when a hostile tribune proposed to the sage that he should submit himself to the ordeal of decapitation in order that his claims to divinity might be proved or disproved. It was rumoured in Islamic tradition that a Jew called Batruni once beheaded a man and then put him together again by one stroke of his sword; thirteenth-century magicians in Europe were frequently credited with performing this marvel; and by the sixteenth century, if not earlier, what Reginald Scot called the Decollation of John the Baptist had become a well-known juggler's trick. It may have had its inception in this story about Simon Magus, in which magic and imposture were combined. It certainly marked a turning-point in the legendary lives of magicians. In the future their resurrection, like their ascension, dwindled to a sporadically appearing feat.

Before analysing the list of marvels ascribed to or claimed by Simon Magus, it should be emphasised that both in the apocryphal writings and in the Clementine documents, the marvels which the magician was able to perform were tacitly attributed to the power of deluding men's minds, a power which always forsook him when one of the apostles appeared.

For in dining-chambers he made certain spirits enter in which were only an appearance and not existing in truth...he made lame men seem whole for a little space, and blind likewise, and once he appeared to make many dead to live and move, as he did with Nicostratus. But Peter followed him throughout and convicted him always unto the beholders.[1]

Then Simon reluctantly drew near to the dead person; and they set down the bier before him; and he looked to the right hand and to the left, and gazed up into heaven, saying many words: some of them he uttered aloud, and some of them secretly and not aloud. And he delayed a long while, and nothing took place, and nothing was done, and the dead person was (still) lying upon his bier. And forthwith Simon Cephas drew near boldly....And as soon as the word of Simon was spoken, the dead man came to life and rose up from his bier.[2]

[1] *The Apocryphal New Testament*, p. 331; *Acts of Peter*.
[2] Palmer and More, op. cit. pp. 34 ff.; *Acts of the Holy Apostles Peter and Paul*.

As the anti-Simonian writings were so largely aimed against magic, the marvels reported of Simon Magus probably represent the kind of claims which the apostles had to contend with from the many wonder-workers in their midst. The arch-magician certainly possessed great power over the minds of men, since he was acclaimed as a god. Moreover, miracles of healing were attributed to him, and also the raising of the dead. The spirits too were believed to be obedient to him, although they were wicked spirits. He boasted himself that he could turn stones to bread, cause trees and sprouts to grow, bear leaf and produce fruit in a moment of time; that he could command a sickle to reap, and it would cut ten times more than any other. Clearly therefore the blood of the primitive medicine-man had been inoculated into his veins. It will be noticed that this wicked magician did not scruple to perform one of the miracles suggested to Christ by Satan. He also bragged that he could perform the other, and fling himself uninjured from lofty summits. He further possessed the gift of invisibility, of flight and of transformation in a very high degree. He could change both himself and others into any shape or form he chose. He was immune from fire, could burst through prison bars and bonds, pass through rocks as if they were clay and bore his way through mountains. Or so he frantically boasted, and many enemies testified to his powers of transformation. He further claimed that he could animate statues, making them laugh and dance, and he had caused a brazen serpent to move. There were already rumours of such gifts about. The Brahmans visited by Apollonius had robot cup-bearers; but the Greek sage, although he praised these and similar marvels, disclaimed any wish to imitate them; Solomon's throne came to be equipped by the legend makers with animated and speaking metal images of men, beasts and birds of all kinds; the works of Daedalus, the statue of Memnon, the oracular heads of antiquity, and Prometheus' living men of clay, were probably familiar to the Middle Ages; but the claim of Simon Magus seems to have directed the attention of medieval magicians and legend writers towards the construction of automata. This creative aspect of their functions had hardly figured at all in the lives of the ancient magi; in fact the Christ-child's sparrows are the first definite sign of it, for Solomon's throne was a later addition. But the moving statues are by no means the most important of the creative innovations of Simon Magus.

Doctrinally speaking he played, as has become evident, the part of Antichrist, that is to say, of the Gnostic redeemer, come to free the souls of men, saying among other things:

There is no resurrection of the flesh, but that of the spirit *only*: and that the body of man is not the creation of God; and also concerning the world, that God did not create it, and that God knoweth not the world, and that Jesus Christ was not crucified, but it was an *appearance* (i.e. but only in appearance), and that he was not born of Mary, nor of the seed of David.[1]

The God in this passage is the transcendent God of the Gnostic cosmos; and it followed logically from this that the soul of man was superior to the being who had created the world.

I would have you know this, that the soul of man holds the next place after God, when once it is set free from the darkness of his body. And immediately it acquires prescience: wherefore it is invoked in necromancy....[2]

A soul that had never owned a human body would, however, be even more potent than a departed and purified soul for magical operations, and Simon maintained:

I have...made the soul of a boy, unsullied and violently slain, and invoked by unutterable adjurations to assist me; and by it all is done that I command.... I, by my power, turning air into water, and water again into blood and solidifying it into flesh, formed a new human creature— a boy—and produced a much nobler work than God the Creator. For He created a man from the earth, but I from the air—a far more difficult matter; and again I unmade him and restored him to air, but not until I had placed his picture and image in my bedchamber, as a proof and memorial of my work.[3]

The characteristically Gnostic twist introduced by Simon Magus into the art of necromancy, the fashioning of a purer soul than belongs to normal mortals, derived from the critical attitude felt by the Gnostics towards God the Creator. The belief, also held by Paul, that matter is inherently evil naturally led to speculations about the nature of the deity who had created it, resulting in his assignment to a low place in the celestial hierarchy. It also increased to fever pitch that dissatisfaction with humanity as such, and the desire to ameliorate it which is such a constant feature of all developing religions.

[1] *The Apocryphal New Testament*, p. 288; *Acts of Paul.*
[2] Palmer and More, op. cit. p. 16; *Clementine Recognitions.*
[3] Ibid. p. 18.

Simon's attempted rectification by means of a being composed of purer elements was made in the interests of magic, and particularly of foreknowledge. It seems to have been the starting point for the ceaseless endeavours of medieval magicians and natural philosophers to produce living organisms without resorting to procreation. Paul, also deprecating sexual intercourse, paved the way for monasticism. The medieval alchemists for their part were aiming at discovering the secrets of nature; and some of them believed that this could be accomplished by hatching out in the laboratory male and female *homunculi* from human blood.[1] Astoundingly intricate experiments of this nature were advocated if not undertaken by ingenious, learned and disordered minds. Paracelsus was one of them. And the hope behind such venturers was the never-abandoned, ever-deluded hope to attain to foreknowledge.

Another aspect of Gnosticism apparent in the legends about Simon was his association with the woman called Helen, the fallen divinity also known as Sophia.

And Thought was made prisoner by the Powers and Angels that had been emanated by her. And she suffered every kind of indignity at their hands, to prevent her reascending to her Father, even to being imprisoned in the human body.... So she, transmigrating from body to body, and thereby also continually undergoing indignity, last of all even stood for hire in a brothel; and she was the 'lost sheep'.[2]

This myth accounts for the sneers of Simon's enemies, who said that the woman was a common prostitute from Tyre. But there was a more poetical conception of her too:

...brought down from the higher heavens.... Wisdom, the mother of all things, for whom...the Greeks and barbarians contending, were able in some measure to see an image of her; but of herself, as she is, as the dweller with the first and only God, they were totally ignorant.[3]

Although all that is known of this shadowy companion is that she was once seen by a great number of people simultaneously to lean forward and look through all the windows of a tower at the same moment, the fact that she was called Helen as well as Luna and

[1] J. Scheible, *Das Kloster*, Stuttgart 1845ff., III, pp. 524ff. prints in *Magia Divina* an account of this process.
[2] Mead, *Fragments of a Faith Forgotten*, p. 169.
[3] Palmer and More, op. cit. p. 15; *Clementine Recognitions*.

Selene, and was identified by the Clementine Simon with Helen of Troy, sheds the waning glory of Greek mythology round the figure of the unhappy heretic who gave his name to the sin of simony, set himself up against Christ and came to such a pitiable end. If he was the first of a long line of wicked magicians to contend unsuccessfully with the pale Galilean, he was also the first, and for a very long time the last, to honour a symbol of beauty only darkly understood.

Part II. THE DARK AGES

CHAPTER I

UNDER THE CHRISTIAN CLOUD

(a) Cyprian

During the age of Christ, of his apostles, and of their first disciples, the doctrine which they preached was confirmed by innumerable prodigies. The lame walked, the blind saw, the sick were healed, the dead were raised, daemons were expelled, and the laws of Nature were frequently suspended for the benefit of the church.[1]

If we pass from the Fathers into the Middle Ages, we find ourselves in an atmosphere that was dense and charged with the supernatural. The demand for miracles was almost boundless, and the supply was equal to the demand. Men of extraordinary sanctity seemed naturally and habitually to obtain the power of performing them, and their lives are crowded with their achievements, which were attested by the highest sanction of the Church. Nothing could be more common than for a holy man to be lifted up from the floor in the midst of his devotions, or to be visited by the Virgin or by an angel. There was scarcely a town that could not show some relic that had cured the sick, or some image that had opened and shut its eyes, or bowed its head to an earnest worshipper. It was somewhat more extraordinary, but not in the least incredible, that the fish should have thronged to the shore to hear St Anthony preach, or that it should be necessary to cut the hair of the crucifix at Burgas once a month, or that the Virgin of the Pillar, at Saragossa, should, at the prayer of one of her worshippers, have restored a leg that had been amputated. Men who were afflicted with apparently hopeless disease, started in a moment into perfect health when brought into contact with a relic of Christ or the Virgin.... Glorious visions heralded their discovery, and angels have transported them through the air. If a missionary went abroad among the heathen, supernatural signs confounded his opponents, and made the powers of darkness fly before his steps. If a Christian prince unsheathed his sword in an ecclesiastical cause, apostles had been known to combat with his army, and avenging miracles to scatter his enemies.[2]

[1] E. Gibbon, *The Decline and Fall of the Roman Empire*, ed. Bury, London 1897, I, pp. 69 ff.
[2] W. E. H. Lecky, *History of the Rise and Influence of the Spirit of Rationalism in Europe*, London 1865, I, pp. 153 f.

This cloud of witnesses to the supernatural power vested in the Church is the cloud under which mere magicians feebly strove to exist. Mythology, hardening into theology, cracked under the strain irrevocably into angelology and demonology, with their human counterparts, the saints and the sinners of the early and medieval Christian Church. These stereotyped figures in the conflict between good and evil were almost indistinguishable from the battleground trampled over by the contending forces, always with the same result; whilst marvels became so excessively cheap as to be hardly worth performing. How could a sorcerer hope to cut any kind of figure in a world where hosts of holy persons could, without the smallest effort, beat him at his own game? The only course open to him was the one Simon Magus had tried to adopt, to creep into the bosom of the Church.

Among the throng of repentant sinners attaining to sainthood who crowd the pages of *The Golden Legend*, St Cyprian and St Justina were outstandingly popular in legend from the fourth to the fifteenth centuries; and although I can see little or no justification for regarding Cyprian as in any special way a forerunner of the sixteenth-century Faust, still the state in which his legend is found shows earlier conceptions clinging to it, and also illustrates the rapidity of the descent from Simon Magus downwards; for, though Calderón was later to set the seal of his genius on the man whom he called the marvellous magician, that was not exactly the light in which he was originally regarded.

It is true that lip-service was paid to his magical powers before his conversion, but only to make the latter more striking, and to show that Cyprian of Antioch (who almost certainly never lived outside the pages of story) was a signal prize for the Church. Early initiated into the mystery religions of Apollo, Mithras, Demeter and Dionysos, he was also widely travelled, and had studied magic in Egypt and among the Chaldaeans. *The Golden Legend* interpreted his initiations as an act of consecration to the devil, made by his parents when he was seven years old. He was reputed to be a master of the elements, of demonology, and of prophecy, and could raise infernal spirits. He could transform himself and others into birds and beasts, was an adept at necromancy; and, as the slaughter of victims and the cutting open of pregnant women were attributed to him, he evidently practised nigromancy, too. A prayer for rain, fathered upon him after his conversion, is a link in the chain between the medicine-man and the Christian priest.

A man so powerful would therefore readily undertake the commission entrusted to him by his friend Acladius (Aglaidas), to soften the heart of the virgin Justina whose hand he was seeking in marriage. But Justina was a convert to Christianity and had embraced the life of chastity. This gave her such superhuman power that she had, after making the sign of the cross, beaten her suitor black and blue, like her model, the virginal Thekla. Supernatural aid was obviously indicated, and Cyprian invoked it, first in his friend's interest, and later in his own. He summoned up a demon, put the case before him, and was assured of speedy success.

I became an apostate from God [the evil spirit boasted] in obedience to my father; I threw the heavens into confusion; I cast down angels from on high; I deceived Eve; I deprived Adam of the delights of Paradise; I taught Cain to murder his brother; I stained the earth with blood; I caused thorns and thistles to grow; I assembled theatres; I caused adulteries; I taught the people to make a calf; I prompted the crucifixion of Christ; I made cities to tremble; I tore down walls; I divided houses. Having done these things, how can I be powerless against her? Take, therefore, this philtre and besprinkle the house of the maid from without and I will go and instill in her the spirit of my father and straightway she will give ear unto thee.[1]

But he was reckoning without his host, and so was Cyprian, 'not knowing, poor wretch, that the power of Christ is insuperable'.[2] The maiden countered by voluble prayers as well as the sign of the cross all the wiles and machinations and sophistries of one demon after the other, finally overcoming even the prince of them all. *The Golden Legend* attempted to give some dramatic interest to this foregone conclusion by the sufferings which not only Justina but all Antioch were then called upon to endure.

And then by the sufferance of God she was vexed with axes and fevers. And the devil slew many men and beasts and made to be said by them that were demoniacs that a right great mortality should be throughout all Antioch, but if Justina would consent wedlock and have Cyprian. Wherefore all they that were sick and languishing in maladies lay at the gate of Justina's father and friends, crying that they should marry her and deliver

---

[1] Palmer and More, *The Sources of the Faust Tradition*, pp. 45 ff.; quoting from the Greek version of *The Conversion of St Justina and St Cyprian*.
[2] Ibid. p. 45.

the city of the right great peril. Justina then would not consent in no wise, and therefore everybody menaced her. And in the sixth year of that mortality she prayed for them, and chased and drove thence all that pestilence.[1]

It seems a pity, in view of the number of dead, that she did not offer up her prayers at the beginning of the plague. The desperate assumption by Cyprian and Acladius of female or even ornithological form in order to get near Justina was of course doomed to failure, as was also the devil's forlorn attempt to beguile Cyprian into the belief that he had prevailed over the virgin by appearing to the frenzied lover in her guise. As soon as Cyprian uttered the name of the maiden, the would-be succubus vanished like smoke. Finally it came to a show-down between the magician and the fiend.

Deeply ashamed, the demon appeared before Cyprian. Cyprian says to him: 'Thou wast conquered by one girl. What power is the source of her victory?' The demon says: 'I cannot tell thee, for I saw a sign and I trembled with fear. Wherefore also I withdrew. If thou wilt know, swear to me and I will tell thee.' Cyprian said: 'How shall I swear to thee?' The demon said: 'By the great powers which abide in me.' Cyprian says: 'By thy great powers, I will not depart from thee.' The demon, taking courage, says: 'I saw the sign of the crucified One and I trembled with fear.' Then Cyprian says: 'Is the crucified One then greater than thou?' The demon says: 'He is greater than all. For whatsoever mistakes we make or whatsoever things we bring to pass here we shall receive our reward in the world to come. For there is a brazen fork and it is heated and placed on the neck of the sinner, whether angel or man; and thus with the hissing of fire the angels of the crucified One lead him to the tribunal and render unto each according to his works.' Cyprian says: 'Therefore I will also make haste to become a friend of the crucified One in order that I may not be subjected to such condemnation.' The demon says: 'Thou hast sworn to me and breakest thou thine oath?' Cyprian says: 'I despise thee and fear not thy powers.'[2]

He was thereupon converted, burnt his books on magic, and, according to some accounts, he and Justina rose high in holiness and ended, he as a bishop, she as the mother of a convent; according to other versions, both were persecuted, tortured and finally beheaded as Christians.

[1] Palmer and More, op. cit. p. 55; quoting from Caxton's translation of *The Golden Legend*.
[2] Ibid. p. 49; *Conversion of St Justina and St Cyprian*.

But even with the mass-produced martyr's crowns upon their heads, they are not exactly edifying figures. Cyprian was too clearly aware on which side his spiritual bread was buttered to arouse much admiration when he brusquely broke with the fiend after swearing allegiance to him. Moreover, blotting out what was meant to be a cosmic conflict and disfiguring the foreground is a mere vulgar seduction story with its inevitable accompaniment of love-philtres. Tragic implications give way to love-interest, that King Charles' Head of Western European literature; and love-interest into the bargain blighted and blemished by Pauline notions of chastity:

And the devil said to her: What is that then that God commanded when he said: Grow and multiply and replenish the earth? Then, fair sister, I doubt that if we abide in virginity that we shall make the word of God vain.... [1]

(b) Theophilus

Diminished in glory though the magus appears in the rather dreary incarnation of Cyprian, still the hero was a magician wielding the traditional powers. But even this distinction was denied to Theophilus of Adana, whose legend captivated the imagination of all Christendom from the sixth to the sixteenth centuries; and, like that of Cyprian, was recounted in most of the European tongues, finding its way inevitably into *The Golden Legend*. Its most famous literary expression was in Ruteboeuf's dramatic mystery of the thirteenth century. The hero, a worthy but spineless steward of the Church, brought an evil fate upon himself by refusing the offer of a bishopric when it was earnestly pressed upon him; and thereupon found himself oppressed and persecuted by the man chosen in his stead, who actually deprived him of his stewardship. Theophilus at first bore this injustice with resignation and fortitude; but he was not great enough for the calamity which had befallen him; bitterness invaded his soul, bitterness and self-pity. In this clouded state of mind he betook himself to

...a certain wicked Jew, a practicer of all sorts of diabolic arts, who had already plunged many into the deep pit of perdition by his unchristian counsels. [2]

---

[1] Ibid. p. 54; *The Golden Legend*.
[2] Ibid. p. 62; *A Miracle of the Virgin Mary concerning Theophilus the Penitent*, by Eutychianus.

For at this period all sorcerers were held to be Jews; and, worse still, all Jews were suspected of sorcery. Fearful tales (offshoots of the poisoned tree of anti-Semitism), were told of their wholesale slaughter of Christian babes, whose blood was used in horrible rites. These or similar atrocities had previously been circulated by the pagans about the Christians—one of the many ways by which hostility to an alien cult finds its ugly vent. The 'detestable Jew' agreed to help Theophilus, warning him not to be frightened at anything he might see or hear, and on no account to make the sign of the cross. He then conducted him in the middle of the night to the Circus of the city and

...showed him suddenly creatures clad in white robes, with a multitude of candlesticks, uttering loud cries, and, seated in their midst, the prince. It was the devil and his minions. The hapless Jew, holding the steward by the hand, led him to this infamous assembly. And the devil said to him: 'Why hast thou brought this man to us?' He replied: 'My master, I have brought him because he has been falsely judged by his bishop and has asked for thy help.' The devil then said: 'How shall I give help to him, a man serving his God? But if he will be my servant and be counted among our hosts, I will aid him so that he may do more than before and rule over all, even the bishop.' And the perverted Jew said to the wretched steward: 'Didst thou hear what he hath said to thee?' And he replied: 'I have heard and whatsoever he shall say to me, I will do so long as he helps me.' And he began to kiss the feet of the prince and to implore him. The devil said to the Jew: 'Let him deny the son of Mary and those things which are offensive to me, and let him set down in writing that he denieth absolutely, and whatsoever he may desire he shall obtain from me, so long as he denieth.' Then Satan entered into the steward and he replied: 'I deny Christ and His mother.' And making a written statement and putting wax on it, he sealed it with his own ring, and the two went away rejoicing greatly at his perdition.[1]

There followed a succession of events not very difficult to foresee. By satanic agency, Theophilus was reinstated in his former office, and promotion above and beyond his previous dignities followed thick and fast. But fear of hell fire now began to gnaw at what by courtesy might be called his conscience, and he broke out into piteous, lachrymose and lengthy laments in which remorse and terror were almost equally mixed. So loud was his clamour that it attracted the attention of the Virgin Mary. Although wrathful at first when

[1] Palmer and More, op. cit. pp. 62 ff. As early as Ruteboeuf's drama, the pact was signed with Theophilus' blood.

she heard what he had done, she was not obdurate. After several colloquies, in which she put the genuineness of his repentance to the test, she obtained divine forgiveness for him, and the miraculous restoration of the pact. Theophilus thereupon made a public confession of his hideous sin before the bishop and the whole congregation; the pact was burned, and the sinner made an edifying end three days later in the place where he had seen the visions of the Virgin.

Meanwhile the real magician, the execrable Jew, came to a bad end, for he was tried and condemned; but his fate was only of minor importance. Sunk to the status of a pariah, he had also shrunk to the proportion of a mere go-between and was not the hero of the story. The Theophilus legend represents the ancient magus at the nadir of his career. If Cyprian had already been shorn of divine origin and sanction, the Jew had not even a proper name nor a single miracle to his credit. The traces of the original tradition which remain hover round Theophilus, who was not a magician at any period of his chequered career. The initiation was the sinister act of homage to Satan. The desperate dialogues with the Virgin Mary, in which he implored and finally obtained her mediation, are a weak and undramatic form of that ultimate trial before some court of appeal which few, if any, magicians escape. And the last scene, a pendant to Cyprian's martyrdom, took the form of a confession, followed by the solemnisation of the mass and the transfiguration of the countenance of the penitent. But the conflict or contest, the great wrestling match with a rival in pretensions whom the hero overcomes, was not really fought out by Theophilus. It was a tussle for his soul, in which Satan and God were the protagonists. Dimly one sees him, crouching in the portico of the Church, overshadowed by the wings of Apollyon, then irradiated by the glory of the Virgin, and completely dwarfed by both.

And yet, paradoxical though it may sound, medieval magicians would have been lost without Theophilus, who was not a magician at all. For he brought back the coherence of dramatic action into their rapidly disintegrating lives. The situation into which he blundered and from which he was extracted by Mary became the stock situation in magic: a battle royal waged between demons and sorcerers round the infernal pact. The ancient practitioners evoked and controlled spirits and were often reputed to be in league with them; the idea of a blood-bond with spirits had already made its appearance in Jewish magical literature before the birth of Christ. Cyprian, however, although he had an alliance with Satan, was able to repudiate it with impunity, by simply breaking his given word. The notion of a formal bond with the devil, admitted by St Augustine and other Fathers of the Church, crept into legend with the tale of a certain Proterius delivered from the consequences of such a pact by St Basil in the reign of Julian the Apostate. It swept all before it, once the legend of Theophilus had taken root. A written pact, renouncing Christianity for services to be rendered at the price of the signatory's soul and signed with his blood, became as indispensable a part of the sorcerer's equipment as the book, the wand, and the circle. It gave rise to innumerable situations, to an unending series of variations upon the one pregnant theme. The wiles of the devil to obtain the bond in its proper 'legal' form; his wicked sophistries about the time and the place when it was to fall due; the guile exerted by his adversary to leave a loop-hole he might wriggle through; the frantic efforts to get possession of the document before his time was up; the frequent successful intervention of a *deus* or *dea ex machina* on his behalf; the rites prescribed for the making and the unmaking of this unholy deed; copies of specimens; the inevitable absorption of the notion into the parallel stream of witchcraft and the disorders, not to say havoc, it created there;—all this is a story in itself, profusely illustrated by many a dismal or hair-raising occurrence in the life-histories of those medieval magicians who attained to legendary fame.

(c) Gerbert

The scandalous legends about nigromantic popes were in the main products of the late fourteenth and fifteenth centuries, and originated in schismatic circles; much capital was later made of them by Lutheran writers. They point to the gradual loss of spiritual prestige of the Roman Catholic Church, but are not otherwise very interesting in themselves. Benno, a schismatic cardinal, who seems to have been the worst traducer, declared that there were eighteen black popes in unbroken diabolic succession from John XII (965–972) to Gregory VII (1073–1085). Others were added later, including of course Pope Joan; and Alexander VI (1492–1503) was generally

PLATE IV

The Miracle of Theophilus

believed to have outdone all the others in wickedness. Bartholomew Platina, assistant librarian of the Vatican, gave the weight of his authority to many of the legends in his *Opus in Vitas Summorum Pontificum*, 1479, and altogether the belief obtained wide credence in the sixteenth century, an obvious sign of the times. The tales told about Gerbert who became Sylvester II (999–1003) derived from a different stratum of ideas, however, for some of them were recounted by William of Malmesbury (1095–1142). Two things came together to earn for this pope the reputation of sorcery. In the first place he was evidently an unusually gifted and learned man, and in the second he was believed to have studied in Spain, either in Toledo or Cordova; and Spain, under the Saracens or Moors, was at that time the heir to the wisdom and magic of the East.

Among those infidels, acknowledged past-masters of the art, there was one, in whose house Gerbert lodged, who possessed a book of magic unrivalled for the power it communicated to subdue the devil to its master's will. Gerbert resolved to obtain this treasure, but the Arabian philosopher refused to part with it, and hid it away at night under his pillow. Gerbert discovered this hiding-place by making love to the Saracen's beautiful daughter. It was then a simple matter to make his host drunk, steal the book and take to flight. But the magician followed him, and, deeply versed in astrology, was able to discover Gerbert's whereabouts either on earth or in the water by consulting the stars. The fugitive thereupon baffled him by suspending himself for some time under a bridge in such a manner that he touched neither earth nor water, and finally arrived safely on the coast. Hastily opening the book, he called up the arch-fiend by means of its powerful incantations, and the spirit carried him safely to the opposite shore. From that moment there was no looking back for Gerbert. He had worsted his powerful rival and now set his heart on the papacy. For this purpose he signed his soul away to Satan, and was rewarded by becoming pope. Raised to power and shockingly abusing it, Sylvester II was naturally anxious to know how long he would live to enjoy the sweets of office. The answer was on the face of it reassuring in the extreme. As long as he abstained from celebrating high mass in Jerusalem, he had nothing to fear. Forewarned was forearmed. Sylvester II had little difficulty in passing a self-denying ordinance on the subject of visiting the Holy Land, and gave himself up whole-heartedly to a wicked and luxurious life. But he who would sup with the devil needs a long spoon. Dispensing the sacrament in an unfamiliar church in Rome, the wicked pope felt his strength rapidly ebbing and also realised that he was surrounded by demons on all sides. On hearing that the name of the church was the Holy Cross of Jerusalem, he knew that he had been tricked and that his hour was at hand. The shock broke him. There and then he made an open confession of his guilt, and uttered the most solemn and touching warnings against commerce with evil spirits. He then commanded that his body should be hacked to pieces, and that after his death it should be placed upon a bier of green wood drawn by two virgin horses, one white and the other black. The horses were to be left to go wherever they would, and the spot at which they halted should be chosen as his burial-ground. Great must have been the sensation when this strange funeral procession drew up at the Lateran church; greater still the terror when loud cries and groans were heard proceeding from the coffin. Then a deathly silence fell, and Sylvester II was laid to rest in the Lateran. But rest is not the right word for his perturbed spirit, which was doomed to a banshee post-mortem existence. His tomb wept regularly at the approaching downfall of every pope, and his bones shook and rattled whenever one of them was about to die. Yet it seems unlikely that he was really damned to all eternity as everyone assumed. For it was presumably under divine guidance that the horses brought his mortal remains to consecrated ground.

The real Gerbert, of whom this dreadful tale came to be told, appears to have been eminent as a philosopher and mathematician. Outstanding gifts, with their aura of the abnormal or the supernatural, had almost automatically been attributed to magic as far back as one can think. But now that the golden age of magic was over, a sinister interpretation clung round the notion: learning and science were suspect arts. Gerbert was believed to have carnal intercourse with the devil, and to be accompanied by a familiar spirit in the form of a shaggy black dog. He was supposed to be able to blind his adversaries and to divine hidden treasure by the much-execrated practice of necromancy. This was the darker side. Tradition also asserted that he was the first to introduce Arabic numerals into North and West Europe and credited him with the introduction of clocks. It was a short step from this modest claim to assert that he had actually invented them. A marvellous timepiece erected by him in Magdeburg was said to register all the motions of the heavens and the times when the sun rose and set. For it goes without saying that astronomy with its twin-sister astrology were among the sciences Gerbert was supposed to have studied in Cordova, where they notoriously flourished. It was the age of heady mechanical dreams; and William of Malmesbury testified to Gerbert's construction of a set of miraculous hydraulic machines in Rheims, in which the water executed symphonies and played enchanting airs. This historian further related his own visit to a magical underground palace which was dazzling and glorious beyond compare, just as Gerbert had built it, but vanished away at the slightest touch. Moreover, this extraordinary pope, a lineal descendant of Simon Magus, seems to have been the first of the many medieval magicians who, by unlawful arts, made brazen heads. These, like the Brains Trust, would give spontaneous answers to any questions, and, what is more, foretell the future. But, like the oracles of old which they had come to replace, their utterances were ambiguous. It was Gerbert's brazen head which misled him about Jerusalem; and naturally so, since it had been made with the devil's aid.

Otherwise it is difficult to see any wickedness in the spate of ingenious contrivances attributed to Sylvester II. His unsavoury reputation was probably due to the possession of a mind above the ordinary. But if he is merely one representative amongst many of the desperate spiritual wickedness which was popularly supposed to dwell in high places, he is also a fairly typical specimen of the legendary black magician of those days.

CHAPTER II

POST-PAGAN SHADES

(a) Virgil

The one-track minds of Christian writers continued during this and subsequent periods to transform the legendary material about magicians into edifying stories of repentance, conversion and salvation, or cautionary tales of wickedness and damnation, such as those of the saints and sinners described in the previous chapter. An orthodox uniformity was thus imposed upon myths which had sprung from ritual in prehistoric times, and had then gone their own way, adapting themselves without much effort to changing conditions, customs and beliefs. This natural growth, consciously tended by Christianity, was pruned and lopped; and, enclosed by the forcing-house of religious fervour, it developed luxuriantly in an artificial atmosphere of stifling piety. If humanity as a whole could ever be completely enslaved by a spiritual tyranny, all the stories about sorcerers from now onwards until the dawn of enlightenment would have been mere illuminated arabesques on the pages of devotional books, and this was in fact the main trend of the literary development both before and after the Reformation. Yet pagan notions of magic were never quite eradicated. They persisted underground, hardly, if at all, coloured by the prevalent creed; they persisted and continued to exercise their perdurable fascination over the human mind: yet the gleams of light which they cast over legend and literature were like fire-flies at night or will-o'-the-wisps over marshlands, not like the stars in the sky.

The stubborn nature of the belief in potent personalities endowed with superhuman powers together with their shrinking religious significance are well illustrated by the curious emergence of Virgil in the guise of a magician towards the beginning of the eleventh century. Granted that the lapse of a thousand years between the death of the poet and his magical rebirth seems a remarkable phenomenon in itself, the form which the legend took is no less unexpected. If Virgil was to be transformed into a medieval magician, his poetical works, if not his actual life, might seem to provide some reason for it; all the more so as the reverence felt for his genius had led to his later deification in Rome, and to the use of his works for divinatory purposes. The *Sortes Virgilianae*, already in vogue among the Antonines (A.D. 96–192), continued to be consulted until the eve of the Renaissance, as Rabelais knew.[1] Bearing this in mind, and considering the beautiful and wonderful *katabasis* in the *Aeneid*, the magical funeral rites of Dido, the love charms described in the eighth eclogue and the 'prophecy' of Christ in the fourth, one would expect something comparable in legend to the august presence in the *Divina Commedia*. But this is far indeed from being the case. The medieval myth, retaining some faint traces of the hero's real life, ignored the *Sortes Virgilianae* and made no use of the descent into Hades or of Dido's invocation of the powers of darkness. The 'prophet' of Christ naturally came off rather better. In this guise Virgil figured in several versions of his legend, and also trod, indeed haunted, the boards of mystery plays, sometimes accompanied, and sometimes replaced, by the Cumaean Sibyl. But otherwise his name proved to be one of those magnets round which disconnected stories gather; in his case fantastic and often very puerile tales deriving from Eastern folklore and strongly reminiscent of the *Arabian Nights*.

This almost total indifference to the historical and literary importance of the hero, who is not even mentioned as a poet, suggests a popular origin; and Comparetti, in his scholarly study of Virgil in the Middle Ages, has traced the legends recounted by Conrad of Querfurt, Gervase of Tilbury, Alexander Neckam, John of Salisbury and others in the twelfth century and later back to their local Neapolitan source. This was the superstitious fancy surrounding the tomb of the poet which survived all memory of his real existence and personality for hundreds and hundreds of years; and which, the curiosity and questions of visitors aiding and abetting, was gradually amplified to include other local monuments, found its way into literature, grew and developed by accretion until, in the sixteenth century, it was fashioned into a fairly coherent whole. But the biographical details were superimposed upon the collection of miracles which had gathered round Virgil's name and had no other function than to bind them together; they are not the result of organic growth, although ritual elements cling to them.

[1] *Gargantua et Pantagruel*, Book III, Chapter X.

The divine origin claimed for the magi of old, and conspicuous by its absence from the truncated lives of Cyprian, Theophilus, Gerbert and their kind, made a modest reappearance in some of the Virgilian legends, according to which he was of royal descent, being the son of the King of Bugia in Libya. Nor were miraculous portents at his birth altogether forgotten, since Rome trembled when he was born, and great precocity marked the early years of the future magician. His initiation into the occult arts came about accidentally. The favourite version has it that he stumbled across an evil spirit imprisoned in a boarded-up hole, who offered as the price of his deliverance the magic book of Solomon, or of Zabulon the fiend. Virgil accepted the bribe, and then, frightened at the proportions of the spirit he had released, tricked it back into captivity again, *à la Arabian Nights*. This very ungentlemanlike disregard of a gentleman's agreement would have caused his poetical namesake to turn in his grave; but (as Cyprian and countless others had discovered) one cannot afford the luxury of finer feelings when dealing with the fiends. And Virgil was shortly to need all the help that magic could give him in his struggle with the Emperor of Rome to regain his mother's property unjustly withheld from him. Prosaic though the *casus belli* might be (based probably on the autobiographical character of the first eclogue), it developed into a full-dress magical contest, in which the Emperor's sorcerer also played a part. First appropriating his rightful crops by magical means from the usurpers of his property, Virgil then defended his castle from attack by an insurmountable wall of air, managed to counter the spell cast upon the defendants by the rival sorcerer who was overpowering them all with sleep, beglamoured his assailants into the belief that they were surrounded and submerged by deep waters, thus paralysing the whole army, and finally coming off victorious. Although the passage of the Red Sea may have served as a model for this last feat, the whole fantastic *agon* is as utterly devoid of Mosaic grimness as of any human interest.

This was supplied for contemporary minds by Virgil's numerous affairs of gallantry, none of them redounding to the credit of the fair frail sex, nor (from the modern point of view) to the hero's either. First in popularity was the tale of Phoebilla, taken bodily from a *fabliau*, and famous in medieval literature long before it became associated with Virgil. The treacherous young woman pretended to lend a favourable ear to the magician's suit, the better to make a fool of him by leaving him suspended in a basket half-way up the wall to her bedroom for the whole city to mock at in the morning, unhappily for him a market-day. But the sorcerer, who had been unable either to foresee the trick or to escape from the snare, was powerful and ruthless enough to take a most unpleasing revenge. He by his arts deprived the whole town of fire, which could only be procured individually by the citizens from between the legs of Phoebilla, suspended from a scaffold in a smock. Thereupon he made off, having so arranged matters that Phoebilla's punishment should last for three days.

He next became entangled and absorbed in a long amorous affair with the daughter of the Sultan of Babylon, visiting her and transporting her to Naples by means of a magic bridge of air. Finally he built her a marvellous palace; but, refusing to marry her himself, gave her hand in wedlock to one of his knights. His real marriage which followed upon his Eastern amours was evidently not very successful to judge by his later attitude towards women. This reflected fairly faithfully the notions engendered by the combination of Christianity and chivalry and everywhere current at the time:

...there never was a time in the world's history in which women were more grossly insulted, more shamefully reviled or more basely defamed than they were in the middle ages.... The number of anecdotes, trivial or obscene, that drag women in the dirt is simply infinite.[1]

It is the meaninglessness and triviality of Virgil's legendary life as a whole which helps to measure the distance between the medieval magicians and the magus of antiquity, a distance only slightly diminished by the variant accounts of his demise. Those legend makers who tried to synthesise the sorcerer with the prophet of Christ allowed him to repent of his evil practices before his end. Making a public confession of faith in Christianity at a farewell banquet, he died in a most edifying manner, with a book of theology in his hands and seated in an arm-chair on which he had carved all the events described in the New Testament. To this school of thought also belongs the tale of St Paul's search for the body of the pagan prophet, which he discovered in a subterranean chamber

---

[1] D. Comparetti, *Vergil in the Middle Ages*, tr. Benecke, London 1908, p. 326.

seated between two tapers and surrounded by books. An automatic mechanism of flails guarded the uncorrupted remains; St Paul put the machinery out of action in order to approach the body, whereupon everything crumbled to dust before his eyes.

The Christianising of Virgil's legend was, however, only sporadic. According to other accounts, he disappeared mysteriously during a storm at sea; or again, misunderstanding the warning of his brazen oracle, he contracted sunstroke and died. This shows knowledge of the real life of Virgil and of the account of Gerbert's end, also brought about by a misinterpretation of the words of the brazen head he had constructed. Virgil's automaton told him to take care of his head, but he took this as a warning to guard the oracle. The version which finally prevailed over all the others told a dreadful tale of thwarted rejuvenation. As old age approached, Virgil resolved to cheat death by renewing his youth. The means were both horrible and dangerous, deriving in all probability from the tales of Medea's operations on Aeson, Jason and Pelias. A faithful, although protesting, servant was persuaded to cut his master into small pieces and place them in a cask with salt for the space of nine days, during which time a lamp hanging over the barrel must be daily fed with oil. The success of the experiment depended on leaving the cask untouched for the whole period. Unhappily the emperor, who had now become much attached to the magician, missed him after seven days, wrung the whereabouts of his friend from the servant, forced him to wreck the automatic mechanism guarding the castle and to lead him to the barrel. He disturbed the contents, recognised Virgil's head, and slew the servant. Whereupon he and his suite beheld the body of a naked child which ran three times round the cask crying: 'cursed be the tyme that ye cam euer here',[1] after which he disappeared and was never seen again.

The naked child is a medieval addition to the Medean 'cauldron of apotheosis', and figured later in the legendary end of Paracelsus who spoke in his works of Virgil the magician. It reflects whilst distorting the tradition of resurrection or regeneration, and ended disastrously, as was also the case with Simon Magus, probably because the possibility of such a miracle wrought by a mere magician no longer seemed credible; but it remains much the most interesting feature in the story; and moreover a species of immortality was

[1] *Early English Prose Romances*, ed. Thoms, London 1858, II, p. 58.

attributed to the bones of the sorcerer, which were held to protect the city of Naples and to cause violent storms if exposed.

For it was in the guise of a protector that Virgil was chiefly honoured in Naples, strewn, according to tradition, with marvels of every kind, both for defence and offence, passive or active in their scope. The traditional connection with the food supply was evident in the trick by which he charmed the enemy's crops into his own manor; he also possessed a magic garden where no rain fell, protected by a wall of air, so that the birds could not fly away; he boasted that he could make fruit trees bear three times a year; and his spirits fetched dishes for his banquets from the feasts of his foes. But these miracles were marginal, and much less characteristic of Virgil than his wonderful devices to avert evil. A bronze fly and a golden leech preserved the city from the presence of these pests; and a brazen horse constructed by his magic art ensured all the steeds in the town, however heavily laden, from broken backs.[1] His healing baths at Puteoli prevented or cured all the diseases known to man, so that one way and another he was certainly behaving as an honest medicine-man should. On the other hand the statue, twice overthrown by his wife, which inhibited sexual passion in the Neapolitan women, shows him hindering fertility instead of promoting it, a maleficent warlock rather than a white magician, but true to the same warped tradition which made Justina into a saint. Women to-day may perhaps forgive Virgil when they hear that he was the first inventor of the refrigerator, a magic butcher's block, warranted to keep meat fresh for an indefinite period.

These ingenious devices and others of the same kind were thrown into the shade by the marvellous automata he constructed, machines anticipating the robots of the future by acting intelligently. Mechanical horsemen on mechanical steeds kept midnight thieves, rogues and murderers off the streets; and the fearful *bocca della verità* (known earlier, but now attributed to him) did even more than the inanimate statue to promote virtuous behaviour among the women. For this gruesome marble head automatically bit off the hand of any wife who swore falsely to her fidelity with her arm in those merciless jaws, a terrible test of chastity, which, however, the wit of woman was able to circumvent on one occasion, to the impotent disgust of Virgil. The *salvatio Romae*, more pleasing to contemplate,

[1] Similar talismans were attributed to Apollonius of Tyana.

was terrible only to the enemies of Rome. It consisted of an elaborate mechanism erected upon the Capitol by means of which the statue of any province or kingdom contemplating treachery against the Eternal City rang a bell and pointed in the direction whence the peril was coming. This contrivance, which probably derived from the legend of the geese, was finally destroyed by a cunning Carthaginian wile. Pretending to be digging for gold under the Capitol, enemy emissaries brought it down; and one after another all Virgil's wonderful talismans met the same kind of fate after he himself was no more.

The tale of his marvellous inventions and miraculous powers is far from being exhausted by the few examples I have given. But enough is enough. This medieval Solomon reared palaces too, and was in fact the master-builder of the Middle Ages, greatly outshining Gerbert. But it has all vanished away; for there was no reality behind the fantastic figure of the marvellous magician and no religious, historical or poetical sanction.

(b) Merlin

A totally different impression is produced by Merlin, the most famous in story of all the medieval magicians. It is like entering another world to turn from the account of Virgil's bustling life and optimistic activities to the dim, mysterious figure regarding the reader with wild and melancholy eyes in the *Vita Merlini*. This Latin poem, now by common consent attributed to Geoffrey of Monmouth, and written about 1148, distils that universal appeal which vouches for its emotional if not its historical truth; and indeed it derives ultimately, whether by direct borrowings or not, from the probably historical Welsh bard of the sixth century, Myrddhin Willt, or Merlin the Wild. According to tradition this unhappy poet lost his reason during a battle, overwhelmed by sorrow at the slaughter of his friends. A vision of intolerable brightness was said to have unhinged his mind during the affray, accompanied by a voice roaring in his ear that he was guilty of the blood shed on the battlefield, and must thenceforth live in the forests among the wild beasts. To this tragic figure Welsh poems of the twelfth century or later refer; others reproduce dialogues between Myrddhin and Taliesin and Myrddhin and his sister Gwenddydd; others again are attributed to him. Slight and obscure as the details are that can be gathered from these sources, they contribute to the picture of a mournful poet haunted by remorse and sorrow, living in natural solitudes, bewailing past glories, having intercourse with spirits, and uttering strange prophecies in a state of ecstasy:

> Ten years and forty, as the toy of lawless ones,
> Have I been wandering in gloom and among sprites.[1]

This Celtic bard, gifted with a weird second-sight as well as prophetic powers, recovered his reason in Geoffrey's poem by drinking the waters of a magical spring, and his death, like his birth, was passed by without mention. But in the *Historia Regum Britanniae*, 1135–47, Geoffrey gave further and more concrete details of Merlin, and in fact described him from a different angle, which was to be the point of view of subsequent romancers. His source for the *History* was the ninth-century *Historia Britonum* of 'Nennius', who introduced a prophet-king, Ambrosius, born without a father; at least his mother declared that she had never lain with a man; but Ambrosius himself claimed to be the son of a Roman consul. Geoffrey identified Ambrosius with Merlin, born of a demon-father, he said, who had seduced a nun. Satan himself was later credited with the paternity of the prophet, the devils in council having agreed to bring forth Antichrist by this species of counter-incarnation. The mother, however, repented and confessed her sin; the infant was baptised by St Blaise; and, whilst retaining miraculous powers, escaped the stigma of evil; indeed the marvellous salvation of his mother at his birth was the first revelation of his supernatural origin. But, whatever the rights or the wrongs of his begetting, the fact that he was the child of no ordinary sire loomed large in literature. And altogether the Merlin of the *History*, which included a series of prophecies, overshadowed the hero of the *Vita Merlini* in the many prose and verse romances written about him, and also in the other works belonging to the Arthurian cycle in which he appears incidentally. This was in harmony with the spirit of an age which loved marvels more than mystery and melancholy; and the actual romances of which Merlin is the title-hero have their tedious and

---

[1] From the Welsh poem *The Avallenau* attributed to Myrddhin; cf. Parry's edition of Geoffrey of Monmouth, *Vita Merlini*, in *University of Illinois Studies in Language and Literature*, Illinois 1925, p. 129.

prolix side. Yet he never quite lost that indescribable charm with which Celtic imagination working through Geoffrey first endowed him, and on which Malory, Spenser, Tennyson and Swinburne have set the seal of great poetry. There is in truth no magician in history so deeply imbued with glamour. The posthumous poetical career of the great world-wizards have blazed a trail through literature whose ramifications are endlessly fascinating; Merlin's track slides into the haunted forest of Broceliande where magic is freed from the bonds of ritual, the reverence due to religion and the burden of moral or philosophical questions, and where enchantment reigns supreme.

Supernaturally begotten as he was, he needed and underwent no specific initiation into the mysteries of his art; but he showed his mettle at a very early age in a contest with the magicians of King Vortigern. These gentry, totally unable to prevent the disasters which the King of Britain was sustaining at the hands of the Saxons under Hengist, counselled the monarch to build a fortress in Wales which might keep his enemies at bay. Although the site chosen was the summit of a hill, the earth swallowed up the foundation stones as soon as they were laid. The bards and wizards, summoned in haste to account for this inexplicable disaster, were naturally at a loss, but by no means anxious to say so. They announced instead that the stones could never be laid together, nor the place built upon, until they were cemented with the blood of a man-child born of a human mother, but owning no mortal father. The search for this prodigy ended in the discovery of Merlin, who was lured to the court of Vortigern, together with his mother, by promises of great riches. When the king beheld this beautiful boy, he behaved as Astyages had behaved hundreds of years before when Cyrus was brought into his presence. Touched by the child's grace, gravity and nobility, he could not bring himself to slay him. Instead of sentencing him to death, he laid the situation before him, and asked for his advice.

To which words...Merlin...thus replied, Royal Sir, blind were your bards, witless your wizards, and silly and simple your soothsayers; who showed themselves averse to art, and altogether unacquainted with the secrets of nature, as altogether ignorant, that in the breast of this hill lies a vast moat, or deep pool, which hath ingurgitated and swallowed all these materials thrown into the trenches. Therefore command them to be digged deeper, and you shall discover the water in which your squared stones have been washed, and in the bottom of the lake you shall find two hollow rocks of stone, and in them two horrible dragons fast asleep....[1]

He had divined correctly; moreover, when the dragons were uncovered, they issued forth and engaged each other in mortal combat, the white dragon (standing for the Saxons) finally overcoming the red, an ominous sign for Vortigern. Beginning his career in this fashion as a seer, Merlin continued to aid by his counsels and supernatural powers Vortigern, Uther Pendragon and Arthur. The bard gradually became lost in the magician as his legend grew and developed, and as such a mysterious or tragic ending inevitably awaited him. Many rumours were afloat on the subject. Some said that he entered the Glass House at Bardsey with nine bards, taking with him the thirteen treasures of Britain, and was never seen again. Others said that he retired to a self-erected edifice, *Esplumeor*, and vanished away, as Moses, Pythagoras, Empedocles and Apollonius had vanished before him. The favourite version, however, brought in the notion of romantic and fatal love, as well as the ritual tradition of doom at the hands of a rival and more potent spirit. If the story of Virgil and the basket throws an unpleasant light on the 'chivalrous' attitude towards women, the tale of Merlin and Nimiane, based too on female guile and treachery, is beautiful and sad. From another angle, it reproduces Virgil's adventure with the imprisoned spirit in reverse. Virgil met this demon at the beginning of his career, outwitted it and bottled it up. Merlin, towards the close of his life, succumbed to the same kind of trick. Nimiane or Viviane (probably derived from the nymph-like companion called Chwimbian in Welsh legend) was thought by some to be a king's daughter, others believed that she was a water-fairy, and Malory called her one of the Ladies of the Lake. Whoever she was, she loved the great enchanter, and hopelessly enslaved him; it was to keep him in her bonds that she wooed from him the secret of the magic tomb hewn in the rocks, lured him thither and imprisoned him there to all eternity, lost forever to the world, yet still alive. This catastrophe, combining the features of the *pathos* of the year-daimon with the *katabasis*, also allowed for a species of immortality or resurrection. For in some

[1] T. Heywood, *The Life of Merlin*, London 1813, p. 40. First edition 1641. Heywood, who used the *Vita Merlini* by Geoffrey on which to hang prophecies about the history of England, here follows his source closely, whilst amplifying it slightly.

accounts the prison was of air, so that Merlin could see and hear everything in his vicinity, himself unseen, and even hold converse with passers-by, as he was reputed to have done with Gawaine. Spenser seems to have been the first, as he was certainly the greatest, to attribute to Merlin the feat by which Solomon ensured that the work on the Temple should continue after his death.

> Forthwith them selves disguising both in straunge
> And base atyre, that none might them bewray,
> To Maridunum, that is now by chaunge
> Of name Cayr-Merdin cald, they tooke their way:
> There the wise Merlin whylome wont (they say)
> To make his wonne, low underneath the ground,
> In a deepe delve, farre from the vew of day,
> That of no living wight he mote be found,
> When so he counseld with his sprights encompast round
>
> And, if thou ever happen that same way
> To traveill, go to see that dreadful place.
> It is an hideous hollow cave (they say)
> Under a Rock that lyes a litle space
> From the swift Barry, tombling downe apace
> Emongst the woody hilles of Dynevowre:
> But dare thou not, I charge, in any cace,
> To enter into that same balefull Bowre,
> For feare the cruell Feendes should thee unwares devowre:
>
> But standing high aloft low lay thine eare,
> And there such ghastly noyse of yron chaines
> And brasen Caudrons thou shalt rombling heare,
> Which thousand sprights with long enduring paines
> Doe tosse, that it will stonn thy feeble braines;
> And oftentimes great grones, and grievous stownds,
> When too huge toile and labour them constraines,
> And oftentimes loud strokes and ringing sowndes
> From under that deepe Rock most horribly rebowndes.
>
> The cause, some say, is this: A litle whyle
> Before that Merlin dyde, he did intend
> A brasen wall in compas to compyle
> About Cairmardin, and did it commend
> Unto these Sprights to bring to perfect end:
> During which worke the Lady of the Lake,
> Whom long he lov'd, for him in hast did send;
> Who, thereby forst his workemen to forsake,
> Them bownd till his retourne their labour not to slake.

> In the meane time, through that false Ladies traine
> He was surprisd, and buried under beare,
> Ne ever to his worke returnd againe:
> Nath'lesse those feends may not their work forbeare,
> So greatly his commandement they feare,
> But there doe toyle and traveile day and night,
> Untill that brasen wall they up doe reare;
> For Merlin had in Magick more insight
> Then ever him before, or after, living wight.[1]

The great Welsh enchanter outdid Solomon in this respect, since the latter's bodily presence was necessary to keep the fiends at work, whilst Merlin's command was enough to guarantee enduring obedience. In fact something of the golden age of magic permeates this legend: a supernatural origin, miracles performed at birth, perils menacing his early years, a contest with rival magicians, a subsequent supreme trial (Nimiane), a mysterious death embodying a kind of descent into the underworld with an invisible continued existence; only the initiation, the distant journeys and the farewell scene are absent from the ten stock features of a complete legendary life; and many a magician has less; but in Merlin's case the gold is fairy gold; he has been absorbed back into the poetry from whence he emerged.

Prophecy ranks supreme among the gifts attributed to the magical bard. Indeed, he had no peer as a diviner in medieval times until the days of Nostradamus.

> The Sibyl foretells a tale that will come to pass—
> A golden rod of great value, will, for bravery,
> Be given to glorious chiefs before the dragons;
> The diffuser of grace will vanquish the profane man,
> Before the child, bold as the sun in his courses,
> Saxons shall be eradicated, and bards shall flourish.[2]

Geoffrey first published a book of Merlin's prophecies, and then included them in his *History*; and the popularity of this and other collections is illustrated by the fact that they were put on the Index by the Council of Trent (1545–63). Heywood gave great publicity to Merlin the soothsayer by printing a great many of his *soi-disant* prophecies in rhymed couplets in 1641; and his name was used for

[1] Spenser, *The Faerie Queene*, Book III, Canto 3.
[2] *The Avallenau*. Parry's edition of the *Vita Merlini*, p. 129.

109

almanacs as late as the eighteenth century, much as Old Moore is used to-day. But he had many other powers besides foreknowledge. Spenser maintained that he could sway the course of the sun and moon, turn night into day, the land into sea and the sea into land; so that power over the forces of nature was strongly marked; this ensured control of the food supply, and one learns without surprise from Heywood that he caused whatever game King Vortigern desired to fall immediately into his lap. As a medicine-man or healer he made use of music, charming the melancholy of Vortigern by sweet sounds produced by invisible hands. It was by the power of music too, said some, that he magically transported the monoliths of Stonehenge from Ireland to their present position on Salisbury Plain. Many Welsh wizards were credited with similar miracles, as were Amphion and Orpheus in Greece; and this seems natural enough when one remembers the musical genius of the Celts. Like Simon Magus before him Merlin was also a past-master in the art of transformation. He disguised Uther Pendragon miraculously so that he appeared to be Gorlais, the husband of Igerna, and lay with her in that shape, as Zeus had lain with Alcmena; whilst Gorlais, like Uriah, was slain in battle. This is the only shabby trick associated with Merlin's name. Otherwise the magician presiding over the Round Table, the most famous magic circle in history, used his powers to protect his friends. He cast a spell upon Pellinore, when the latter would have slain Arthur, by sending him into a trance and also by rendering Arthur invisible. He could produce phantom armies, and manufacture or discover magical swords. In fact he was almost a second Virgil in craftsmanship. In Welsh legend he was famed for that magic mirror which, according to Spenser, played the part of the *salvatio Romae* for King Ryence.

> Such was the glassy globe that Merlin made,
> And gave unto king Ryence for his gard,
> That never foes his kingdome might invade,
> But he it knew at home before he hard
> Tydings thereof, and so them still debar'd.
> It was a famous Present for a Prince,
> And worthy worke of infinite reward,
> That treasons could bewray, and foes convince:
> Happy this Realme, had it remayned ever since! [1]

[1] *The Faerie Queene*, Book III, Canto 2.

PLATE V

Merlin

The Welsh also spoke of a house of glass which he had formed round a mistress, which probably led to the story of Nimiane and Merlin's prison of air, again reminiscent of the wall of air with which Virgil surrounded his castle and his magic garden; whilst the bridge in the *Morte Darthur* which no knight could pass unless he were without treachery or villainy, is the male counterpart of the *bocca della verità*. Heywood finally credited Merlin with prophesying an invention already circulating in the streets of Naples.

> All by a brazen man shall come to passe,
> Who likewise mounted on his Steed of brasse,
> Both night and day will *Londons* prime Gate keep,
> Whether the carlesse people wake or sleep.[1]

But in spite of these similarities, or even borrowings, Virgil and Merlin are poles apart. The great Latin poet, one of the greatest poets of all times, has degenerated into a magical mountebank whose ingenious inventions and amorous discomfitures make the lightest of light reading. The shadowy Welsh bard, who may even never have existed, lives the intenser life of poetry, but has no solid ground beneath his feet. It is the loss of all feeling of reality which, even more than the spiritual and intellectual degradation, represents the downfall of the magus after the coming of Christ. Cyprian and Theophilus are pure figments of pious imaginings; the real Gerbert has vanished behind the black magician almost as completely as the real Virgil behind his medieval namesake; Merlin is to all intents and purposes the creation of Geoffrey of Monmouth. Even the mythical Zoroaster has a greater hold on reality than these post-pagan shades. An urgent desire to come across the tracks of a flesh-and-blood practising magician is aroused at this juncture, a desire which can now be fulfilled.

[1] Heywood, op. cit. p. 75.

CHAPTER III

BENEATH A BLACK SUN

(a) Zyto

There were, of course, professional magicians in medieval times, for there always have been and always will be such gentry. But their existence was on the whole obscure, their tracks were hidden, and they practised the ancient craft for the most part furtively under the rose. Nevertheless, at the court of some superstitious nobleman or prince, they sometimes enjoyed patronage and immunity. Amongst such favoured few, the Bohemian sorcerer Zyto stands out at the end of the fourteenth century as the most renowned for his tricks and feats. Nothing is known of his origins; and all that was rumoured of the course of his life was the presence of a Schotek or familiar spirit at his beck and call, and his final carrying off by the devil. This sinister personage doubled the parts of court jester and court magician to King Wenceslas IV of Bohemia, and was much in the society of the public executioner who was also a member of the royal suite. His position, although a privileged one, was in the nature of things precarious; and it fell to his lot on one occasion to maintain it in the teeth of a rival sorcerer with whom he became involved in a magical contest. According to the chronicler Dubravius, this occurred in the year 1389, during the ceremonies attendant on the marriage of Wenceslas to his second wife, Sophia of Bavaria. Her father, Duke John, well knowing how much his relative-to-be delighted in displays of magic, brought a whole wagon-load of conjurers in his train for the wedding festivities at Prague. Great was the pressure round the platform raised to accommodate the troupe, great was the wonder and applause at the marvels they wrought: making ropes of sand, eating fire, and transforming themselves into terrifying monsters; and great too was the vexation of spirit Zyto underwent at seeing himself eclipsed and losing prestige rapidly with the fickle public. At last he could stand it no longer, and obtained permission from Wenceslas to teach the foreign interlopers a lesson. Approaching their leader, Gouin, and stretching his mouth from ear to ear, he thereupon swallowed him whole with all his apparatus, only rejecting the shoes which were too muddy for his taste, much as Mount Aetna rejected the sandals of Empedocles. The gasp which went forth from the multitude swelled into a roar when, after a remonstrance from Duke John, he spewed the wretched conjurer up again into a tub of water. Memories of Jonah and the whale and of the race of ogres headed by Polyphemus flash by and make way for memories of those sacrificial meals in which the god was eaten either actually or symbolically. The contest between Zyto and Gouin went according to that ancient custom; and the restoration of Gouin is a medieval and messy version of ritual resurrection. Moreover, by coughing him up again, when he must have seemed to the onlookers to have gone for good, Zyto entered the ranks of those relatively rare magicians who were thought to be able to resurrect the dead.

If this feat were performed in self-defence, the same cannot always be said of the many mischievous tricks the Bohemian sorcerer played on his fellow-courtiers, although they were sometimes in the nature of reprisals, and often show traces of great antiquity. His revenge for a piece of mockery for instance took the form of crying 'Fire! fire!'; and when the jokers poked their heads out of the windows to see where it was, he conjured stag's horns on their foreheads so that they could not draw them back. The Palaeolithic stag-man, the most impressive of the horned figures of that period, is ocular proof of the connection between magic and the assumption of animal shape, still closely connected in England in the seventh century, when Theodore, Archbishop of Canterbury from 668–90, issued a declaration to the effect that anyone who

goes about as a stag or a bull; that is, making himself into a wild animal and dressing in the skin of a herd animal, and putting on the heads of beasts; those who in such wise transform themselves into the appearance of a wild animal, penance for three years because this is devilish.[1]

Devilish the courtiers will certainly have thought Zyto's trick to be, when he played it on them seven hundred years later; and the respectable antiquity of its origin would probably not have appeased them, nor reconciled them to the shock of finding

[1] From the *Liber Poenitentialis*, quoted by M. Murray, *The God of the Witches*, London n.d. p. 22.

their hands transformed into hoofs at mealtimes, thus hindering them from enjoying the supply of food whilst Zyto gobbled it up.

Zyto may have amused Wenceslas, but the courtiers must have disliked and dreaded him inexpressibly, since he was able to strike them dumb and motionless at the slightest provocation and thus deprive them of the power of retaliation. There was no getting even with him, as the peasant who bought a herd of swine from the magician learnt to his cost. Rather naturally disregarding the warning not to drive them into water, he discovered by doing so that they were mere bundles of hay which could not withstand that test. He returned to the inn where the bargain had been sealed, maddened by the sorcerer's duplicity, and determined to have it out with him. He found Zyto apparently sunk in deep slumber; pulling him roughly by the leg to awaken him, he nearly fell backwards as the limb came away in his hands. This unnerving experience proved to be wreckingly expensive, and the cruellest of illusions into the bargain; for, no sooner had the peasant been mulcted of a large sum in compensation than Zyto was a whole man again.

It seems from the nature of nearly all the tricks Zyto was said to have performed that he was a past-master at creating illusions. Everyone gaped when he harnessed a bantam cock to a massive beam of wood and caused it to drag this burden through the street without the slightest effort. In the midst of the general amazement, however, a servant girl happened to pass with a four-leaved clover in her basket, and she cried out that the cock was only pulling a wisp of straw. Zyto punished her for showing him up by conjuring forth an illusory flood of water, through which she waded with her skirts waist-high amidst the derisive cheers of the onlookers, who for their part saw no water at all, because Zyto did not want them to. Why the four-leaved clover, still in her basket, did not function on this occasion, history does not relate.

Although the name Bohemian applied to the gypsies has probably nothing whatever to do with their origin, which, to judge by their language is thought by some to be Indian, nevertheless this particular story combined with Zyto's general faculty for deluding and beguiling inclines me to believe that he sprang from gypsy stock. The power of the gypsies to beglamour those who are not of their race is notorious;

and it is surely more than a coincidence that Scott relates the following tale of a gypsy who

'exercised his glamour over a number of people at Haddington, to whom he exhibited a common dung-hill cock, trailing...a massy oaken trunk. An old man passed with a cart of clover. He stopped and picked out a four-leaved blade; the eyes of the spectators were opened, and the oaken trunk appeared to be a bulrush.'

The quatrefoil, owing to its cruciform shape, acted as a powerful antidote to witchcraft. Moreover, in the face of this sign of the Cross, the Gypsy was bound to desist from the exercise of what was an unlawful art.[1]

Both the language and the physique of the gypsies suggest affinities with Hindustan; and this description of an illusion from which, in Zyto's case, one person was immune, has a strong family resemblance to the myth of the Indian rope-trick. This by the way was put into circulation again by Madame Blavatsky in *Isis Unveiled*, and she probably took it from Wier's *De Praestigiis Daemonum*. In nearly all accounts of this legendary feat, there is someone, either a notoriously difficult person to hypnotise, or else too far away, or placed too high above the magician's head to come within the range of his glamour, and who sees nothing remarkable except a gaping crowd. Indeed, so constant a feature is this of rope-trick yarns that an American journalist made capital out of it in 1890 by a description in the *Chicago Tribune* of witnessing the performance with a friend who made sketches of it, whilst he took snapshots. The sketches reproduced the whole process, the snapshots showed only a gesticulating fakir and an excited audience. This article caused a sensation; and Hodgson, a keen member of the Society for Psychical Research, who had vainly inquired after the rope-trick throughout India, wrote to the author, pressing for details. The latter was then forced to acknowledge that he had invented the whole incident under the transparent pseudonym S. Ellmore (sell more) as a piece of mystification. This world-famous legend has now become as fabulous as the unicorn, but not as extinct as the dodo. In a much less sensational way, Zyto played the fakir in the cock and clover story. It suggests that he practised hypnotism, even though the theory of mass hypnotism must be excluded. In fact he possessed that power over

[1] The quotation from Walter Scott and the note to it are taken from David MacRitchie's article on 'Gypsies' in Lewis Spence's *Encyclopaedia of Occultism*, London 1920.

the minds of men without which no magician can function. But magic, it must be remembered, is an art which demands collaboration between the artist and his public. Whether any other kind of collaboration, either from above or from below, is ever involved must remain a moot question, which the case-histories about to follow will hardly help to solve.

(b) Joan and Gilles

However exaggerated and even legendary the stories about Zyto may be, he was certainly a real person, practising his art at a royal court. His value to Wenceslas was purely as a jester, which shows once more how greatly the whole conception of magic had shrunk; but in so far as he provided amusement, he contributed to the well-being of his *entourage*; whilst the malice and spite to which he gave vent show him in the light of a blackish practitioner. In all probability this mischievous rogue had already ceased to exist when two very different victims of magic regarded as a black art came to a dreadful end in France: Joan of Arc in 1431 and Gilles de Rais, nick-named Bluebeard, in 1440. The first suffered martyrdom because any form of magic not practised by the Church was believed to be diabolic; the second because he became involved in its most sinister practices. Both the saint and the sinner paid the penalty for living under the black sun of magic which darkened the Christian skies.

Although the bottomless gulf which seems to separate white magic from black yawns between them, they were friends and comrades-in-arms during the glorious days of Joan's triumphs; and even to-day they seem linked together by a mysterious bond, as if they were the obverse and the reverse of the same medal. Miss Murray, in her important anthropological studies on witchcraft, has claimed for both the status of substitutes for the divine or royal victim of a primitive pagan cult, still very prevalent in Europe then and later, or so she believes. This interesting theory helps to explain so much otherwise inexplicable in the history of witchcraft that one is strongly tempted to accept it, or at least to make use of it as a fruitful hypothesis. It certainly simplifies the problem of the witch-craft trials held in such numbers from the fifteenth to the eighteenth centuries, which bear witness to a spiritual epidemic unparalleled in history, accompanied by mass hysteria, mass delusions or perhaps even mass manifestations on an incredible scale. If they were the death-throes of a religion *in extremis*, the case seems less baffling as Miss Murray maintains:

The only explanation of the immense number of witches who were legally tried and put to death in Western Europe is that we are dealing with a religion which was spread over the whole continent and counted its members in every rank of society, from the highest to the lowest.[1]

It has been accepted for some time that witchcraft, when genuinely present, is a survival of pagan notions and rites improperly understood by its adversaries and even by its practitioners. Miss Murray believes, although perhaps on insufficient evidence, that it was still an organised religion as late as the fifteenth century, an open secret among the populace, a secret vice among the better educated, and fiercely persecuted by the Church. The fearful stigma of heresy attaching to witchcraft and the monstrous stories told about it were due to the spirit of the Church Militant inspiring the judges and demonologists against a rival creed. This seems likely enough. It is more difficult to feel sure that Miss Murray is right in maintaining that the custom of claiming a divine victim or a substitute periodically was still alive in those days in Western Europe. She makes some very plausible deductions from this hypothesis, however, and amongst them is her interpretation of the trial and execution of Saint Joan.

Joan of Arc, as mysterious to-day as she was during her short and tragic life, was perhaps the heroic prototype of all those unfortunates called witches among whom she was finally classed, and who in their hundreds and thousands suffered torture and death for their god and their faith. With this difference that, whereas they were mere martyrs, she was a chosen sacrificial victim. That was why no one raised a finger to save her in the whole of France; and, if Miss Murray is right, her Christian judges were justified from their point of view in condemning. her; for she certainly again and again refused to acknowledge the authority of the Church. Yet the question was obscured by her undoubted piety and the saint-like voices she invoked; so that her canonisation in our own day is justified too. Yet she may have been neither a 'witch', nor a 'divine victim', nor a 'saint'; but that rarest of all rare phenomena, a genuine magician. She certainly underwent the traditional initiation, victorious contest, persecution, trial, violent death, and a personal, although probably spurious, resurrection as Jeanne des Armoises. Whatever inter-

[1] M. Murray, *The God of the Witches*, p. 48.

pretation is put upon the facts, the facts themselves are not in doubt, and run an exactly parallel course with the 'facts' of legend. A person claiming supernatural powers and guidance and performing seemingly miraculous feats suffered publicly the traditional fate depicted by the actors of primitive sacrificial rites: the lot of the incarnate god, of the king-magician-priest. If Miss Murray's theory is correct, the old god, impersonated by a girl not yet out of her 'teens, was actually on this historic occasion tragically vanquished by the new. Reading her story to-day (even in the blinding light of common sense shed by Shaw in his preface to *Saint Joan*), it certainly appears as if real magic had at one period been involved: ambiguous as usual, transient as always, and ending catastrophically for the practitioner. Supernatural, or at least supernormal, gifts seem to have been granted her. Shaw calls it genius, I prefer the word *mana*; something neither good nor bad in itself; potent, rare, tricky, and unreliable; always deserting its instrument in the hour of need: 'My power, *my* power, thou hast forsaken me'; a bitter cry, ringing down the centuries.

Joan died too young for any of the more questionable qualities generated by *mana* to develop; her chosen protector in battle, Gilles de Rais, peer and marshal of France, became, if we are to believe his own confession, the most iniquitous and depraved of human kind. Although, like the rest of France, he made no effort to save the Maid, he seems to have taken her fate to heart; for he wrote *The Mystery of Orleans* in her honour, mounted and produced it with unheard-of splendour and acted the part of Gilles de Rais himself. The great valour he had shown in battle took the form in peace of magnificence, display, luxury and extravagance run riot. The descriptions of his mode of life both at home and when travelling abroad stagger the imagination, suggesting inordinate, insensate vanity, if not something worse. And there may have been something worse behind this frantic prodigality; although the accusations against him which led to his trial may also have been framed in order to preserve what his squanderings had left of his riches for his clamorous presumptive heirs; in which case the trial of Gilles de Rais would bear a close resemblance to the proceedings against the Knights Templar.

Whether based on facts or not, ominous rumours of infant murders, black magic and appalling atrocities began to circulate about Bluebeard; and soon an avalanche of accusations made it

imperative to bring the suspect to trial before an ecclesiastical and a
civil court. Arrogant and offhand with his judges at first, Gilles was
clearly shaken when members of his household testified against him,
accusing themselves of complicity in his crimes; he was a changed
man when threatened with excommunication, and pleaded piteously
against that sentence; but he did not break down and confess to the
crimes of which he had been accused until after the threat of torture
had been made. Then indeed a spate of words came tumbling out,
revealing such depths of degradation, such indescribable cruelties,
such inhuman atrocities that the Bishop of Nantes rose and veiled
the crucifix hanging over the judges. Gilles' repentance, as sensational as everything else in his extraordinary life, was so heartfelt and
genuine that he died in the most heroic and exemplary fashion,
consoling his two accomplices with promises of paradise until the last
moment, when he was hanged before being burnt. Indeed, it was
such a saint-like ending that one is hardly surprised to hear that
a temple was erected at the place of his execution; although its
visitation by nursing mothers to make their milk flow abundantly
is an ironic turn of fortune's wheel, considering how Gilles had
massacred the innocents, or so it was said, whilst he was alive.

Although his 'spontaneous' confession, made under the threat of
torture, is naturally suspect, the accounts given in it of his many
attempts to enter into an agreement with the devil are convincing,
because, however often and however earnestly he attended the
ceremonies, he never saw or heard anything at all. He attributed this
to God's mercy; it seems more likely that the Italian magician
Prelati, who drew the circles, made the sacrifices, and reported
progress to Gilles, was deceiving him throughout with his tales of
the spirit called Barron, who never manifested when Gilles was there.
Bluebeard himself was not a magician, although he employed
magicians and took part in the revolting ceremonies they implemented on his behalf. In this he resembled Theophilus; but how
innocuous that milk-and-water saint appears when compared with
Gilles de Rais. The latter may have been criminally insane; and
although reason boggles at the number of crimes he confessed to and
the incredible sadism they imply, Buchenwald and Belsen have an
answer to that. Yet, in spite of his own confession and those of his
confederates; in spite of the circumstantial evidence, and the plausible
descriptions of unavailing invocations to the devil, the fact that the

threat of torture preceded all these revelations invalidates them. The horrible document read out at Bluebeard's trial may have been a legendary document, whether composed by himself or another. It certainly embodied all the dark dreams which had haunted the minds of men for many a century and had begun to obsess society since the so-called discoveries about the rites of the Templars. It was in fact the product of the most depraved type of imagination, whether a mere paper product or a record of facts. For that mind could conceive such loathsome performances is as serious a symptom of moral and mental disorder as that man should enact them. And Gilles de Rais, or whoever was responsible for his 'spontaneous' confession, gave added sensational substance and a yet more lurid light to the myth of black magic.

This outweighs in importance for the history of sorcerers his possible status as substitute for the divine victim, confessing to imaginary sins in order to be slain. His story does not lend itself so well to Miss Murray's interpretation as that of Joan. She did seem at times to be provoking her own doom during the course of her trial. She certainly hedged on questions of faith; she was obviously holding something back. Gilles, who declared that in all the 'grants' he had prepared to give to the devil, signed with his blood, he had always reserved his 'life and soul', was as orthodox as they come; and this makes his crimes, if crimes there were, all the more sinister. His later identification with the Bluebeard of folk-lore has been most picturesquely supported by Lévi; but Perrault's tale, and the documents of Gilles' trial have little in common except the atmosphere of horror and the smell of blood. Meanwhile the dark and ambiguous allure of Bluebeard of Orleans continues to exercise a fearful fascination over the minds of men. Huysmans' *Là-bas* and the highly poetical description in Charles Williams' study of witchcraft bear witness to that.

If Joan possessed *mana*, Gilles displayed *panache*. Both knew glory and fame at their zenith; both gave proof of gallantry and courage; both were tried for witchcraft, found guilty and executed. One of them may have been a magician, the radiant and immaculate one; the other, a desperate criminal, was not. Yet somehow they belong together, and both transcended human limitations; therefore neither of these two demonstrably historical persons seems to belong entirely to the world of common men.

(c) Doctor Faust

It was emphatically to that everyday world that the real Faust belonged, and to a very low stratum of it, since he affected by preference those German inns of which Erasmus painted such a vivid picture. Crowded to suffocation, noisome and filthy, they were frequented for the most part by a society the reverse of polite; sullen and morose before food, brawling and indulging in horse-play when the wine had gone the rounds. Jugglers, charlatans and quacks of all kinds thrived in this atmosphere, the ideal breeding-ground for those crass deceptions and those knavish tricks associated with the real Faust, whose fame would probably have mouldered away where it sprang up if he had not been such an unconscionable braggart. For the future hero of Marlowe, Goethe and countless other poets was a big name in magic only in his own estimation. There, however, he reigned supreme, and must be given the credit of being the first begetter of the Faust legend. His silly vauntings irritated, and sometimes maddened, his learned contemporaries, the humanists; who, being themselves all more or less absorbed in occult speculations and experiments, knew that his claims were preposterous. Tritheim, popularly supposed to be a necromancer, spoke of Faust almost with venom; and reported sardonically that the latter had hastily fled from Gelnhausen on hearing of his presence in that town, fearful of meeting him. Rufus, Camerarius and Melanchthon, who had some slight personal contact with Faust, despised him utterly. Yet he continued to publicise himself as the fount of necromancy and chief of astrologers, as the most learned alchemist of all times, as the second magus, palmist, water-diviner and crystal-gazer; as the philosopher of philosophers. He declared that Christ's miracles were nothing to his; and that he could out-do Ezra's restoration of the lost Scriptures by reproducing all the works of Plato and Aristotle, should they ever be forgotten, and what is more, improve on them. No wonder that the epithets braggart, babbler, rogue and fool were often bestowed on him.

The tricks he performed seem to have been as petty and fraudulent as his impudence was great; certainly the only feat any of Faust's actual contemporaries left on record was both paltry and mean:

This wretch, taken prisoner at Batenburg on the Maas, near the border of Geldern, while the Baron Hermann was away, was treated rather leniently by his chaplain, Dr Johannes Dorstenius, because he promised the man, who was good but not shrewd, knowledge of many things and various arts. Hence he kept drawing him wine, by which Faust was very much exhilarated, until the vessel was empty. When Faust learned this, and the chaplain told him that he was going to Grave, that he might have his beard shaved, Faust promised him another unusual art by which his beard might be removed without the use of a razor, if he would provide more wine. When this condition was accepted, he told him to rub his beard vigorously with arsenic, but without any mention of its preparation. When the salve had been applied, there followed such an inflammation that not only the hair but also the skin and the flesh were burned off. The chaplain himself told me of this piece of villainy more than once with much indignation.[1]

A minimum of pharmaceutical knowledge applied with a maximum of malice: this is typical of the shaky foundations of Faust's future magical fame, which was not reared on reality, to judge by the fragments collected and industriously pieced together of the story of his life. These raise the insoluble question as to whether or not there was more than one Faust, a better and a worse one. From the point of view of legend, it is immaterial; but I have sometimes wondered if George (spelt Jörg) and John may not have been brothers, and possibly even twins. The scanty and often scandalous facts about this seemingly dual personality do not preclude such a theory, although they by no means demand it.

In 1507 a man calling himself George Sabellicus, Faust junior, the fount of necromancy and so forth, obtained towards the end of Lent the post of schoolmaster at Kreuznach. This was owing to the good offices of the famous Franz von Sickingen, 'a man very fond of mystical lore'. His *protégé*, however, grossly abused the trust placed in him by indulging in 'the most dastardly kind of lewdness with the boys'.[2] When his sins found him out he fled from punishment. Two years later, on 15 January 1509, a certain Johannes Faust was granted the degree of B.A. in the Faculty of Theology of the University of Heidelberg, was placed first on the list of fifteen and duly paid his fees. It seems in the highest degree unlikely that this scholar was George; but the next reference suggests that he may have been; for in October 1513 George Faust 'Helmitheus Hedebergensis' (? Hemitheus Hedelbergensis, the demi-god of Heidelberg) was heard by the humanist Rufus bragging and talking nonsense in an

---

[1] Palmer and More, *The Sources of the Faust Tradition*, p. 106; translating from the fourth edition of Johannes Wier, *De Praestigiis Daemonum*.

[2] Ibid. p. 86; Tritheim in a letter to Johannes Virdung in 1507.

PLATE VI

Dr Faustus. From an etching by Rembrandt

Erfurt inn. On Sunday, 12 February 1520, Doctor Faust received ten gulden for casting the horoscope of the Bishop of Bamberg; and George Faust of Helmstedt was heard to proclaim on 5 June 1528 that prophets were born when the sun and Jupiter are in the same constellation, and that he was the commander or preceptor of the Knights of St John at Hallestein on the borders of Carinthia. Ten days later, on 15 June 1528, Dr George Faust of Heidelberg was banished as a soothsayer from the town of Ingolstadt; and Doctor Faust, 'the great sodomite and necromancer', was refused a safe conduct by the city of Nuremberg on 10 May 1532. On 25 June 1535 'the famous necromancer Dr Faust' was in Münster, where he prophesied accurately that the bishop would recapture the city that same evening. And in 1540 'the philosopher Faust' correctly foretold 'a very bad year' for the European armies in Venezuela.[1]

Scandalous misconduct and a good theological degree (if George and John are one); insensate boastings and a sinister reputation; horoscopes cast and the future foretold; this, with that shabby trick played on Dorstenius, is all that is really known about the historical Faust. But hardly had he disappeared from his accustomed haunts before rumours of a more sensational sort began to go the rounds. The reputation he had been determined to achieve survived his braggings. Others now took up the tale, crediting him with 'many marvels about which a special treatise could be written';[2] and declaring him to be 'as remarkable a sorcerer as could be found in German lands in our times'.[3] And it was now discovered that he had acquired 'such a celebrated name among the common people that there can hardly be found anyone who is not able to recount some instance of his art'.[4] He had blown his own trumpet to some purpose; but he must surely also have performed, at least before the 'common people', some tricks more showy than the mere singeing of a chaplain's beard. One thing seems certain, if we are to believe Wier, who is a conscientious reporter; it was Faust himself who started the rumour that he was in league with the devil:

When another acquaintance of mine, whose beard was black and whose face was rather dark and showed signs of melancholy (for he was splenetic),

[1] Cf. for all these details Palmer and More, op. cit. pp. 87–96.
[2] Ibid. p. 103; from the sixteenth-century *Zimmersche Chronik*.
[3] Ibid. p. 104.
[4] Ibid. p. 123; from the *Operae Horarum Subcisivarum* of Philipp Camerarius, the son of Joachim.

approached Faust, the latter exclaimed: 'I surely thought you were my brother-in-law and therefore I looked at your feet to see whether long curved claws projected from them'; thus comparing him to the devil whom he thought to be entering and whom he used to call his brother-in-law.[1]

This bad joke could hardly fail to be taken literally in the devil-minded sixteenth century. A Swiss Protestant clergyman, Johannes Gast, had actually once dined with the notorious nigromancer; therefore when he described in a popular sermon how Faust was finally strangled by the devil and how (gruesome to relate) the corpse kept on turning face downwards although five times placed on its back, the outline of the legend was there. This terrible end lost nothing in the retelling: the premonitions of the victim; the shaking of the house at midnight; the discovery of the body next morning near the bed with the face twisted to the back: all this soon became common gossip and found its way into print. Gast also reported that when he had dined with Faust in Basle, the magician had contributed some game to the meal not then in season, and therefore obviously supernatural; and that the horse and dog who accompanied him were demons 'ready for any service'. Indeed the clergyman had been told that the dog often assumed the form of a servant and waited at meals. Worse still, this malignant sorcerer had revenged himself upon the monks of 'a certain very rich monastery' for giving him inferior wine by sending a *Poltergeist* to plague them. This spirit proved so outrageous that they finally had to quit the monastery and leave it under the protection of the Count Palatine. This may be a development of the beard-story; but it is also possible that Faust himself was accountable for his posthumous connection with the hardiest annual among ghost-stories. For a Wittenberg tradition reported that he had threatened such reprisals on Melanchthon for sermonising him:

Faust replied: Sir, you continually rebuke me with abusive words. One of these days, when you go to the table, I will bring it about that all the pots in your kitchen will fly out of the chimney, so that you and your guests will have nothing to eat. To this Melanchthon replied: You had better not. Hang you and your tricks. Nor did Faust carry out his threat: the devil could not rob the kitchen of the saintly man....[2]

[1] Palmer and More, op. cit. pp. 106 ff.; from Wier, op. cit.
[2] Ibid. p. 122; from A. Lercheimer, *Christlich bedencken und erinnerung von Zauberey*, Heidelberg 1585.

The tales put into circulation by Gast were founded on Faust's
own sayings and doings, interpreted according to the lights of the
time. They had all the authority behind them which words from the
pulpit, backed by a dining acquaintance with the necromancer,
could give. Even greater prestige attached to the anecdotes of
Melanchthon, Luther's colleague and collaborator in the Reformation. He spread the story that Faust had devoured a rival magician
in Vienna, the latter being discovered a few days later in a cave
(shades of Zyto); and also that he had attempted to fly in Venice, but
had been 'sorely dashed to the ground' (shades of Simon Magus).
Luther's two authentic references to Faust in his Table-talk also
show that, if the humanists did their best to deflate the magician's
claims, the Reformed clergy helped to confirm them; and it was the
mythopoeic tendency and not the rational opposition which finally
won the day.

Faust's personality and possibly his own deeds conditioned the five
tales told about him in Hogel's *Erfurt Chronicle*. This was copied in
the seventeenth century from a mid-sixteenth-century source which
is now lost; and the stories in question are also to be found *verbatim*
in the 1589 edition of the Spies Faustbook. They seem so legendary
at the first glance that one is naturally drawn to credit the story-
book with their invention. Nothing can be proved either way; but
they reflect so many of Faust's characteristics that they may well have
been founded on fact. His parade of learning, his inordinate conceit,
his love of good cheer and trickery, his unregenerate heart confront
the reader in these anecdotes. Even the first tale, harking back to
antiquity, is not inconsistent with the view that Faust made use of
the tradition. While he was in Erfurt, so the story runs, the magician
brought it to pass by his ceaseless boastings that permission was
given him to give a course of lectures to the Erfurt students about
Homer. During these expositions, he whetted their appetite so
much that they petitioned him to produce the heroes of the poems
in person. Having appointed a time for the performance, Faust did
in fact summon forth one after another of the ancient Greek heroes.
Each entering separately, shook his head at the audience as if in
action against the Trojans, and then retired. Last of all the one-eyed
giant Polyphemus made a terrifying appearance, with a flaming red
beard, and in the act of devouring a man whose legs were dangling
from his mouth. This monster proved easier to summon than to

dismiss, made as if he would eat a couple of students, hammered on the floor with his great iron spear, and struck terror into all hearts until he was finally induced to depart. The 'fount of necromancy' here made good that boast, and seemed almost like a second Odysseus. Actually classical necromancy, a facet of the reawakening enthusiasm for Greek poetry, had already made its appearance in Italy in the fifteenth century; for John Franciscus, a nephew of Pico de la Mirandola, reported the conjuring up of Achilles and Hector by a sorcerer, who also displayed the siege of Troy and was thereafter carried off by the devil. Faust was therefore only following this predecessor's lead, although contributing the grotesque incident of Polyphemus.

Granted that such stories were current at the time, what was to hinder Faust from stage-managing the performance with the help of confederates? He had had time to prepare, and the audience was doubtless in the right mood. It may be attributable to the matter-of-fact style of the chronicle, but the description of the evocation reads exactly like a scene in *Dumb Crambo*; and, especially with the entry of Polyphemus, a feeling of realism creeps in. At the very least, the permission to lecture about Homer, wrung from the authorities by Faust's bragging, may well have been a fact.

The next story has Faust written all over it, being another version of his well-authenticated boast about the works of Plato and Aristotle. At a banquet held to celebrate the commencement for masters in Erfurt, the theologians and councillors present were bewailing the lost comedies of Plautus and Terence. Faust offered to produce them entirely for a certain number of hours, during which time they could be hastily copied by an assemblage of students and scribes. Fearing that the devil might insinuate offensive matter into such texts, the city fathers and the theologians refused this handsome offer. Had they accepted, something no doubt would have been forthcoming for the clerks to transcribe. But what?

The third story is also susceptible of a natural explanation, granted collusion with the host of the inn and his son. During a carousal at the Anchor Inn in Erfurt, a company of Faust's friends were regretting his absence and enquired his whereabouts of the host, who declared that he was in Prague. One of the band jestingly summoned him to join them, and lo, he appeared instantaneously on a *soi-disant* magic steed, to whose supernatural voracity the landlord's son appeared at intervals to bear sensational witness. After copious toasts had been brought to the magician, he treated the company to Rheinfal, Malmsey, a Spanish and a French wine as called for, by boring holes through the table, plugging them up, and then tapping the wine from the holes. This trick, which took Goethe's fancy, is naturally one of the most popular in the conjurer's stock-in-trade. I have seen several variants of it on the halls, and could even explain it at need. No magic is involved. Faust's cronies, now nicely lit-up, thereupon 'saw' Faust mount his horse, which rose quickly into the air, and transported him back to Prague. How many of them, one wonders, were under the table by then?

The fourth, which was to have a highly interesting development, deserves to be quoted in full:

After several weeks he comes again from Prague to Erfurt with splendid gifts which had been given him there, and invites the same company to be his guests at St Michael's. They come and stand there in the rooms but there is no sign of any preparation. But he knocks with a knife on the table. Soon someone enters and says: 'Sir, what do you wish?' Faust asks: 'How quick are you?' The other answers: 'As an arrow.' 'No,' says Dr Faust, 'you shall not serve me. Go back to where you came from.' Then he knocks again and when another servant enters and asks the same question, he says: 'How quick are you?' 'As the wind,' says he. 'That is something,' says Dr Faust, but sends him out again too. But when he knocked a third time, another entered and, when he was asked the same question, said he was quick as the thoughts of man. 'Good,' said Dr Faust, 'you'll do.' And he went out with him, told him what he should do, and returned again to his guests and had them wash their hands and sit down. Soon the servant with two others brought in three covered dishes each, and this happened four times. Thirty-six courses or dishes were served, therefore, with game, fowl, vegetables, meat-pies and other meat, not to mention the fruit, confections, cakes, etc. All the beakers, glasses, and mugs were put on the table empty. Soon Dr Faust asked each one what he wished to drink in the way of beer and wine and then put the cups outside of the window and soon took them back again, full of just that fresh drink which each one wanted to have. The music which one of his servants played was so charming that his guests had never heard the like, and so wonderful as if several were playing in harmony on harmoniums, fifes, cornets, lutes, harps, trumpets, etc. So they made merry until broad daylight.[1]

---

[1] Palmer and More, op. cit. pp. 114 f.; from Hogel's *Erfurt Chronicle*.

It was certainly a noble banquet, even by sixteenth-century standards; but there is hardly even a suggestion of magic about it. A little play-acting at the beginning, a little hanky-panky during which the window was used as a hatch, a royal feast and charming music. The only wonder is how Faust was able to afford it; but its grandeur was probably exaggerated. There being little or nothing of the marvellous in this tale, it was left unnoticed in the Spies Faust-book of 1589 for nearly a hundred years. But when Faust was introduced on to the popular German stage, the possibilities latent in those self-satisfied domestics was recognised; they were transformed into fiends, and the scene became a favourite one in the puppet-plays, capable as it was of indefinite variations; it even found its way into the Black Books. As far as I know the incident itself is peculiar to Faust; so is the tale about Plautus and Terence, though deriving from the feat attributed to Ezra. Since the course of Faust's life as it came to be shaped by ritual followed traditional lines; and since nearly all the phenomena later attributed to him were at second, third, fourth and even nth hand, one is the more inclined to deduce an historical basis for the small residuum of individual matter that remains.

The fifth episode in the *Erfurt Chronicle* is biographical rather than anecdotal. It may have been an elaboration of the heated arguments Faust was rumoured to have had with Melanchthon, or it may have been an embroidery of an actual occurrence in Erfurt. There is certainly nothing at all unlikely in the intervention of a Franciscan monk called Dr Klinge, urged on by the authorities to convert Faust to better ways, lest he should lead the youth of Erfurt and 'other simpletons' astray. The conversation between them is given mostly in dialogue form; Klinge urged the necromancer to repent, but without avail; for the latter took his stand on the blood-pact he had signed with the devil, impatiently rejecting the monk's opinion that it was not yet too late to amend and obtain divine pardon, especially if a mass were said for him in the Franciscan cloister:

'Mass here, mass there,' said Dr Faust. 'My pledge binds me too absolutely. I have wantonly despised God and become perjured and faithless towards Him, and believed and trusted more in the devil than in Him. Therefore I can neither come to Him again nor obtain any comfort from His grace which I have forfeited. Besides, it would not be honest nor would it redound to my honour to have it said that I had violated my bond and seal, which I have made with my own blood. The devil has honestly kept the promise that he made to me, therefore I will honestly keep the pledge that I made and contracted with him.'[1]

Brave words, but misleading ones. Here, in embryo, is the crux of the situation which was to be the very soul of the Faustbook; the case of the hardened sinner who cannot and will not repent. If this conversation had a biographical genesis, Faust himself was responsible for the legend of his obduracy; and it may be biographical, for his predecessors were represented as repenting in the nick of time, or else they were whisked off to perdition without warning. If the *Erfurt Chronicle* predated the first Faustbook (1587), this passage also contains the first explicit reference to the infernal pact, in which case Faust once more figures as the architect of his posthumous legend. However that may be, the flippant but sinister reference to his 'brother-in-law' made to Wier's friend would have been enough to start the shuttle flying that was to weave him into the sombre tapestry of sixteenth-century magic. He was caught up into a web, the strands of which running up and down, over and across, gradually obliterated the unprepossessing features of the real man until he became a stereotyped figure in the baleful pattern of contemporary infernal mythology. This was dominated by malignant fiends escorting whole cohorts of the doomed and the damned towards the gaping jaws of hell. He had hardly deserved it. He was not big enough nor wicked enough. He was not a Gilles de Rais. He had merely thrown his weight about and played some silly tricks and said some very foolish things. But he had entered into a league with the devil, whereas Bluebeard had never accomplished that, and even if he had would never have forfeited his life and his soul.

The student of magic discovers without much astonishment that Faust plays a very small part indeed in the history and theory of the art. The contemporary demonologists wasted few words upon him. Wier despised him; Bodin did not even mention him in his exhaustive work *De la démonomanie des sorciers*, 1580. Lavater, Hondorff, Reginald Scot and Guazzo only allude to him casually.

---

[1] Palmer and More, op. cit. pp. 117 ff.; from the *Erfurt Chronicle*. It has been suggested that this episode may derive from the *Confessions* of St Augustine.

In fact only Lercheimer gave some space to Faust in his defence of witches, in which he attacked the sorcerers and Faust among them. As time went on his name figured even less in the works of writers on magic. Burton, in the profusely documented 'Digression on Spirits' in the *Anatomy of Melancholy*, never mentioned him once. Naudé naturally did not classify him in 1625 with the great men falsely accused of magic, referring contemptuously to the stories about him as mere fables. When Francis Barrett attempted a rehabilitation of the arts of magic in *The Magus* in 1801, he ignored Faust altogether in the main body of the book, and did not include him in his biographical appendix. Eliphas Lévi had nothing to say about him in his exhaustive *History of Magic* in the eighteen-fifties. Sax Rohmer saw no reason to include him in his lively monograph, *The Romance of Sorcery*, 1914. And he was right. Students of the occult arts still consult the lives and works of Hermes Trismegistus, Solomon, Nostradamus, Paracelsus, Agrippa, Roger Bacon and John Dee in order to learn about the tradition or to discover magical secrets. No one to-day would dream of seeking any light from Faust, even though the Black Books attributed to him had a certain vogue among the smaller magical fry in Germany in the seventeenth and eighteenth centuries. But compared with *The Key of Solomon*, this hardly even counts.

Expert opinion has never been taken in by Faust; but he did not appeal in vain to the popular mind of his own day and later. And during his lifetime, he managed to impose himself upon a few of the educated as an astrologer who could predict events. The Bishop of Bamberg paid good money for a horoscope; and the famous classical philologist Joachim Camerarius, whilst deriding Faust's 'juggler's tricks', suggested almost in the same breath that he might with advantage be consulted about the future. As for the University students, it would seem that they were his to a man. Always dabbling in magic and playing tricks on their own account, they kept his memory green after he had gone; repeating and embroidering the stories current about him and others, and preserving them in writing. Later these were loosely strung together on a pseudo-biographical thread in the Wolffenbüttel Manuscript which underlay the first Faustbook. The tales were the same old chestnuts which had been religiously handed down from generation to generation and were now gathered together under the name of Faust. Book-making of the crudest kind was therefore one of the elements in the Spies Faustbook which appeared in 1587. To this the author contributed a certain amount of book-learning, culled from Wier, Lercheimer and others, where supplementary tales were to be found both about the hero of his book and about fellow-sorcerers. Everything seemed set fair for a compilation à la sixteenth-century Virgil. But the author of the biography had a serious purpose in compiling it. He was a deeply religious man of the Lutheran persuasion, so religious that it generated in his fervent mind a sombre streak of poetry. It was because of this that Faust, who had been propelled into the Wolffenbüttel Manuscript under the steam of his own publicity, was to slip through the golden gates of poetry almost before you could look round. Elizabethan prose and Elizabethan verse were the two portals through which he passed on his way to immortality; and never surely did any human being deserve it less. I am reserving this aspect of Faust's posthumous life for a special study. At the moment his place in the tradition of magic is my main concern.

'Spies'[1] said that Faust was of humble but respectable parentage, but so precociously clever that a wealthy relative adopted him and paid for his schooling and university studies. The shades of Moses and Pharaoh flicker past and vanish to make way for an aspiring, arrogant and perverted mind, turning from theology to black magic. So quickly did Faust advance in this unhallowed art that he was soon in a position to trace the magic circle of goetia and summon up an evil spirit. Only a few nights later he had signed a pact with him, sealed with his own blood, renouncing Christianity and selling his soul in return for knowledge and power. So he went sliding down the well-worn track, cleared by Proterius and Theophilus, trodden smooth by a monstrous regiment of popes, and made more slippery still by a host of other black magicians, one of whom, William de Line, had been condemned to death in 1453 for having perpetrated this deed. Grotesque and terrifying manifestations preceded the materialisation of the spirit before the circle. They were not due to the inventive genius of the author, but embodied current notions, which have been wonderfully described by Benvenuto Cellini. Yet one innovation there certainly was, though whether due to 'Spies' or

---

[1] Spies was the publisher of the first Faustbook which appeared anony-mously with a preface by him. I sometimes use his name in inverted commas when referring to the author.

his authorities it is impossible to say. This was the proper name of the attendant devil or familiar spirit: Mephostophiles, who did not become Mephistopheles until the eighteenth century. It is a name remarkable both for its euphony and for seeming to mean something, although no one has yet discovered what, or even what language it derives from, Persian, Hebrew, or Greek. A sinister ambiguity haunts the syllables and seems to mock such conjectures as 'no friend to light' (Mephotophiles) or 'no friend to Faust' (Mefaustophiles), or 'destroyer-liar' (Mephiz-Tophel); whilst also transcending those barbarous and meaningless names which were being invented by the score for contemporary lists of the infernal hierarchy. It was, on the other hand, a new feature to give the familiar spirit of black magicians a proper name; the baptism in 'Spies' made the demon more real and favoured the interesting effort to endow him with an individual character. This psychological attitude both to the magician and his control, embryonic though it is, was a factor in the survival of the legend; for something torn and Titanic is present in the hero, something terrible and ruthless in the fiend.

Faust's desire for illicit knowledge played a large part in impelling him to sign the pact, the fatal act of initiation; fear and remorse contributed their quota to those distressful and ever-recurrent questions about heaven and hell, the wicked and the damned, to which Mephosto returned such gruesome and despair-inducing answers in the first part of the book. Aspiration to absolute knowledge was the key-note of Solomon's legendary life; and in the same tradition are the journeys up into the sky, down in a dream into the infernal regions, and round what with the help of geographical compilations did duty for the earth in the second part. The dream about hell is a grotesque version of the *katabasis*. The main *agon* was between the hero and the evil spirit, perpetually at war in the questions and answers; coming into fierce prominence when Faust expressed a desire to marry, or was overcome with remorse, or attempted to repent, as he did rather feebly after the admonitions of a good old man, evidently the Dr Klinge of the *Erfurt Chronicle*. But in one of the stories of his magical feats (for the most part grouped together in the third section of the biography) traces of the earlier form, the contest with a rival magician, are discernible. It goes back to the tale of the mock death and resurrection of Simon Magus, if not still farther. For it is a decapitation story of a kind by now widely disseminated. The Celtic heroes Cuchulainn and Gawaine were both supposed to have met a stranger on their travels who challenged them to behead him. When they complied, he went off carrying his head and reappeared later none the worse. A Jewish sorcerer called Zedechias, attached to the court of Louis the Pious (814–49), a Master Theodo and a Johannes Teutonicus, in the thirteenth century were also said to be adepts at this particular art, and Lercheimer reported a circumstantial story of a certain A. v. Th. in his own day. This magician had overpersuaded the young 'boots' of an inn where he was staying to subject himself to this dangerous and delicate experiment. When it came to replacing the head, he was unable to do so, because someone in the audience was hindering him by strong counter-magic. After two solemn warnings to the unknown to desist, the magician miraculously caused a lily to grow out of the table at which he sat, whose flower he then decapitated; thereupon one of those present fell headless beneath the bench and A. v. Th. was able to resuscitate the 'boots'. In Germanic folk-lore, the lily is the symbol of the immortal soul, which accounts for its appearance here. Rigorous moralists will probably feel that the wicked magician got his deserts; and all will agree that it was a happy outcome for the poor young 'boots'. 'Spies' adopted the story as it stood, wrote it up a little, and attributed it to Faust. Not satisfied with that, however, he invented another and uglier one.

Doctor Faustus came during Lent to the Frankfort fair; and his spirit Mephostophiles told him that there were four magicians in an inn in the Jews' Alley who were cutting off each other's heads and sending them to the barbers to be shaved with many people looking on. That angered Faustus, who considered himself the only cock in the devil's basket, and he made off to the inn to have a look. There were the magicians all together, ready to cut off their heads, and the barber was with them to shave and wash them. But on the table they had a glass vessel with distilled water, and one amongst them, the chief magician and leader, conjured a lily into the vessel which bloomed in it, and he called it the root of life. After that, he operated on the first one, let the head be shaved and put it on the body again, after which the lily disappeared, and the head was whole on his shoulders.... And when it now came to the chief magician and leader, and his lily was also blooming and blossoming in the water, his head was struck off; and whilst it was being soaped and shaved in Faust's presence, whom such glaring roguery deeply offended, together with the arrogance of the chief magician who had thus impiously and with laughter allowed his head to be cut off, he, Faustus, went to the table on which stood the vessel with the lily, and cut the flower, slitting the stem apart, the which no one noticed. And when the other magicians became aware of the damage, all their art was in vain, and they could not restore the head to their comrade. So that wicked man had to die in his sins and be damned, as indeed the devil gives all his servants such an end at the last and makes away with them. But none of the magicians knew how the stem had been slit and had no idea that Faustus had done it.[1]

This diabolical mixture of malignancy and sanctimoniousness puts this contest in a class apart in the annals of sorcery. It was not even done in self-defence; it was not done openly; it was not a trial of magical skill. Anyone could have slit the stem. There is no precedent in the conflicts among magicians for anything so uncalled for and so cowardly as this. Zyto swallowed a formidable rival whole, but restored him when his patron protested, little, if any, the worse. Merlin was content with showing up the ignorance and folly of Vortigern's wizards, although they had plotted against his life; Virgil defeated his enemies in the open field and left it at that. Simon Peter certainly dealt cruelly with Simon Magus and encompassed his death, but it was in order that truth might prevail. Apollonius of Tyana confounded his opponents and vanished away; Zoroaster had the Kigs and Karaps destroyed; but they had tried to do the same to him, and were the enemies of light. Only 'Dionysos' and Moses can fairly be called malignant; and it is impossible to mention them and their fearful ruthlessness in the same breath with the spiteful little sorcerer called Faust.

This tale is only an episode in Faust's life, significantly enough the darkest one, whereas the victory over the rival magician is otherwise apt to be the highlight in the hero's career. The real contest was greater: the struggle for Faust's soul. This came to a climax when the sorcerer tried to repent after his interview with the old man. Terrorised by the infuriated fiend, he signed a second pact, even more binding than the first. After that, there was no looking back. He sank ever deeper into vileness and debauchery, obtaining through the good offices of Mephostophiles a whole harem of mortal women to cohabit with him (shades of Solomon), also many succubae, and among them the spirit whom he believed to be Helen of Troy.

[1] Scheible, *Das Kloster*, II, pp. 1043 ff. 'Spies' may have found the story ready-made and used it; but it looks as if he had invented it on the model of Lercheimer's tale.

Once the Homeric heroes had become again the object of necromantic spells, it was inevitable, in an age deeply preoccupied with
women, that the incomparable Helen should emerge with them from
the long twilight of the gods of Greece which was now beginning to
lift. They returned by the ambiguous power of magic, wraith-like
and eerie, for they were devils in disguise. The Nigromant in the
Historia of Hans Sachs (identified by Lercheimer with Tritheim),
produced Maria of Burgundy for Maximilian I, and also summoned
up Helen of Troy for the imperial edification. She was evidently in
demand; the Spies Faustbook conceived the further complication of
mating her with Faust. It was not the first time that her shade had
been imagined to renew her earthly life of love. She and Achilles
were supposed by the Greeks to have lived together on the island of
Phera after they had left this life; and Simon Magus had offered
a more obvious precedent by identifying the Gnostic Helen who
accompanied him with Helen of Troy, and describing her in
memorable words. 'Spies' was not at the height of the idea he
rediscovered or reintroduced. Nor did he handle the theme with the
tragic intensity which the medieval poets had lavished on the
bondage of Tannhäuser to Frau Hölle, whose other name was Venus.
This striking poetical symbol for the overpowering fascination of
pagan beauty and joy and the havoc it could wreak is on a very much
higher plane of poetry than the Helen of the first Faustbook.
Described almost entirely by diminutives as if she were a beautiful
doll with the wanton glances of a minx, she will stir no pulse to-day.
But this inadequate representation of a meant-to-be glamorous fiend,
translated into English prose, set the imagination of Marlowe aflame.
She also inspired such a passion in Faust that he could not bear her
out of his sight. From this strange union there issued a child called
Justus Faustus, born with prophetic gifts, as Merlin had been before
him; and also like that mysterious boy formed by Simon Magus for
mantic purposes. Both mother and son vanished away when the
magician died.

Wallowing therefore (to adopt the tone of his first biographer) in
every kind of lewdness with his paramours and succubae, Faust
approached his predestined end, and the nearer he approached the
oftener he began to wallow in despair. When he had a bare month to
run before his contract with Satan fell due, weepings, wailings and
gnashings of the teeth became the order of the day. These piteous

plaints maddened Mephostophiles (as well they might) and he retorted with a counterblast in which he spoke, and by no means for the first time, like the great Reformer himself. The voice was the voice of Mephosto, but the words were the words of Luther. In that racy, nervous, popular idiom, based almost entirely on current proverbs and sayings, with which Luther was wont to drive his points home; with the same boisterous verve, the same inexorable moral judgements, and the same blistering wrath, he berated his weak-kneed dupe for his apostasy from God and for his evil life. Now, said that ruthless and triumphant voice, let him reap where he had sown. 'God is the Lord; the devil is only an abbot or a monk.'

This handsome tribute, together with other pointers in the same direction, Mephosto's hatred of marriage, sneers about the celibacy of monks and nuns, the disrespectful attitude towards the Pope, and the fact that the evil spirit waited on Faust in the guise of a monk, are always used as evidence of the anti-Catholic tendency of the book. This is true enough, but trifling in comparison with the great inspirational force intermittently apparent, which emanated directly from Luther. This intensified the drama of the conflict between the two antagonists, whilst rendering it completely hopeless. For Luther, and for all the countless minds he swayed, the notion of the might and malignancy of the devil amounted to an obsession. This went a good deal beyond the conceptions entertained hitherto, which still survived in popular literature in comic or stupid devils. Luther was to change all that and open up disastrous prospects, a fearful and sinister view of life, entangled with the wiles and snares of the devil which were almost impossible to circumvent.

Under this blackest of black suns the question of the eventual salvation of a necromancer could hardly arise in earnest. 'Spies' was at pains to show that Mephosto's power over his victim's mind was such as to debar him from seeking divine forgiveness and grace. It has generally been allowed that the greater leniency shown to earlier sorcerers was due to mariolatry; as witness the legends of Theophilus and of his shadowy successor Militarius, who could not be brought to deny the Blessed Virgin and so escaped perdition. But the damnation of Faust and his contemporary colleagues in magical crime is even more clearly a form of diabolatry: the Lutheran belief in the almost unlimited powers of Satan, with no mediating saints and no merciful Mother of God to counteract it.

Nevertheless, faint verbal traces of the Catholic tradition are discernible in the first Faustbook. They are audible in the speeches of the old man, but the evil spirit made very short work of the hopes he held out. Quite unconsciously, however, an ambiguity crept into the account of Faust's end, which closely resembles that of Gerbert. The latter, it will be remembered, commanded that his body should be mutilated before and after death, and that his burial should take place wherever the horses dragging the bier should halt. As they drew up outside the Lateran church, it would seem that he had been forgiven, and that his soul was saved. Opinion on that matter was divided, but no one ever doubted Faust's eternal damnation, or would have thought of altering the legend until Lessing character-istically did so. Yet Faust's last night on earth followed the precedent set by Gerbert. Summoning all his dearest student-friends together to partake of supper with him about half a mile from Wittenberg, the unhappy magician opened his heart to them. He told them of his wicked life, of his pact with the devil, and of his approaching end. Like Gerbert and like Gilles de Rais, he warned them in most moving terms to avoid a similar destiny. After refusing all comfort and all hope, he begged them to retire to bed and not to be afraid at whatever noise they might hear, but to bury his body if they should find him dead in the morning. He concluded with these words:

For I die both as a bad and a good Christian. A good Christian, because I feel true repentance and cease not to pray for mercy in my heart, so that my soul might yet be saved. A bad Christian, for I know that the devil will have my body, and that I will willingly give him, if he but leave my soul in peace. Wherefore I beseech you to retire to your beds, and I wish you a good night; but for myself a vexed, bad and terrible one.[1]

He was granted his wish. Between midnight and one o'clock in the morning a terrible wind arose which seemed like to destroy the house, and a fearful whistling and hissing was also heard as if the building were full of adders, snakes and other dangerous serpents. Faust's door flew open, and the terrified students heard him feebly calling 'Murder! Help!' But soon all was still. Next morning his mangled body was found near the manure heap in the yard; his room was full of blood, brains and teeth, and his eyes were found adhering to the wall. The devil had certainly seized his body. But what about his soul? Surely the mutilation presented a loophole through which it

[1] Scheible, op. cit. II, p. 1066.

might have escaped? Perhaps the students, who succeeded in obtaining burial for him, cherished some hopes in this direction; but they must have been sorely dashed when the ghost of the dead man appeared at night to Wagner and made sinister revelations; and was also seen by others looking out of the window of his house.

Though Faust's damnation is not textually self-evident, yet in spite of the piety of his last words, it cannot be said that he made an edifying end. He persisted in his evil ways until the eleventh hour; and, having already corrupted his servant Wagner, he not only left him all his books on magic, but made arrangements for this depraved youth to inherit his devilish skill and to have a familiar spirit to serve him after his master's death. This cynical assistance in leading another to perdition lessens the value of the piercing laments he uttered when the fear of eternal torment began to shake his morale. He was ruthless in the hour of his might, and steeped in self-pity when the day of reckoning came. Zyto, impenitent to the last, was fetched off by the devil from a banquet. Tradition does not recount how he behaved at this crisis. Robert of Normandy, nicknamed the Devil, had been consecrated to Satan by his mother before his birth, and was a demon of carnage and slaughter incarnate in his early manhood. He came to his senses when he realised that all people fled from him, questioned his mother and learnt the terrifying truth. In great anguish of spirit he went to Rome, confessed to the Pope and was assoiled on condition of performing the most fearful penances. He underwent these ordeals manfully and was saved, although the merciless denied this. Virgil, according to the Christian version of the legend, repented his sins and died prophesying the advent of Christ. Merlin, the Antichrist, faded from view after he had been baptised. Gerbert, whose manner of death closely approximates to Faust's end, seems to have been genuinely remorseful when his hour struck, and more shattered than cringing. Theophilus did penance in dust and ashes; Cyprian was converted. Gilles de Rais welcomed death and died heroically. All those who felt convicted of sin renounced the fruits of their unholy alliances in order to make their peace with God. Faust sat wailing on the fence until it was too late. His lachrymose and poor-spirited ending forms a striking contrast with that of his Polish double Twardowski. The latter, whose pact with Satan was not to fall due except in Rome, found himself tricked like Gerbert into a hostelry of that name in Poland. He was furiously preparing to fight the matter out, when the devil appealed to his honour as a Polish gentleman to stand by his given word. Twardowski gallantly surrendered at once. His is one of the few fine endings of magicians in post-Christian times. The two most tragic are Simon Magus, falling like Lucifer from heaven, and Joan of Arc, dying the death of a sacrificed saviour-god.

The course of Faust's life, dispensing with a supernatural origin and portents and perils at birth, has all the other features of the magus-myth, including a highly detailed last scene. All this part, barring the celestial, infernal and terrestrial journeys, is written with a kind of fearful conviction as well as with a fearful interest in the state of mind of the sorcerer and the nature of his control which gives emotional reality to the account. This is not so with the description of Faust's feats. For the most part bundled together in the third section of the biography, they are so baldly narrated and so carelessly arranged that they automatically suggest a vision of scissors and paste. Such as they are, however, they show all the familiar features. The magical power over the elements, and especially over rain on account of its importance for the food supply, had become, as in medieval stories generally, a pretext for mystification or display. An illusory flood of water was produced on one convivial occasion in order to make the ladies present pick up their skirts and show their lovely legs to the men, who had no idea why they were thus favoured, an elaboration of Zyto's, and a variant of Virgil's feat. A glorious summer garden miraculously conjured forth in the frozen depths of winter was a reminiscence of a circumstantial tale told about Albertus Magnus, another sophistication of the rain-maker's influence on crops, as were also the magical banquets, produced in the twinkling of an eye, which all medieval magicians revelled in. Faust conjured forth no less than seven during his career, all provided with the choicest and rarest foods, fruit out of season and exquisite wines. His tenuous kinship with the medicine-man of old was manifest in love-charms, and the power to render inconvenient persons temporarily blind, dumb or paralytic. As with Zyto, remnants of ritual resurrection flicker round the story of an impertinent young 'boots' whom the conjurer swallowed alive and then restored in a sopping condition under the stairs. Like Gerbert, he erected a dazzlingly beautiful palace; and like Simon Magus he was responsible for a prophetic sprite, his son Justus Faust. Many feats of seeming transformation were also put down to his credit. He deluded a party of drunken students into the belief that their noses were clusters of grapes and only disillusioned them in time as they were about to hack them off; he repeated Zyto's pranks with the stag's horn and with the bundles of hay disguised as swine and disintegrating in the water, with its sequel, the luckless leg-pull of the dupe. He could render himself invisible at will, and did so with great effect in the Vatican, snatching savoury dishes and goblets of wine from his startled Holiness the while. He also surrounded the harem of the sultan in Constantinople by a thick fog, during which time in the guise of Mahomet he disported himself with the inmates. He possessed a magic steed, a magic cloak and a magic ladder for flights through the air, produced phantom armies, as Merlin was also said to do; and foretold the future by means of astrological observations as he had done in real life. He added to these many and various powers the capacity to swallow anything whole: the 'boots' aforesaid, a load of hay, and a cart-horse and wagon.

It will be apparent from the foregoing list that Faust also swallowed Zyto whole and brought him up again rather the worse for wear. Like the lean kine eating the fat kine in Pharaoh's dream, he was little, if any, the better for it; and these borrowings are only a fraction of the tale of plagiarisms of which the author of the first Faustbook was guilty. His hero in fact is the veriest daw arrayed in peacock's feathers. All tales of magic are by their nature traditional. But in Faust's case incident after incident has been simply lifted out of other books and transcribed *verbatim* merely altering the hero's name. This underlines the fact that there was precious little substance behind this man of straw. An odious piece of Jew-baiting for instance, which strikes one as possibly original, turns out to be taken from a story told by Hondorff about a sorcerer in the year 1274. This man, and Faust after him, fooled a Jewish creditor by pretending to saw his leg off and persuading him to take it in pawn for his debts. The Jew, on second thoughts, threw it away as valueless. Whereupon Faust demanded it back, saying that he could now redeem it. The wretched Jew then had to pay through the nose for a pound of flesh he had never really received. The story of the noses and grapes, which owing to Goethe now seems peculiarly Faust's own, was originally told by Lercheimer about somebody else. Moreover, some of these curious tales are singularly marred in the telling, whilst the most important, the feats of necromancy, are explicitly attributed to Mephostophiles. When the Emperor Charles V asked to see Alexander the Great, Faust consulted apart with his spirit and solemnly warned the emperor not to address the apparition, nor to ask any questions; for, as he frankly owned, like any other good contemporary Lutheran, what Charles was about to witness was a diabolic impersonation:

But Your Majesty must know, that their mortal bodies cannot rise from the dead, nor be present, for this is impossible. But the primeval spirits, who have seen Alexander and his consort, they can take on their shape and form themselves into those persons. Through these spirits I will show your Majesty Alexander in very truth.[1]

The real point of necromancy, from the days of the Witch of Endor downwards, had been the questioning of the spirits raised. The rite was performed for mantic reasons and therefore had a serious purpose. It had here degenerated into a mere show in *Dumb Crambo*, as in the Erfurt tale; its original meaning was lost. Worse still, it was a garbled replica of Lercheimer's description of the raising by Tritheim of all the great pagans and emperors to delight Maximilian I. Finally, the phantom of his dead wife, Maria of Burgundy, was conjured up. The inconsolable widower, intently regarding her, recognised a tiny black mole on the nape of her neck, by which he recognised her in very truth. 'Spies' clapped a great black wart on the neck of Alexander's consort, of which Faust had read or heard. The little beauty-spot in the original adds pathos to the tale. Magnified into an ugly wart it looks exceedingly silly on the neck of a lady who probably never had one. But no sillier than the brazen head which Gerbert and Virgil had made famous appearing incongruously and without explanation, not to utter oracles, but to produce those floods of water which caused the ladies such inconvenience. It is quite meaningless where it stands. One could go on for much longer giving similar instances of unintelligent plagiarisms. But it is probably enough to say that, after wading through all the tales and tracing them back to their near or remoter sources, only the incident of the chaplain's beard belongs exclusively to Faust. He 'improved' on the decapitation trick; he cohabited with Helen of Troy and produced Justus Faust, thus going one better than

[1] Scheible, op. cit. II, p. 1012.

Simon Magus; and he also conjured the four wheels off the wagon
of a surly peasant who had refused him a lift, and sent them flying
to the four gates of the town. But what is that feat in comparison
with Merlin and the monoliths of Stonehenge?

The general impression gained of Faust as a conjurer is a pitiable
one; for the traditional feats have become petty and trite; the
actual borrowings on the other hand are made unintelligently, or else
they show up the performer as a spiteful and disagreeable person.
In fact, tales of magic wrought reach their lowest level in the biography of Faust. Had this been the only element in the book, its
hero could not long have survived the sixteenth century. But the
strong religious fervour in the biographical portions gave a cosmic
nature to the conflict and reality to the sorcerer and his familiar. It
was this which carried them both with breath-taking speed into
Elizabethan drama, and thence down the centuries to us.

Faust himself, cutting the poor figure he does, is a telling symptom
of the times and of the great change for the worse Christianity had
effected in the status of magicians. Yet the foundations of their lives
still held firm, though much of the superstructure had crumbled
away. The divine origin with its attendant portents and perils was
barely recognisable in the royal descent of Virgil and darkly
disguised in the demon-father of Merlin. Distant journeys died
away after Cyprian and reappeared with Faust. The initiation was
symbolised by the infernal pact; and the main conflict was between
good and evil externalised, rather than the conquest of an old god
by a new one or a sacrifice consummated. Sporadic encounters
between rivals in magic, however, witness to the tenacity of the
original tradition in the lives of Virgil, Merlin, Zyto and Faust. The
trial and persecution were merged for the most part with the main
conflict between the hero and the evil spirit; but the last scene, often
taking the form of plenary confession, in Faust's case made at a last
supper (and Zyto was fetched away from a banquet), emphasised the
sinful nature of sorcery as such. The *pathos* retained and made more
gruesome the feature of violent dismemberment in the endings of
Gerbert, Virgil and Faust as well as in Cyprian's martyrdom; but
Merlin's final fate was poetical and mysterious. The descent into
Hades was represented by eternal damnation in hell, although Faust
also undertook a dream-journey into the nether regions, thus
reviving the *katabasis*. The resurrection was now whittled down to

banshee wailings and hauntings and romantically conceived as deathlessness for Merlin, whilst Joan of Arc was also supposed by some to have escaped the faggots. Whatever the elements omitted, retained or added, the myth of the magus as retold by 'Spies' was now an unsightly ruin with parts very badly restored and a general appearance of Gothic gloom. Only the evilly disposed could feel at home in its purlieus. This is one of the reasons why the tales of age-old magic crystallised round Faust at the close of the Middle Ages, and not round Joan of Arc, the sacrificed saviour, nor yet round Martin Luther, the teaching-god of those days. One need only state the situation in this way to realise fully how debased the whole conception had become; for Saint Joan and Luther would have been great magi in antiquity. That they did not become so now was partly due to the fact that they were not wicked, partly too because they were outstanding and well known. Only the lowest and the last of mortals would do to represent magic in the sixteenth century.

The spirit of the age therefore chose Faust rather than his more distinguished predecessors and contemporaries. Legend had been at least equally busy with Albertus Magnus, Thomas Aquinas and Peter of Apono in the thirteenth century, but they did not become myths. Tritheim, Agrippa, Paracelsus and Nostradamus in the sixteenth century were much more famous than Faust and enjoyed an equally sinister reputation; yet they were never completely mythologised. Granted that an incalculable element enters into the mythopoeic process, it is yet true that certain circumstances militate against it. Mahomet for instance, although many legends surround his name, and although tradition began shaping him into a Zoroaster or a Moses, resisted complete transformation, because his real life was too well known. The same contention applies to Luther. He gave his enemies a handle by confessing to frequent assaults by the devil; and they obligingly labelled him Antichrist, in return for the compliment he had paid to the Pope; all kinds of legendary stories were told about him; but his life was too publicly lived to favour a coherent myth. And even if this had not been so, he was too great to become a magus during this period, when the heart had gone out of magic.

Leaving temporary fashions aside, it would seem that what Goethe once said of poetry also applies to mythology: only insufficient knowledge is productive. Magicians must either be enveloped in obscurity and mystery in their own times, or belong to days that are dim before they can be reborn into myth. Virgil, Merlin and Faust all point the same moral. And so does a man, the deliberate omission of whose name until now must have been perplexing, the Englishman Roger Bacon.

(d) Friar Bacon

Although Bacon lived in the thirteenth century, he came of age as a hero of legend in the sixteenth century, and must be regarded as Faust's contemporary in the history of magic. This is all the more inevitable, because the popular version of his life and deeds reads like a deliberate answer to the lamentable tale of the hero of 'Spies', almost as if the spirit of England were up in arms against German magic and recommending a national brand. Yet the bibliographical data seem to point in the opposite direction. Greene's comedy, *The Honourable History of Friar Bacon and Friar Bungay*, which provides the absolutely fixed point, was produced in February 1592. In all probability it was based on a prose version of the legend. But the earliest extant edition (reprinted in the first volume of Thoms' *Early English Prose Romances*) cannot have been published before 1597, since it quotes from Bacon's *Epistle on the Secret Operations of Art and Nature and the Nullity of Magic*, first translated in that year from Latin into English. Marlowe's *Tragical History of Doctor Faustus*, on the other hand, was written after May 1592, when the English Faustbook first appeared; for this is now generally agreed to have been his one and only source. Greene therefore certainly had the priority over Marlowe; and it looks as if the Bacon legend must have got into print before the Faust legend in this country. Yet, both in the story-books and in the plays, though less strongly in the latter, one has the vague but persistent impression that Bacon is being manœuvred into playing the part of anti-Faust. To put it in another way, neither 'Spies' nor his English translator, P.F., shows the slightest sign of being aware of the Bacon legend; whereas whoever wrote *The Famous Historie of Fryer Bacon* seems to be preoccupied with Faust. And one is justified in the supposition that the preoccupation was present in Greene's source, because it has coloured his comedy, and is one of the elements of a definite anti-German bias discernible in the   lay. Whatever the odd, unaccountable and baffling relationship between the Faust and Bacon legends may be, and however it arose, it seems to be there. As it is not explicit, for Faust is never mentioned in the Bacon legend, the contrast may not have been intended, and may be due to the fact that the real Bacon was the very antithesis of the real Faust.

Roger Bacon (*c*. 1214–*c*. 1292) was a very remarkable man; so far ahead of his times in many respects that he suffered persecution for his views. In the heyday of scholasticism, he deprecated and openly attacked its very basis: the settling of all disputed questions by appeals to authority, often made at second or even third hand, and often too in utter ignorance of the language of the writers appealed to. A knowledge of Greek, Hebrew and Arabic was one of his reiterated demands, backed up by the compilation of grammatical treatises. Even more insistently he advocated the search for truth by means of experimental science, and sketched a method for its procedure. Three hundred years later, his namesake Francis was more successful in impressing his contemporaries with the importance of this approach to knowledge. Roger, who had been a student at the University of Oxford from the then usual age of twelve or thereabouts, graduated at Oxford, became a lecturer there, and then removed to Paris, according to the prevalent custom. At what period he entered the Franciscan Order and became a Friar is not known; but he came under the unfavourable notice of the Superior, and was placed under strict surveillance in Paris, writing thus about his treatment to Pope Clement IV:

...the Prelates and Friars have kept me starving in close Prison nor would they suffer any one to come at me, fearing lest my Writings should come to any other than the Pope and themselves.[1]

This was in 1267, when (luckily for Bacon) Guy de Foulkes, previously Papal Legate in England, and Pope since 1266, wrote to the Friar asking him to send him an account of his scientific theories. Bacon in a very short time dispatched his *Opus Majus*, *Opus Minus* and possibly his *Opus Tertium* (1267–68). Clement, who died in 1268, can hardly have read them; but Bacon was released from confinement and returned to Oxford in 1268. Ten years later, he fell out of favour again because of the suspect 'novelties' in his writings. This

[1] Quoted in the Preface to Roger Bacon, *The Cure of Old Age*..., tr. R. Browne, London 1683.

imprisonment, again in Paris, was even harsher and more rigorous than the first. It lasted from 1278 to 1292, in which year he was released, returned to Oxford and died; although some writers place his death two years later.

It was rumoured at the time, and seems more than likely, that the real reason for his persecution was the charge of practising magic, in spite of his declaration of its 'nullity' in his essay on the wonders wrought by art and nature:

...there is a more damnable practice, when men despising the Rules of Philosophy, irrationally call up wicked Spirits, supposing them of Energy to satisfie their desires. In which there is a very vast errour, because such persons imagine they have some authority over Spirits, and that Spirits may be compelled by humane authority, which is altogether impossible, since humane energy or Authority is inferiour by much to that of Spirits. Besides, they admit a more vast mistake, supposing such natural instruments, as they use, to be able either to call up, or drive away any wicked Spirit. And they continue their mistake in endeavouring by Invocations, Deprecations, or Sacrifices to please Spirits, making them propitious to their design. Without all question, the way is incomparably more easie to obtain any thing, that is truly good for men, of God or good Angels, than of wicked Spirits. As for things which are incommodious for men, wicked Spirits can no further yield assistance, then they have permission, for the sins of the sonnes of men, from that God, who governs and directs all humane affairs.[1]

Concerning those Secrets, which are revealed in Magicians writings, although they contain some truth, yet in regard those very truths are enveloped with a number of deceits, as it's not very easie to judge betwixt the truth and the falsehood, they ought all worthily to be rejected. Neither must men be believed, who would assure us, That *Solomon*, or some other of our sage Progenitors were Authors of such Books, because those books are not received either by the Churches Authority, or by any prudent men, but only by a few cheating Companions to be the work of such men. Mine own experience assures me they compose and set forth new works and inventions of their own, in lofty high flown expressions, the more colourably to make their lies pass under the shelter of the Text: prefixing some specious titles, the better to set them off, impudently ascribe such bastard births to famous Authors.[2]

[1] Frier Bacon, *His discovery of the Miracles of Art, Nature and Magick*. Faithfully translated out of Dr *Dee's* own Copy, by T.M. and never before in English, London 1629, p. 3. [There was an earlier translation in 1597, which I have not been able to see.]

[2] Ibid. pp. 6 ff.

Although Bacon then goes on to show that the miracles of art and nature far exceed anything that can be produced by magic, nevertheless it will be noticed that he had investigated magic with an unbiased mind, and had come to the conclusion that there was something in it. He was not altogether certain for instance that there was no power in incantations and charms, for he was aware of the power of words. 'All the miracles since the world began, almost, have been wrought by words', he once stated. Moreover, like everyone else in his day, he included astrology in the study of astronomy, and thought that certain predispositions in the characters of men were due to the aspect of the heavens at their birth; but he insisted on the free will of the individual and condemned the kind of astrology which

. . . usurps a consideration of the heavenly bodies which is marred by characters, incantations, conjurations, superstitious practices, and various frauds.[1]

His *Mirror of Alchemy* reflects the same attitude. He regarded it as an experimental science, one of the means of penetrating to those secrets of nature and art with which he was always primarily concerned; art standing of course for the inventions and discoveries, mechanical and other, made by a close study of nature. And sharing with his age the strong expectation of the imminence of Antichrist, he also believed that this wicked spirit would certainly know and use all the secret powers of nature and art for the confusion of the world as well as the magical sciences.

And yet it is true that these magnificent sciences, through which great good can be wrought as well as great evil, should only be known by certain persons authorised by the Pope. . . so that the Church in all its tribulations can have recourse to these powers, and at last Antichrist and his followers would be met and—as miracles like his were done by the faithful—it would be shown that he was not God and his persecution would be hindered and mitigated in many respects by measures of this kind.[2]

This passage, probably later in date than the *Discovery*, seems to be referring to the wonders magic can produce, and looks as if Bacon had become more impressed by them; but he still regarded them as essentially inferior, since he went on to state that Antichrist would

---

[1] W. Winthrop, *Roger Bacon*, London n.d. p. 108; quoting from the *Opus Majus*.

[2] A. G. Little, 'Roger Bacon', *Proceedings of the British Academy*, London 1928, XIV, p. 289; quoting from the *Opus Tertium*.

also use mechanical inventions, works of mathematics and geometry, in which there is no magic, and which show the inferiority and indignity of magical powers to that of nature and art:

...such as burning glasses which operate at any distance we can choose, so that anything hostile to the commonwealth may be burnt—a castle, or army or city or anything; and the flying machine, and a navigating machine by which one man may guide a ship full of armed men with incredible speed; and scythe-bearing cars which full of armed men race along with wondrous machinery without animals to draw them, and break down or cut through all obstacles.[1]

Here, as also in the *Discovery*, Bacon clearly foresaw the coming age of mechanisation; he described poison gas, diving-suits, and other inventions as well, generally stating that he had found them in some ancient author. Whether or not he was correct in these scholastic attributions, he had a forward-looking mind, and certainly experimented with magnifying glasses, spectacle lenses and telescopes. Some time before 1571 Leonard Digges constructed a reflecting telescope according to the instructions found by him in 'one old written book of the said Bacon's experiments'. He was not the first to discover gunpowder, it would appear; but he evidently hit on the formula independently, and seems to have hidden it in cypher in the alchemical chapters at the end of the *Discovery*. More astonishing still, a passage in his work on geography which was incorporated by the Cardinal Pierre d'Ailly in his *Imago Mundi* so much impressed Columbus that he annotated it fully in a letter to Ferdinand and Isabella. So that the *Opus Majus* (which contains the work on geography) became at second hand one of the authorities which inspired Columbus to undertake his great voyage of discovery. Bacon's proposal to reform the calendar, taken up later by Dr Dee, and based on astronomical calculations, is also said to have influenced Copernicus through the medium of Paul de Middleburg.

Roger Bacon's undoubted greatness as a thinker, a man of vision and a pioneer in experimental science seems to have been allied as well to nobility of mind.

Authority may impel belief, but cannot enlighten the understanding, he once said, and

The end of all true philosophy is to arrive at a knowledge of the Creator through knowledge of the created world.

[1] A. G. Little, op. cit. p. 290; quoting from the *Opus Tertium*.

The Admirable Doctor passed his life and wrote his works in the precincts of two great universities, in humble Minorite cells, and for more than a decade in the harsh confinement of prisons. The atmosphere surrounding his studious life is as different as possible from that pothouse odour which tenaciously clings to the real Faust, in spite of his later traditional association with the University of Wittenberg. And though Faust, like Bacon, had some experience of the inside of prison walls, how differently he passed his period behind them, if Wier's tale is to be believed! On the one side, in thirteenth-century England, a persecuted devotee of science and learning; on the other side, in sixteenth-century Germany, a bragging charlatan and an evil liver to boot.

There can be little doubt that Bacon's experiments made no small stir in his own day, and were accountable for the unenviable reputation of dabbling in magic which had such unhappy results. Less than a century after his death, his legend was beginning to take shape. In 1385 Peter of Trau wrote thus about him from Zara in Dalmatia:

> By natural condensation [of the air] he sometimes made a bridge 30 miles long over the sea from the Continent to England, and after passing over it safely with all his retinue, destroyed it by rarefying the air by natural means.[1]

Bacon had not protested quite in vain therefore that the miracles he described were brought about by the power of nature, a claim not put forward for Virgil's similar feat; Bacon's bridge, on the other hand, irresistibly brings the passage through the Red Sea to one's mind. His own optical experiments, however, obviously inspired the following tale:

> He...made two mirrors in the University of Oxford: by one of them you could light a candle at any hour, day or night; in the other you could see what people were doing in any part of the world. By experimenting with the first, students spent more time in lighting candles than in studying books; and seeing, in the second, their relations dying or ill or otherwise in trouble, they got into the habit of going down, to the ruin of the University, so by common council of the University both mirrors were broken.[2]

This legend later played an important part in the story-book of the sixteenth century, at which period it seems probable that the various tales about Bacon were first collected and strung together

---

[1] Winthrop, op. cit. p. 14.   [2] Ibid. pp. 14 ff.

into what Thoms calls a prose romance. This is not biographically integrated to anything like the same extent as the Spies Faustbook. It lacks the centre round which Faust's life revolved, for no contract signed with the devil figures in Bacon's career. This omission appears to have been deliberate. For there was a tradition that Bacon had entered upon such a pact, promising his soul to the devil, provided that he died neither in the Church nor out of it. This seemed fair enough to Satan. But Bacon outwitted him by making a cell in the wall of a church and dying there, not within and not without. Neither Greene's comedy nor the tale given by Thoms makes any use of this piece of sophistry, although the prose legend shows Bacon exercising that gift in favour of another, and incidentally playing the part the Erfurt Franciscan monk Dr Klinge and the Old Man in 'Spies' tried to play for Faust. An unhappy gentleman, deeply in debt, had promised his services unconditionally to the arch-fiend (cunningly disguised as a usurer) if he would relieve him of his financial burdens. The contract was to fall due when all the debts were paid; and the horror of the miserable debtor can be imagined when he discovered that he had unwittingly signed his soul away to the devil in person. Putting him off with transparent excuses, he got rid of the menacing spirit for the space of a day, and was just about to commit suicide when Friar Bacon chanced to pass by, and urged him to desist from such a sin:

Sir, should I leave you to this wilfull damnation, I were unfit ever hereafter to weare or touch any robe that belongeth to the holy order, whereof I am a brother: you know (I doubt not) that there is given power to the church to absolve penitent sinners, let not your wilfulnesse take away from you that benefit which you may receive by it: freely confesse your selfe (I pray you) unto me, and doubt not but I shall give your troubled conscience ease: Father (said this Gentleman) I know all you have spoken is truth, and I have many times received comfort from the mother church, (I dare not say our, for I feare that shee will never receive me for a childe) I have no part in her benediction, yet since you request so earnestly the cause, I will tell you, heare and tremble. Know then that I have given my selfe to the Devill for a little wealth, and he tomorrow in this wood must have me: now have you my griefe, but I know not how to get comfort. This is strange (quoth Fryer Bacon), yet be of good comfort, penitentiall teares may doe much, which see you doe not spare; soone I will visit you at your house, and give you that comfort (I hope) that will beget you againe to goodnesse: The Gentleman with these words was somewhat comforted and returned home. At night Fryer Bacon came to him, and found him full of teares for his haynous offences, for these teares he gave him hope of pardon....[1]

In the *Erfurt Chronicle*, Faust impatiently sent Dr Klinge about his business; in the Spies Faustbook, he began to repent, but Mephostophiles frightened penitence away and forced him to sign a second pact. Bacon's *protégé*, having sincerely repented, was saved by a clever piece of casuistry. All three coming together next day, Bacon as a 'chance' passer-by was appealed to by the contracting parties, and ruled that since the improvident gentleman was still in debt to the devil, his soul would not be forfeit until he had repaid him the moneys lent. This neat solution is in harmony with the light and almost sunny tone prevailing throughout. The ever-looming danger, which gives so much emotional colouring to the Faustbook, is entirely absent. By an odd twist of the wheel of legend a graceless and sorry swindler was transformed into a doomed soul; whilst the high-minded and persecuted Bacon shrank to the proportions of a benevolent, urbane and successful magician, who went about doing good, allowing himself at most an occasional Puckish trick against evildoers. Moreover, his humaneness was such that it finally caused him to abjure magic altogether. He was already grievously depressed in spirits by the news of the terrible end of his crony Bungay (with reason as will be seen later), when two youths begged him to let them look into his magic mirror, the famous 'perspective glass', in order to see how their fathers fared at home. Unfortunately these parents were discovered to be fighting a duel. High words arose between the sons as they looked on impotently. Finally, drawing their swords, they stabbed each other to death. Overcome with sorrow and remorse, Bacon shattered the glass; and then, calling his friends and scholars together, he addressed them in this wise:

My good friends and fellow students, it is not unknowne to you, how that through my art I have attained to that credit, that few men living ever had: of the wonders that I have done, all England can speak, both king and commons: I have unlocked the secret of art and nature, and let the world see those things, that have layen hid since the death of Hermes, that rare and profound philosopher: my studies have found the secrets of the starres; the bookes that I have made of them, doe serve for presidents to

---

[1] *The Famous Historie of Fryer Bacon*, ed. Thoms, *Early English Prose Romances*, London 1858, I, p. 202.

our greatest doctors, so excellent hath my judgement been therein. I likewise have found out the secrets of trees, plants and stones, with their several uses; yet all this knowledge of mine I esteeme so lightly, that I wish that I were ignorant, and knew nothing: for the knowledge of these things (as I have truly found) serveth not to better a man in goodnesse, but onely to make him proud and thinke too well of himselfe. What hath all my knowledge of natures secrets gained me? Onely this, the losse of a better knowledge, the losse of divine studies, which makes the immortall part of man (his soul) blessed. I have found, that my knowledge has beene a heavy burden, and has kept downe my good thoughts: but I will remove the cause, which are these bookes: which I doe purpose here before you all to burne. They all intreated him to spare the bookes, because in them there were those things that after-ages might receive great benefit by. He would not hearken unto them, but threw them all into the fire, and in that flame burnt the greatest learning in the world...then caused he to be made in the church-wall a cell where he locked himselfe in, and there remained till his death. His time hee spent in prayer, meditation and such divine exercises, and did seeke by all means to perswade men from the study of magicke. Thus lived he some two yeares space in that cell, never coming forth: his meat and drink he received in at a window, and at that window he did discourse with those that came to him; his grave he digged with his own nayles, and was laid there when he dyed.[1]

One cannot help remembering the legend of how Solomon burnt his books before the end; and indeed there is much of Solomon in Bacon; his wisdom, his learning and his contrivances, not to mention the fact that one of the Solomonic judgements in the *Gesta Romanorum* was attributed to the English magician in the prose romance. Even more obvious, however, is the contrast with that hardened sinner Faust who bequeathed all his magic books to Wagner, and set his successor's feet on the road to evil he had trodden himself; nor can one fail to compare Bacon's farewell speech to his friends and students with Faust's last oration to an audience similarly composed; and one can hardly avoid the conclusion that the contrast was intended. It runs threadlike through all the tales told about Bacon in his collection, many of them borrowed from earlier sources; but all of them chosen, or so it seems, for their humane, even humanitarian character. Now this was far indeed from being an Elizabethan characteristic, as the literature of the period bears eloquent and at times startling witness. The moral aim of the *Historie* reprinted by

---

[1] Thoms, op. cit. I, pp. 248–50.

Thoms is indubitable, and at times even oppressive; not, however, or at least not until the end, in the delightful account of the conflict between Bacon and Bungay on the one hand and the German sorcerer Vandermast on the other. Bacon had succeeded by natural means (in fact by his famous burning-glass) in reducing a long beleaguered city in France at the request of the King of England. The latter had then shown such clemency to the conquered (clemency again) that the French ambassador designed a marvellous entertainment for him to show his gratitude, and of this entertainment Vandermast, the famous German magician, was to be the outstanding feature. The fact that he was a German does not necessarily imply that the author had Faust in mind; for as Herford puts it, to the average Englishman of that day Germany 'was famous only as a land of magicians and conjurers, as the home of Albertus and Agrippa, Paracelsus, Tritheim and Doctor Faust'.[1] Any continental conjurer would therefore be apt to be represented as a German. The King of England, however, had no mind to see his country outshone in the art of magic any more than in the art of war, and privately ordered Friar Bacon and his inseparable friend Friar Bungay to attend the proceedings and hold a watching brief for England. Vandermast led off in fine style, producing Pompey attired as if for the battle of Pharsalia at the king's request and to everyone's amazement. Bacon, however, thereupon raised the spirit of Caesar who engaged Pompey and inevitably vanquished him, as the English monarch had obviously intended.

My lord ambassadour (said the king) me thinks that my Englishman has put down your German: hath he no better cunning than this? Yes, answered Vandermast, your grace shall see me put downe your Englishman ere that you goe from hence; and therefore Fryer prepare thy selfe with thy best art to withstand me.[2]

Bacon nonchalantly told the German to try conclusions with Bungay first; and the latter seemed to be paving the way for a German victory by conjuring forth the tree of the Hesperides laden with its golden apples and complete with its guardian dragon. It was child's play for the rival magician to summon up the ghost of Heracles from the shades and bid him re-enact his traditional feat of

[1] C. H. Herford, *Studies in the Literary Relations of England and Germany in the Sixteenth Century*, Cambridge 1886, p. 165.
[2] Thoms, op. cit. I, p. 218.

daring. But just as he was about to pluck the fruit, Bacon waved his wand and the shade of Heracles faltered. Urged on by the German with threats of torment, he showed great fear, and said:

I cannot, nor I dare not: for great Bacon stands, whose charms are farre more powerful than thine, I must obey him Vandermast. Hereat Vandermast curst Heracles, and threatened him: but Fryer Bacon laughed, and bid not to chafe himself ere that his journey was ended: for seeing (said he) that Heracles will doe nothing at your command, I will have him doe you some service at mine: with that he bid Heracles carry him home into Germany. The Devill obeyed him, and tooke Vandermast on his backe, and went away with him in all their sights. Hold Fryer, cried the ambassadour, I will not loose Vandermast for half my land. Content yourself my lord, answered Fryer Bacon, I have but sent him home to see his wife, and ere long he may returne.[1]

Although in all the conflicts between rival magicians, the assumption that the spirits with whom they are in league are assisting them underlies, even if only implicitly, the trial of magical strength, this account shows a further development in presenting the spirits fighting it out visibly before all. The phenomenon of necromancy has here been drawn into the ritual encounter, making it more spectacular and dramatic, whilst detracting from its greatness. For one need only think of Moses before Pharaoh, or of Simon Peter destroying Simon Magus to realise the depth of the fall from ancient to medieval magic. The spiritual grandeur and significance of the earlier encounters show up the playfulness of Bacon, the befooling of Vandermast and the whole pseudo-classical entertainment for the mere amusing nonsense they are. On the other hand, the harmlessness of Bacon's victory is in pleasing contrast with the malevolence shown by Faust to his unfortunate rival in the decapitation scene. Was it therefore only by chance that Vandermast is represented as vindictive in the extreme? Smarting under his defeat, he determined to avenge himself by the death of Bacon; and for this purpose he engaged a Walloon soldier to cross over to England and, for the sum of a hundred crowns, to slay his hated rival. Luckily the Friar had been apprised of threatening danger by consulting his books, and was on the alert when the hired assassin appeared before him with drawn sword. Discovering that the man was an infidel who did not believe in hell, Bacon raised the spirit of Julian the Apostate to

[1] Thoms, op. cit. I, p. 219.

convert him. The latter appeared with his body burning and full of wounds, and confessed that he was being tormented in this wise because of his apostasy. Faced with this terrible object-lesson, the Walloon became a Christian on the spot, and then made off as a crusader to the Holy Wars where he died as a true believer. Here the moral is almost rammed home; but the author wished to leave nothing to chance, and a further episode was added. Believing Bacon to be dead, Vandermast came over to England himself to try conclusions with Bungay. After various tricks played by one upon the other (presided over by the shade of Zyto-Faust), Vandermast challenged Bungay to a magical contest in form, and to the field they went.

There they both spread their circles some hundred foot from one another: and after some other ceremonies did Vandermast begin: hee by charmes did raise up a fiery dragon, which did runne about Fryer Bungyes circle, and did scorch him with his heat so that he was almost ready to melt. Fryer Bungye tormented Vandermast in another element: for he raised up the sea-monster that Perseus killed, when he did redeem the faire Andromeda. This sea-monster did run about Vandermast, and such flouds of water did he send out of his wide mouth, that Vandermast was almost drowned. Then did Fryer Bungye raise a spirit up like saint George, who fought with the dragon, and killed it: Vandermast (following his example) raysed Perseus, who fought also with his sea-monster, and killed it, so they were both released from their danger.

They being not contented with this tryall of their skill went further in their coniurations, and raised up two spirits each of them one. Bungye charged his spirit for to assist him with the greatest power hee had, that by it he might be able to overcome Vandermast. The Devill told him he would, if that he from his left arme would give him but three drops of blood; but that if he did deny him that, then should Vandermast have power over him to doe what he would: the like told Vandermasts Devill to him: to this demand of the spirits, they both agreed, thinking for to overcome each other; but the Devill overthrew them both.

They having given the Devill this bloud, as is before spoken of, they both fell againe to their coniurations: first Bungye did rayse Achilles with his Greekes, who marched about Vandermast and threatened him. Then Vandermast raised Hector with his Troians, who defended him from Achilles and the Greekes. Then began there a great battell between the Greekes and Troians, which continued a good space: at last Hector was slaine and the Troians fled. Then did follow a great tempest, with thundring and lightning, so that the two coniurers wished they had been away. But wishes were in vain: for now the time was come: that the Devill would be paid for the knowledge that he had lent them, he would not tarry any longer, but then tooke them in the height of their wickednesse, and bereft them of their lives.

When the tempest was ended (which did greatly affright the townes there by) the townsmen found the bodies of these two men...breathlesse, and strangely burnt with fire. The one had Christian buriall, because of his order sake: the other, because he was a stranger.[1]

John Franciscus Picus, the nephew of Pico de la Mirandola, had recounted the story of a magician displaying the combat between Hector and Achilles in the fifteenth century and being fetched off by the devil for his pains. Here once more the necromantic feat was wedded to the magical contest, and ended tragically for both rivals, since both had signed a pact with the devil by giving him their blood. Bungay, of whom no other evil is heard, plays the part of scapegoat for Bacon in this tale. The step Bacon scorned to take was luridly illuminated by Bungay's sin and the fate which overcame him. The author by this means was able to eat his cake and have it: to depict the horrible end which awaits sorcerers, and to keep Bacon's virtue intact. It seems possible, too, that this tremendous Homeric display was inspired by Faust's conjuring up of Helen. But, even if these suggestions are wide of the mark, even if Bacon were not intended to be an anti-Faust, and Vandermast were not meant to caricature him, the anti-German bias in the tale of the contest remains, and was even more strongly emphasised by Greene.

This negative kind of patriotism was balanced by the positive love of England that inspired the legend by which Bacon still remains best known to posterity. It has not the symbolical glamour attendant on Faust's central and most famous feat, the calling up of Helen of Troy; but it harks back to the kind of dreams the real Bacon was always entertaining, and it is also of a nature to appeal to our present much-menaced age, when wars and rumours of wars are so constant a feature of daily life. The great ambition of the Bacon of legend was to encompass all England with a wall of brass and thus to make it safe from invasion. His whole mind was set upon that glorious task. Realising, however, that it was impossible to accomplish it by natural means (as the late Minister for Defence would be the first to acknowledge), he fell back upon a favourite expedient of the times when in doubt or difficulty: the construction of a talking head of

[1] Thoms, op. cit. I, pp. 242–4.

brass which would answer his questions. Sylvester II and Virgil had each made one; Grosseteste in the real Bacon's day was supposed to have constructed another. As for Albertus Magnus, another contemporary, he had actually fabricated a talking metal Android, which irritated Thomas Aquinas so much with its eternal chattering that he smashed it into smithereens. Faust too seemed to need a brazen head before he could produce those illusory floods of water in the grounds of Castle Anhalt which so much perturbed the ladies. Indeed, these brass heads were so common that people began to believe that there was nothing supernatural about them.

Some report he made a Brazen Head that spake, and think he did it by the help of the Devil. But Albertus Magnus did the same and Boëthius the like, without any other Magick than Natural. For Cassiodorus writes thus to Boëthius: By the Ingenuity of your Art, Metals roar, Diomede in Brass sounds a hollow Charge, the Brazen Serpent hisseth, Birds are counterfeited: and things that have no voice of their own, are made to sing melodiously.[1]

The Bacon of legend, however, with the help of Friar Bungay, did indeed make a brazen head with the inward and outward parts in all points resembling the human prototype, but could not make it speak.

Many bookes they read, but yet could not finde out any hope of what they sought, that at the last they concluded to raise a spirit, and to know of him that which they could not attaine to by their own studies. To do this they prepared all things ready and went one evening to a wood thereby, and after many ceremonies used, they spake the words of coniuration, which the Devill straight obeyed and appeared unto them, asking what they would? Know, said Fryer Bacon that wee have made an artificial head of brasse, which we would have to speake, to the furtherance of which wee have raised thee, and being raised, we will keepe thee, unlesse thou tell us the way and manner to make this head to speake. The Devill told him that he had not that power of himselfe; beginner of lyes (said Fryer Bacon) I know that thou dost dissemble, and therefore tell it us quickly or else wee will here bind thee to remaine during our pleasures. At these threatnings the Devill consented to doe it, and told them, that with a continual fume of six hotest simples it should have motion, and in one month space speak, the Time of the moneth or day hee knew not; also hee told them that if they heard it not before it had done speaking, all their labour would be lost: they being satisfied, licensed the spirit for to depart.[2]

[1] Roger Bacon, *The Cure of Old Age*..., tr. R. Browne, London 1683; written in the Preface.   [2] Thoms, op. cit. I, pp. 205 ff.

This decidedly sinister interview does not imply any pact between Bacon and the devil; but rather that much sought after and greatly envied power over him without harm to the body and soul of the exorcist which only the really big magicians were capable of wielding. It proved of little practical value in this case, as indeed in many others; and we are still at the mercy of attack from the sea, because there was a catch in it. Forworn with waking and watching after three sleepless weeks, the two Friars put Bacon's servant Miles on guard, and snatched some repose, after having strictly charged him to awaken them the moment the head began to speak. That merry simpleton Miles (hero of some of the most charming tales in the saga) ruined the whole enterprise by trusting to his judgement and ignoring his instructions. For when the head said: 'Time is', and after an interval 'Time was', Miles felt sure that his master would not wish to be roused from slumber to listen to such platitudes. He flouted the automaton with jeering remarks and lewd but tuneful songs. The minutes irrevocably slipped by. The Friars went on sleeping. Miles went on mocking and warbling. Half an hour passed, and then the head uttered the inexorable words: 'Time is past', and exploded with a deafening noise and fearful belch of smoke. This serves as a reminder of Bacon's invention of gunpowder and also as a practical example of the tricky nature of oracles.

Defensive and offensive engines of war figured largely in the works of the real Bacon, and the association of the brazen head with the protective wall of brass was obviously deliberate. Moreover, the speech made by the Friar to the King of England before employing his burning-glass to reduce the besieged French town was copied *verbatim* from the 1597 translation of the *Discovery of the Miracles of Art, Nature and Magick*. The author of the story also used the 'glass perspective' with great effect, and throughout shows knowledge of the historical personage. The connection with Oxford; the association with Friar Bungay;[1] the last years passed in a cell; all these details are founded on fact. The real life and the real works of this great man coloured his legendary existence discernibly. It is all the stranger therefore that the tragic conflict with his Order was omitted and with it the greatness and significance of Bacon's life.

[1] Thomas or John de Bungaye was a distinguished member of the group of Franciscan schoolmen who taught and studied at Oxford in the thirteenth century, and a faithful companion of Bacon in his researches.

In its place is the purely fanciful and on the whole frivolous contest with a rival German magician, dragged in to enhance the prestige and the virtue of the English champion. And whereas the suspicion of magical practices brought tragedy into Bacon's real life; in legend it wins him nothing but universal admiration and esteem. This cheerful colouring splashed on to a very sombre story (of which the writer can hardly have been unaware) is on a par with the dogged determination to stress the highly ethical character of his hero. It gives Bacon a unique position among the magicians of the Christian era. Indeed, only Apollonius of Tyana is his equal in urbanity and philanthropy. Friar Bacon is far enough removed from the sublimity of the Greek sage; but he stands out among his medieval colleagues as much the most agreeable and humane. Among the converts from magic he alone repented because of the harm he had caused to others. Cyprian, Theophilus, Gerbert and Gilles de Rais did so for their own dear sakes. This is perhaps due to a difference between the Christian and humanistic attitudes to life; but an ulterior motive of some sort seems to underlie the legend of Friar Bacon. It may have been an attempted rehabilitation of the man himself, an effort to free him from the odium attached to him in the thirteenth century. It may have been an apology for white magic, made with all due caution, since Bacon renounced even that before he died. It may have been a veiled attack on Faust, impregnated with national and patriotic pride. But, whatever the intention, the English Catholic Friar Bacon faced the German Protestant Doctor Faust and wrested an ethical victory from his triumphant aesthetic foe.

CHAPTER IV

IN THE LIGHT OF COMMON DAY

(a) Dee and Kelley

The legends of Virgil, Merlin and Bacon hardly even pretend to be true in the sixteenth century; and the tales of Virgil and Bacon given by Thoms were not meant to be taken seriously, except for the moral purpose informing Bacon's end. The author of 'Spies', on the other hand, was a red-hot believer; and the emotions he experienced gave to his tale the dynamic force which was to make it immortal in poetry. This coincided with and may have helped to bring about the final break with a tradition which was wearing very thin. The ritual thread stretching back to Zoroaster and beyond snapped in the sixteenth century; and the myth of the magus was rung to its grave, or so it seemed, in the Spies biography. Strange and beautiful flowers of poetry were to spring up from its disintegrating remains, weeds and wild flowers too, a luxuriant wilderness ramping over the earth that covered Faust. But as a living force generating new legends the magus-myth seemed to be finished. Certainly John Dee, 1527–1608, who kept a private and spiritual diary, who wrote several autobiographical tracts, whose letters have been in part preserved, and about whom something can be found in contemporary records, has never imposed himself upon posterity in a mythical guise. And, indeed, what with one thing and another, the invention of printing, the increased facilities of transport and communication, and the general spread of learning and enlightenment, it was growing increasingly difficult and bade fair to become impossible for outstanding men who devoted themselves to occult practices of any sort to fight their way into the shadow of legend through the light of common day. The seeming impossibility was later victoriously achieved; but not by John Dee, whose life and deeds, although presenting many riddles and obscurities, demand psychological rather than ritual interpretation.

The story of Dee's life has now been told from beginning to end, and I shall not repeat it in detail.[1] His learning was great and also

[1] Cf. Charlotte Fell-Smith, *John Dee*, London 1909.

PLATE VII

Dr John Dee

profound. In fact he was probably the foremost mathematician of his day, and certainly an eminent astronomer. He furnished an important preface to the first English translation of Euclid, and was entrusted with the calculations on which to base a reform of the old-style calendar. That he should also have been an astrologer went without saying in those days, when the false assumptions on which the science was based were still believed to be truisms. Being a natural philosopher, he was also inevitably an alchemist, attempting the transmutation of metals and the artificial manufacture of gold. This second scientific blind alley at least gave a great impetus to experimental methods; on the other hand, sorcerers, swindlers and dupes swarmed round this particular subject like flies round honey, and astrology was hardly less popular with such gentry. Moreover, the prestige of great antiquity which surrounded them irresistibly attracted the occultists; for deriving as it was believed from the great Hermes Trismegistus himself (the Egyptian god Thoth), they were by definition hermetic and therefore sacrosanct: two of the secret and hallowed ways of attaining to universal knowledge. It was this aspect in all probability which first attracted John Dee, although later his interest in alchemy for its own sake was reinforced by utilitarian motives. But the lad who devoted eighteen hours out of twenty-four to study when he was a student at St John's College, Cambridge, grew into a man who thirsted after knowledge in the manner of Goethe's Faust, and quite unlike the real one. Cornelius Agrippa, Paracelsus and Dee all present much the same picture: that of men actually generations ahead of their times in learning and science, but real children of their age in following truth down those alluring by-paths which seemed to be royal roads to knowledge and proved to be delusory. It is perfectly possible that posterity may pass the same kind of judgement on the scientists of to-day, and speak pityingly of wasted efforts. For humanity seems to give up one set of false values only to adopt another. And from the point of view of a civilised outlook, the search for an elixir of life and a universal panacea is on a much higher level than the invention of poison gases and gigantic instruments of destruction. Alchemists often laid their own lives waste in their search for the philosopher's stone; but they did comparatively little harm to others; and what little they did dwindles to nothingness compared with the destruction wrought by one atomic bomb.

John Dee was one of those who injured no one but himself and his family in his baffled quest after universal knowledge; yet an evil reputation for practising black magic dogged his footsteps almost from the start. In 1546, being one of the original Fellows of Trinity College, and Under-Reader in Greek, he constructed an ingenious flying-machine for a production of Aristophanes' *Peace*, acted by the students. It would probably be considered crude enough to-day, but it created a sensation then, so much so that diabolical aid must, it was thought, have been invoked. He never lived down that unfortunate construction put upon his cleverness. And even when acting as Astrologer Royal to Queen Mary, he was still so suspect that his tactlessness in casting Elizabeth's horoscope too, and what was worse, letting her compare it with her sister's, led to an accusation of high treason, followed by the deadly charge of having practised against Mary's life with enchantments. He was thrown into prison and eventually brought into the Star Chamber; but he managed to clear himself of both accusations and of the further one of heresy, and was released in 1555. The accession of Elizabeth, gracious but close-fisted, made him an important personage at court; and during all the vicissitudes of an increasingly precarious and even dubious life, he never fell out of her favour, nor lost the parsimonious patronage that went with it. The opening years of that remarkable reign saw Doctor Dee, as he was always called, at the height of his happiness and fame. *Persona grata* at court; very much in the eye of the great ones on the Continent too; solicited by four universities: Louvain, Paris, Oxford, and Cambridge; and already the author of learned books, what more could his heart desire? The answer has tragic implications. He desired universal knowledge. The years passed, and he was no nearer to attaining it. He seemed to have settled down in his mother's house in the village of Mortlake on the Thames. He had married, lost his first wife, and then married again, the gentle uncomplaining Jane Fromond. He had a handsome library and a fine laboratory at his disposal; he was favoured more than once by royal visits. None of this was enough. The middle-aged scholar could not reconcile himself to our human limitations, and was for ever striving to transcend them. Immersed in the labyrinth of mystical numbers, gazing and gazing and gazing again into the liquid depths of the crystal; hearing strange noises and dreaming strange dreams, until on 25 May 1581 he was able to note in his diary, triumphantly but no doubt tremulously too: 'I had sight in Χρυσταλλω offered me, and I saw.'[1]

Although crystal-gazing, like alchemy and astrology, goes back to remote antiquity, Dee's experiments in this line jerk him out of the world of horoscopes and projecting-powders into modern spiritualistic circles. Not that he sought after, or believed that he attained, communication with the dead; he aimed higher than that:

And forasmuch as for many yeres, in many places, far and nere, in many bokes and sundry languages, I have wrought and studyed, and with sundry men conferred, and with my owne reasonable discourse Laboured, whereby to fynde or get some ynkling, glimpse, or beame, of such the aforesaid radicall truthes....And seeing I have read in thy bokes and records...that to Abraham, Isaac, and Jacob, Josua, Gedeon, Esdras, Daniel, Tobias, and sundry other, the good angels were sent, by thy disposition, to instruct them, informe them, help them....Therefore, Seeing I was sufficiently taught and confirmed that this wisdome could not be come by at mans hand, or by human powre, but onely from thee (O God) mediately or immediately.[2]

It was not so much what Dee aimed at, as what he achieved and the company he kept during his endeavours that seem to annihilate the centuries between him and us. Like many other devout seekers after hidden truths, and in spite of the vision granted to him on 25 May, he was not sufficiently gifted psychically to make much progress alone. He needed a seer or 'skryer', and a fairly typical medium called Barnabas Saul seemed for a few months in 1582 to be supplying that want. But he was soon forced to confess 'that he neyther hard nor saw any spirituall creature any more';[3] he left in a hurry, got into some kind of trouble with the laws of the land, disowned his psychic gifts, slandered Dr Dee, and generally gave proof of that moral deficiency which so often accompanies mediumship. But worse was to come in the shape of Edward Kelley, who appeared only a few days after Saul's departure. This most ambiguous person (about 27 years Dee's junior) was either one of the greatest mediums who have ever lived, or the world's most accomplished fraud. He was certainly no saint, having already lost both his ears, or so it was said, as a punishment for forgery. The black skull-cap he always wore gave colour to that belief. He was also

---

[1] *The Private Diary of Dr John Dee*, ed. Halliwell for the Camden Society, London 1842, p. 11.
[2] Fell-Smith, op. cit. pp. 84f.   [3] *Private Diary*, p. 14; 6 March 1582.

rumoured to have exhumed a newly buried corpse, and, by his incantations, to have enforced answers to questions about the future. He himself confessed to dealings with evil spirits and to possession by them. But there is no getting at the truth about Kelley, save in one respect. *Where* he acquired the famous *Book of Saint Dunstan*, an alchemical treatise, and the two powders of projection, said to have been found when digging in the environs of Glastonbury Abbey, we shall never know; but it seems certain that he believed absolutely in them; and so did Dr Dee, whose learning in this abstruse science was as indispensable to Kelley as his skill with the crystal was to his employer. It was a most uneasy partnership. Dee once wrote in his diary: 'The rancor and dissimulation now evident to me, God deliver me! I was not sent for';[1] and as for Kelley, he was always trying to break away. This has been interpreted as hypocrisy; but it seems clear from a perusal of the *True Relation* that Kelley loathed and abominated 'skrying'. Either it bored him, as well it might; or it was too great a strain on his inventive faculties; or he was as genuinely convinced that the spirits who answered to the crystal were evil, as he was constantly declaring them to be. Any one of these three reasons is sufficient to account for those terrifying outbursts of temper and those menacing scenes which the unhappy Doctor bore so patiently. If Kelley were practising guile of such a nature over such a long period of years, the recriminations and threats to go would be in the nature of a release to pent-up emotions; long-drawn-out boredom would have much the same result; as would also fear of the spirits he was raising. But he had gone too far either in fraud or in materialisations to be able to draw back. 'Angelic' voices and visions came thick and fast in and around the crystal whenever he looked into it. Dee sat apart, taking notes, sometimes hearing and even seeing himself; but generally depending on Kelley's word for what was taking place. He had his doubts, but they were rare, and quite unable to shake his almost incredible obstinacy in pursuing the séances despite all Kelley could do to stop him:

Because I have found so much halting and untruth in E. K. [he wrote shortly before their connection came to an end at last] his reports to me made, of the spiritual Creatures, where I have not been present at an Action; and because his memory may fail him, and because he was subject to ill tempters, I believe so much hereof as shall by better trial be found

---

[1] *Private Diary*, p. 29; September 1588.

true, or conformable to truth.... E. K. had this day divers apparitions unto him in his own Chamber, and instructions in divers matters *which he regarded not*, but remained still in his purpose *of utterly discrediting* those Creatures, and not to have any more to do with them.[1]

Actually Kelley rather than Dee seems to me to have been the more signal victim of the two, though whether a victim to his own fraud or to the spirits it is impossible to say. And Dee was probably so deaf to discouragement because of something that had occurred shortly after Kelley was installed as his 'skryer'. This did not take place, as far as one can make out, at one of the regular sittings before the 'table of practice' on which the stone was set with all the elaborate accessories favouring illusion to which crystal-gazers incline; nor was Kelley present at all, unless disguised. It was in November 1582 at sunset time when Dee saw in the western window of the laboratory the figure of a child-angel, later said to be Uriel, the spirit of light. He bore in his hand the famous 'angelical stone'; a thing 'most bright, most clere and glorious, of the bigness of an egg'. And then Michael appeared with a fiery sword and bade Dee: 'Go forward, take it up, and let no mortall hand touch it but thine own.'[2]

It is idle to speculate as to what sober facts lay behind this vision; but easy to understand why Dee persisted with the sittings afterwards. It is clear that Kelley's *technique*, and evidently Saul's too, whether fraudulent or not, were breaking new ground in crystal-lomancy. The traditional gazer sought in the stone for visions of distant or future events, or even of spirits. And Kelley also 'skryed' in this orthodox fashion, describing very lengthy and generally allegorical actions of a highly fantastic nature. There was further a rite to be found in many of the contemporary Black Books, and evidently particularly popular in England, of 'banning' spirits into the stone and keeping them there for mantic purposes. Peter of Apono was supposed to have seven such familiars in crystal vessels. But Kelley's 'table of practice', like the spiritualists' cabinet, was more than anything else a medium for materialisations. Spirits were

---

[1] *A True and Faithful Relation of what passed for Many Years between Doctor John Dee and Some Spirits....*, ed. Casaubon, London 1659, Actio Tertia, p. 13; April 1587.

[2] Fell-Smith, op. cit. pp. 86f.; from the early part of the *Spirituall Diary*, discovered after Casaubon's publication, and still in manuscript. Michael had appeared previously during a sitting with Kelley on 14 March 1582 and given to Dee a ring and a seal.

seen and heard both in the crystal and outside it, in very great abundance, if Kelley is to be believed. The conversations they held through him with Dr Dee are on the whole so long-winded, pious and boring, so repetitive, so platitudinous, so obviously plagiarised from the Bible, and probably from books of sermons too, so high-flown and inane, that, allowing for differences of style, one is irresistibly reminded of the jargon employed by 'spirits' to-day; and asks oneself whether they do not constitute a proof that the same solemn but silly source is everywhere being tapped. Incomprehensible languages were sometimes used (Dee believed them to be the speech of Adam); and occasionally an intrusion of 'merry' spirits, the bane of all serious spiritualists, vexed the good doctor with their ribaldry. Practical or definite questions were answered with vague generalisations; the prophecies made were nearly always false; yet sometimes too there seemed method in all this madness, and then one strongly suspects that Kelley was responsible. After an inane and seemingly pointless interview with a little spiritual creature, babbling nonsense like a brook, and later owning to the name of Madimi, the reason for all this twaddle gradually emerged. Madimi produced a book of gentlewomen, intended to prove the descent of Count Laski from the Plantagenets.

Prince Alasco of Siradia in Poland, a guest at Elizabeth's court in 1583, a respectful admirer of Dr Dee, and a man of reputedly enormous wealth, now entered the spiritual scene. The situation seems to have been this: Dee and Kelley had progressed considerably in the experiments with the powders by which they hoped to transmute other metals to gold; but meanwhile they were in dire straits for money, alchemical experiments, like many others, simply eating up funds. Nor were the spirits, however earnestly interrogated, of any real help on this subject, or on any other, as the following conversation with Madimi shows, typical of many others, whether with Galvah, Murufri, Il, Jubanladace, Nalvage, Ath, Morvorgran, or even Uriel, Michael, Gabriel and Raphael:

DEE. Mistresse *Madimi*, you are welcome in God, for good, as I hope; What is the cause of your coming now?

MAD. *To see how you do.* [There had just been a violent scene with Kelley about his wife.]

DEE. I know you can see me often, and I see you onely by faith and imagination.

MAD. ...[Pointing to E. K.] *That sight is perfecter than his.*

DEE. O *Madimi*, shall I have any more of these grievous pangs?

MAD. ...*Curst Wives, and great Devils are sore Companions.*

DEE. In respect of the Lord Treasurer, Mr Secretary, and Mr *Rawly*, I pray you, What worldly comfort is there to be looked for? Besides that I do principally put my trust in God.

MAD. ...*Madder will staine, wicked men will offend, and are easie to be offended.*

DEE. And being offended will do wickedly, to the persecution of them that meane simply.

MAD. ...*Or else they were not to be called wicked.*

DEE. As concerning *Alb. Laskie* his Pedigree, you said your sister would tell all.

MAD. ...*I told you more than all your Dog painters and Cat painters can do.*

DEE. You spoke of *William Laskie* and *Sir Richard Laskie* his brother, of which *William* going into *France*, and then into *Denmarke*: and his marriage into *Poland*, came this *Albert Laskie*, now Paladine of *Soradia* [sic], etc.

MAD. ...*Those were two pretty men for me to meddle withal. When you set yourselves together, and agree together, I will make all agree together.*

E. K. WILL YOU *MADIMI* LEND ME A HUNDRED POUNDS FOR A FORTNIGHT?

MAD. ...*I have swept all my money out of doors.*

DEE. As for money we shall have that which is necessary when God seeth time.

MAD. ...*Hear me what I say. God is the unity of all things. Love is the unity of every Congregation (I mean true and perfect love). The World was made in the love of the father. You were redeemed in the love of the Father and the Son. The Spirit of God is (yet) the love of his Church.*[1]

And so on for a long time, an unctuous sermon on love, mixed with reproaches levelled at Kelley. Nevertheless, on the subject of Laski the spirits were rather more encouraging; and indeed Galvah gave him quite a build-up as the future king of Poland and the regenerator of the world:

I say unto thee, his name is in the Book of Life: The Sun shall not passe his course before he be a King. His Counsel *shall breed Alteration of this State;* yea of the whole world.[2]

There was a good deal more at intervals to the same heady effect; and it would seem as if Kelley were trying to interest Lord Laski

---

[1] Casaubon, *True Relation*, p. 31; July 1583.   [2] Ibid. p. 17; 1583.

practically in their alchemical schemes by playing on his ambitions.
For the future regenerator of the world would certainly need an
inexhaustible supply of gold. One way and another, Laski fell for
the prophecies, the more readily on account of Dee's brilliant
reputation; and it was finally agreed that the doctor with his family
and Kelley with his wife should accompany him back to Poland.
The journey took place in the autumn of 1585, and the interrogation
of the spirits went on almost uninterruptedly until they all arrived
at the count's estate, the spirits blowing now hot now cold about
Laski's glorious future, and the alchemical experiments still requiring
formidable funds. That they should have persisted in the sittings
seems all the more remarkable, as one of the apparitions, later called
the tempter and announced by Kelley as an evil spirit, gave them
a most solemn warning to desist:

E. K.   NOW IS ONE COME IN VERY BRAVE; LIKE A PREACHER;
        I TAKE HIM TO BE AN EVIL ONE.

DEE.   Benedictus qui venit in nomine Domini.

E. K.   HE SAITH NOTHING; NOT SO MUCH AS, AMEN.

....   *Are you so foolish to think that the power of God will descend into so
base a place?...What greater imperfection, then to imagine much
more believe, that the Angels of God, will, or may descend into so
filthie a place, as this corruptible stone is?...*

DEE.   Who causeth thee to come here?

....   *Thy folly.*

....

....   *He* Albert Laskie *shall come to destruction, as thou and thine to
miserable beggery: Because he hath consented to them that are Ministers
of iniquity, spirits of falshood....Avoid darknesse, avoid darknesse,
avoid darknesse.*[1]

However, as other spirits called this one the tempter, it was easy
to ignore him and his injunctions to Dee to burn his 'blasphemous
books'. Completely innocent in intention, Dee went labouring on
with the sittings, aided unwillingly by an increasingly restless Kelley.
It was a restless time altogether, comprising a great deal of travelling.
From Poland they went to Prague, where the Emperor Rudolph II
had his court; then they returned to Poland to the court of King
Stephen, then back to Prague again and were finally received as the
guests of a powerful and wealthy nobleman called Rosenberg at his

[1] Casaubon, op. cit. pp. 53 ff.; Lübeck in November 1583. The prophecy
about 'miserable beggery' for Dee was fulfilled.

castle of Trebona in Bohemia. The whole party was perpetually on the move, although at times the wives and children would be left behind. But wherever Dee went, there too went Kelley. They were indissolubly bound together, it seemed; not only because of the crystal-gazing, which the doctor craved for as addicts crave for drugs; but also because of the alchemical experiments. And here again, Kelley, so much less learned, seems to have been Dee's superior in skill. Whatever the rights or the wrongs of the case, it was certainly he who finally convinced those about him that he could make gold. The emperor knighted him for this achievement, or so the story goes; which had perhaps better be told in the words of a true believer:

In 1585 we find them in Prague, then the metropolis of alchemy, and the headquarters of adepts and adeptship. Edward Kelly and his companions presently abounded in money, and the owner of the Hermaic Benediction made no secret of his prize or his powers, indulged in all kinds of extravagance, performed continual projections for himself and his friends, as well as for many persons of distinction who sought his acquaintance. Much of the result was distributed. The transmutations of Kelly at this period are attested by several writers, including Gassendus. The most authenticated and remarkable, according to Figuier, is that which took place in the house of the imperial physician, Thaddeus de Hazek, when, by the mediation of a single drop of red oil, Kelly transmuted a pound of mercury into excellent gold, the superabundant virtue of the agent leaving in addition at the bottom of the crucible a small ruby[!]. Dr Nicholas Barnaud, the assistant of Hazek, and an alchemical writer, whose works are as rare as they are reputable, was a witness of this wonder, and subsequently himself manufactured the precious metal, the *désir désiré*, with the assistance of Edward Kelly.[1]

So well authenticated and credibly vouched for was this achievement that Lord Burleigh wrote pressingly to Kelley on more than one occasion urging him to return to England and put his miraculous knowledge at the service of his queen:

Be assured of worldly reward. You can make yr Queen so happie for her, surely as no subject she hath can do the like. Good Knight, let me end my letter conjuring you, in God's holy name not to keep God's gift from yr natural countrie, but rather help make Her Majestie a glorious and victorious power against the mallyce of hers and God's enemies.[2]

[1] A. E. Waite, *Lives of Alchemystical Philosophers*, London 1888, pp. 155f. The 'prize' was of course the famous powders.
[2] Fell-Smith, op. cit. pp. 206f.

Unhappily it was not in Kelley's power to respond to this appeal, probably penned in 1591, two years after Dee was safely back in England. Kelley had been too successful. His secret was too desirable to allow him his freedom. He must not only continue to manufacture gold, he must also reveal the composition of the projecting powders, or philosopher's stone. Neither he nor Dee, strive how they might, could discover that secret. What was worse (according to Waite's account, which may be apocryphal), Kelley had wasted those powders on riotous transmutations, and could therefore no longer produce the *désir désiré*. This being interpreted as a contumacious refusal, he was cast into a dungeon, released under surveillance in order to continue his experiments, gave way to that terrible temper of his, murdered a guard, and was kept in confinement ever after. He spent his time in writing a treatise on the philosopher's stone; at last, unable to bear his incarceration any longer, he attempted to break prison in 1595. He made a rope of knotted sheets and began to let himself down from the window of his prison; but the rope gave, he sustained a terrible fall, and died shortly afterwards as the result of his injuries. This at least is the generally accepted account of his death, which may have been less sensational, but which certainly occurred abroad in 1595. He had been too clever by half; and whether an out and out fraud, or a genuine medium, or (as is most probable) a mixture of both, the *Spirituall Diary* of Dr Dee shows that he was one of those tormented and tormenting persons who often meet a violent end. But his achievements, both spiritualistic and alchemistic, however produced, were notable indeed.

As far as these 'sciences' were concerned, Dr Dee was very much Kelley's inferior, and lost without him. During their sojourn on the Continent, Kelley declared that the spirits were enjoining and urging the pair of them to share their wives in common, at the same time declaring that he was fully convinced of the diabolical nature of the spirits (a constantly recurring refrain), and that he for one would have no more to do with them. This has generally been interpreted as lewdness on his part, masked by rank hypocrisy. I rather incline to believe that it was a final desperate effort to be done with the 'skrying' for good and all, the better to devote himself to alchemy. Be that as it may, Dee himself felt some doubts on this occasion.[1]

[1] See above, pp. 164f.

Kelley flung off, and little Arthur Dee, aged eight years, was installed in his place. This was in accordance with traditional crystallomancy, which advocated a boy of tender years in crystal-gazing experiments. But it did not answer. Arthur, who was supposed to be psychic, as we should call it to-day, saw nothing significant, and heard no voices proceeding from the stone. Kelley returned, was rapturously welcomed, undertook his office again; and the final result was humble acceptance of the extraordinary command laid upon them by the spirits, amongst them Madimi, now grown to womanhood, and shamelessly showing herself naked. This extra-vagant tale proves that Dee would bring himself to do almost any-thing rather than lose the services of Kelley; and that communication with the spirit-world had become a passion with him that nothing could cure. He returned to England in the autumn of 1589, having waited vainly for months at Stade for Kelley to join him. He was never to see his tempestuous 'skryer' again. He travelled across the Continent in great state; but it was the last time that any kind of state was to be his portion. He seems to have presented Kelley with all his alchemical apparatus before leaving Bohemia; but the precious crystal, the 'angelical stone', later in the possession of Horace Walpole and now in the British Museum, accompanied him home; and of course his *Spirituall Diary*, to which he was probably referring when he spoke of 'my terrible dream that Mr Kelly would by force bereave me of my bokes'.[1]

His other books, the valuable library at Mortlake, and the laboratory as well had actually been plundered and wrecked the year he left England by a mob taking safe reprisals against the absent 'wizard'. It was symbolical of the sad story of his declining years. He never again found another medium of the calibre of Kelley. Moreover, poverty, which had always dogged his footsteps, was now his constant and squalid companion. Elizabeth doled out small sums from time to time; she graciously sent two commissioners down to Mortlake to listen to his lamentable and not really *Compendious Rehearsal* of the dignities and indignities, the trials, triumphs and disasters of his life, from which all mention of crystal-gazing was noticeably absent; she even finally procured for him in 1595, the year of Kelley's death, the wardenship of Christ's College, Man-chester. But this proved to be a very doubtful blessing; the exchange

[1] *Private Diary*, p. 31; August 1589.

of one kind of poverty for another, with the added burdens of office and the petty persecutions of the Fellows. He gave up the position in 1603 and retired to Mortlake where he kept the wolf from the door by casting horoscopes and telling fortunes. To the very end his reputation as 'a companion of the Hell-hounds, a caller and a conjurer of wicked damned spirits' added to his griefs as he slowly withered away. James I could not be induced to do anything for him, and ignored the piteous plea of the aged scholar:

to cause your Highness said servant to be tryed and cleared of that horrible and damnable, and to him most grievous and damnageable sclaunder, generally, and for these many yeares last past, in this kingdom raysed and continued, by report and Print against him, namely that he is or hath bin a conjurer or caller or invocator of divels.[1]

Whatever the nature of the spirits raised for him by Kelley, they had finally, as one of them had truly prophesied, brought him and his to 'miserable beggery'. Between them, he and his 'skryer' had also initiated a new kind of necromancy, imbued with that peculiar blend of holiness, phoneyness and feeble-mindedness which surrounds the spiritualism of to-day.

(b) Gauffridi and Grandier

Dee's initiation into magic and his long-enduring conflict with Kelley show that magicians in real life undergo almost inevitably some at least of the triumphs and trials invented for them by legend; for legend derives from ritual, and ritual is an imitation of life. Mythology, however, divides the sheep from the goats and represents magicians as either black or white; whereas human magic-makers have mixed and complex natures; and at times the bogus element predominates to such an extent that magic takes wings and flies away, leaving an ugly stench behind. This was largely the case in the seventeenth century, during which no really great names adorn the annals of magic, although there were a great number of more or less reputable practitioners, such as Dr Lambe and William Lilly in England. But they and their sometimes nefarious doings are completely dwarfed in the history of magic by the ghastly affairs of the possessed nuns of Sainte-Baume, Loudun and Louviers; and altogether obliterated by the sinister scandals of La Voisin and Madame de Montespan

---

[1] Fell-Smith, op. cit. p. 293. The complaint about 'Hell-hounds' occurred in the Preface to Euclid.

and their evil machinations against Louis XIV. This appalling story of murderous rites belongs rather to the realm of witchcraft than of magic proper, and has little to do with the magus-myth. I can therefore by-pass it, and would do the same for the hysterical nuns were it not for the fact that the unhappy wretches supposed to be responsible for their condition were tried and burnt as sorcerers; Gauffridi in 1611, Grandier in 1634, the dead Picart with the living Boullé in 1647. Neither Gauffridi nor Grandier was a saint; but neither were they magicians. They fell as victims to the malignancy of clerical enemies who faked much of the phenomena in a fashion crude enough to be detected at the time, and yet so much in accordance with prevalent beliefs as to ensure the condemnation of the accused. The wretched Gauffridi confessed after torture to visions of Lucifer, to a compact with him, to visiting the Black Sabbath and celebrating the Black Mass. Urban Grandier heroically withstood the most terrible torments, maintained that he was innocent of any form of sorcery and seemed according to all accounts like the only sane man in Bedlam:

The unfortunate Grandier was not therefore delivered into the hands of malefactors but rather of raving maniacs, who, strong in their rectitude of conscience, gave the fullest publicity to this incredible prosecution. Such a scandal had never afflicted the church—howling, writhing nuns, making the most obscene gestures, blaspheming, striving to cast themselves on Grandier like the Bacchantes on Orpheus; the most sacred things of religion mixed up with this hideous spectacle and drawn in the filth thereof; amidst all Grandier alone calm, shrugging his shoulders and defending himself with dignity and mildness; in fine, pallid, distraught judges, sweating profusely, and Laubardemont in his red robe, hovering over the conflict like a vulture awaiting a corpse: such was the prosecution of Urban Grandier...he remained firm, resigned, patient, although confessing nothing....To hide their emotions, the exorcists replied with invectives, and the executioners wept. Three nuns, in one of their lucid moments, cast themselves before the tribunal, crying that Grandier was innocent, but it was believed that the devil was speaking by their mouth, and their declaration only hastened the end....The chief exorcists, Father Tranquille and Lactance, died soon after in the delirium of violent frenzy; Father Surin, who succeeded them, became imbecile; Manoury, the surgeon who assisted at the torturing of Grandier, died haunted by the picture of his victim...the nuns remained idiots. So it is true that the question was one of a terrible and contagious malady, the mental disease of false zeal and false devotion.[1]

[1] Lévi, *History of Magic*, pp. 370ff.

The concluding sentence of this striking description is true enough; but what Lévi does not see is that the hysteria manifested itself also as downright fraud, clearly revealed by Pitaval in his analysis of the documents in 1747, and recognised as such at the time. It was probably because Grandier's personality and indeed charm were much more in evidence than was the case with his fellow-victim of rank superstition and malignant malice that he achieved the greater posthumous notoriety, and an article to himself in Collin de Plancy's *Dictionnaire Infernal* in 1826 with a facsimile reproduction of the bilateral pact he was firmly believed to have signed with the spirits of hell:

My Lord and Master Lucifer, I acknowledge you as God and Overlord, I swear to serve you and obey you as long as I live, I forswear another God, and Jesus Christ, all the saints, the apostolic Roman Church, their sacraments, and all the prayers by means of which the believers might intercede for me. Further I promise you to do as much evil as I am able. I forswear the sacred unction and baptism, as well as the merits of Jesus Christ and the saints, and should I fail to serve you and to worship you and to offer you my homage thrice daily, then I will surrender my life to you as that which belongs to you.

Given in this year and day,
Urban Grandier.

Excerpt from the Hellish Archives.

We, the omnipotent Lucifer, have today with the support of Satan, Beelzebub, Leviathan, Elimi, Astaroth and others received the pact which Urban Grandier has made with us, in return for which we promise him irresistibility with women, the flower of virgins, the honour of nuns, all imaginable dignities, distinctions, pleasures and riches. He will commit fornication every three days, never abstain from drunkenness, proffer us his allegiance once a year sealed with his own blood, spurn the sacraments and address his prayers to us. By means of this pact he will enjoy all earthly pleasures for twenty years, and then enter into our kingdom, in order to blaspheme God in our company.

Given in Hell in the Council of Demons,
       Signed: Lucifer, Beelzebub, Satan, Elimi, Leviathan, Astaroth.
       Visa for the signature and the seal of the Master of Devils and all
       Overlords of Demons.

       Countersigned: Baalbarith, Secretary.[1]

---

[1] Scheible, *Das Kloster*, III, pp. 876f. Pp. 878ff. give Pitaval's analysis of the proceedings against Grandier.

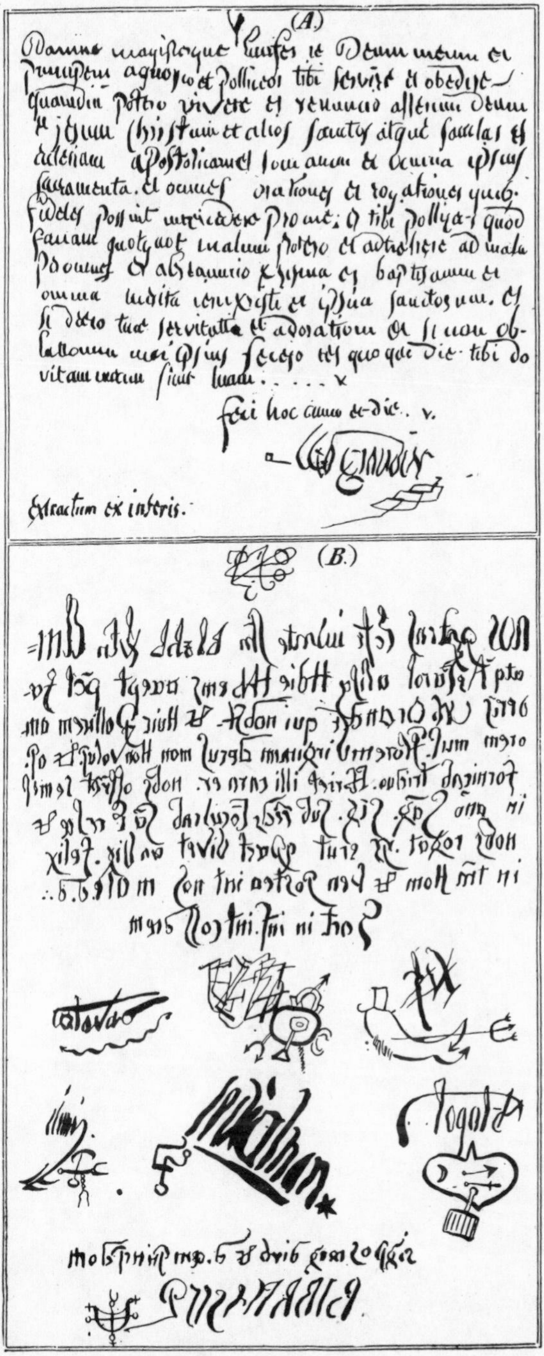

Grandier's Pact

One almost despairs of the human mind in the face of the 'confession' of Gilles de Rais, the *Spirituall Diary* of Dr Dee and the faked pact of Urban Grandier. The senseless depravity of imaginations unhinged by magic appears at this juncture to witness against it as a vicious or silly manifestation of mere fraud. Was it only because the sages of antiquity lived so long ago that their powers seem so stupendous; or was it because they lived in different days? It is with such questions occupying one's thoughts that one approaches the eighteenth century.

PART III.   THE RETURN OF THE MAGI

CHAPTER I

ARISTEAS REDIVIVUS

Both the darker and the more puerile forms of magic had been gaining ground steadily in Europe since the victory of Christianity. Protestantism bade fair to complete its spiritual ruin. The recurrent epidemics of convulsionism have all the marks of a spontaneous reaction against the emotional sterility engendered by the Reformation, which released intellectual curiosity tending to religious scepticism. The result was that the great Catholic rituals ceased to have a universal cathartic effect even within their own now limited sphere of influence, and unbridled emotions arose in protest. But protest was not enough. The dynamic nature of the demand created its supply. Almost before the conscious need was felt, secret societies arose to fulfil it; emerging, not indeed into the full light of day, but into the far more enticing twilight of rumour and romance. And as everyone knows they came to stay, and their name is now legion. They seized and held the imagination of men chiefly by virtue of their ritual mysteries which claimed prehistoric sanction— a claim generically sound, even if it must be disallowed in every single specific instance. What the Freemasons declared about themselves is substantially true of all serious secret societies,

...the royal art has, like the ancient mysteries, no other aim than the knowledge of nature, where all are born, die, and regenerate themselves.[1]

And the three grades representing generation, putrefaction and regeneration are the age-old features in primitive kingship rites, so that the myth of the magus was once more being enacted in its traditional form.

The gradual development of speculative masonry from operative masonry which took place some time between the fourteenth and the eighteenth centuries was of prime importance and probably antedated all other kindred associations, although it is impossible to be dogmatic on a subject so complicated, by its very nature so obscure,

[1] Quoted from Ragon in *The Trail of the Serpent*, London 1936, p. 84. The pseudonymous author calls himself 'Inquire Within'.

and about which so many conflicting opinions and theories are held. It is certain at least that the year 1717, which saw the Grand Lodge of England formed from four London and Westminster Lodges, marks a turning point in the history of magic. For the brotherhood which rapidly spread to the Continent proceeded to elaborate a legend which brought Solomon, one of the master-magicians of antiquity, into prominence again. This is the tale of Hiram, the architect of Solomon's Temple, murdered by three fellow-craftsmen in order to obtain the master-word. The hidden body, according to some versions, has to be found; according to others it has been discovered, and Hiram has risen again as the Grand Master of the Order. Further, by tracing Freemasonry from Adam to the Tower of Babel, Solomon's Temple, the advent of Christ and down through the ages to the Knights Templar, an impressive tradition and a sublime descent were associated with the master-masons. It hardly needed the secrets, the symbols, ceremonials and signs, glamorous though these were, to attract modern magicians into the orbit of the lodges. The ritual and the myth would have generated them spontaneously.

Spontaneous generation was indeed the order of the day as far as secret societies were concerned, and is the only explanation for the mysterious order which materialised inexplicably from nowhere a century before Freemasonry issued out of its obscurity and met at the London Apple-Tree Tavern. Said to have been founded in the fourteenth century, but known at first only by the anonymous manifestoes of 1614-15, it also possessed a fully developed magus-legend, and bore a name so highly symbolical as to fire the imagination whenever it was uttered: the brotherhood of the Rosy Cross. The founder, the original members and their meeting place (the House of the Holy Spirit) almost certainly never existed in reality; but the idea was there, born of the collective consciousness of an age avid for mystery and projecting its theosophical, cabalistic and alchemistical dreams into this esoteric society. It is not too much to say that the Rosy Cross replaced the Crucifix in the minds of mystics and poets during the eighteenth century. Goethe himself was drawn for a time into the radius of this striking symbol and embarked on a religious epic which he never completed, but which has much in common with the legend of Christian Rosencreutz, the mythical founder of the legendary brotherhood. Travelling from the

West to the East in search of occult wisdom and magical lore, this modern magus was following in the footsteps of Pythagoras, Apollonius, Cyprian, and hundreds of kindred spirits, whose traditional journeys eastwards and hard-won initiations into secret wisdom featured in the lives of the foremost magicians of the past. The great age to which he attained; his passing away, less like a death than a translation; the discovery of his body a hundred years later 'fair...whole and unconsumed': these various incidents in his career not only secured for Christian Rosencreutz a place in the main body of magical tradition, but gave new life and glory to it.

The same may be said generally of secret societies as a whole. They restored the vanished prestige of the magicians and gave them a new lease of life. The revival of ritual brought about a renascence of magic. The emblematic rites of the arcane lodges and their legends commemorated lives led on a traditional pattern and filled with a significance, which the spiritual, mystical or pseudo-occult ideals of the confraternities impressed upon initiates and revealed to the adepts. Ritual, mystery and magic united again under a quasi-religious sanction.

Throughout Europe the ritual element was developed along those spectacular lines so dear to the eighteenth century, packed with sensationalism and presented with a splendour and mystery which lost nothing in the telling. Indeed some of the descriptions are clearly influenced by the *Arabian Nights* as well as by such inflamed imaginations as that of the Marquis de Luchet, who probably invented the following almost certainly spurious account purporting to come from an anonymous correspondent in Vienna writing to a M. Rollig:

Your introduction has procured me a very interesting acquaintance in M. N.Z. He seemed to have been informed of my arrival either by you or another. He warmly approved of the harmonica. He mentioned certain special tests, but I did not catch his meaning....He took me out to his country seat yesterday towards evening. Everything, especially the garden, is beautifully planned. Temples, grottoes, cascades, labyrinths, caves offer so much diversity to the eye as to be quite enchanting. The only thing which depressed me was a very high wall surrounding the whole, since it deprives the eye of an enchanting view. I had been obliged to take the harmonica with me and to promise M. N.Z. only to play it for a few moments in a place indicated when he gave me a certain sign. Meanwhile he led me...to a room in the front of the house and left me there saying that the arrangements for a ball and an illumination demanded his presence urgently. It was already late and I was nearly asleep, when I was roused by the arrival of some carriages. I opened the window, but could distinguish nothing; even less could I catch the low and mysterious whisperings of the new arrivals. Soon after sleep overcame me entirely and after I had slept for about an hour I was wakened by a servant who offered to carry my instrument and desired me to follow him. As the servant walked very fast and I very slowly it followed that I had the time (curiosity abetting me) to follow the muffled sound of the trumpets which seemed to me to be issuing from the depths of a cave.

Imagine my surprise when, having descended half the staircase, I saw a cavern in which a dead body was being placed in a coffin to the sound of funeral music. Beside him was a man dressed in white, but all covered with blood, whilst a vein in his arm was being bound up. Except those who were succouring him, all the others were muffled in long black cloaks, and armed with drawn swords. At the entrance to the cavern I saw piles of human skeletons heaped one on top of the other, and the whole was illuminated by lights whose flame resembled burning spirits of wine. This increased the horror of the frightening place and I hastened to withdraw in order not to lose my guide. He was just coming back by the garden gate when I reached it. He hastily seized my hand and dragged me along with him. I have never seen anything which reminded me so much of fabulous fairy-tales as the entry into that garden. Everything was lit up, innumerable fairy-lamps, the murmuring of distant cascades, the song of artificial nightingales, the perfumed air which I breathed, it was all marvellous. I was shown to a place behind a verdant grotto, the interior of which was divinely decorated, and into which soon after a swooning figure was brought, and immediately I was given the sign to play. As I was then more occupied with thinking of myself than of the others, I lost much of what was happening; nevertheless I was able to observe that the fainting man revived after I had been playing for about a minute, and that he asked in great surprise: Where am I? What voice do I hear? Outbursts of joy, accompanied by trumpets and cymbals answered; everyone took up arms and made towards the centre of the garden, where I lost them from view.[1]

Allowing for the long bow of fiction, this fanciful account is symptomatic of the stories current about secret rites; and, however flamboyantly, it embodies the main features of initiation ceremonies from time immemorial: simulated death and resurrection.

This would naturally lead to the belief that partakers in such mysteries could prolong their lives indefinitely, a notion sedulously encouraged by real or pretended members of the Rosicrucian

[1] [Marquis de Luchet], *Essai sur la secte des Illuminés*, Paris 1789, pp. 221–4.

fraternity in particular. Who those mysterious beings really were is not easy to determine, since they were forbidden to proclaim themselves; but at one time or another a great many eminent men were said to have been Rosicrucians: Roger Bacon, Agrippa, Paracelsus, Jakob Boehme, Descartes, Robert Fludd, Thomas Vaughan and Francis Bacon, whose supposed membership of the sect has become inextricably involved with the belief that he was the author of Shakespeare's plays. But whatever the membership, the sect was said to be bound by its rules to cure the sick without charging a fee, and it was claimed that the cures were effected by means of the elixir of life. The personal immortality of such healers would follow as a natural corollary, and lead to many legends. One of the most widespread of these was the story of Signor Gualdi, the so-called 'sober Signor', a lineal descendant of Aristeas the Pythagorean:

There happened in the year 1687, an odd accident at *Venice*, that made a great stir then, and which I think deserves to be rescued from oblivion. The great freedom and ease with which all persons, who make a good appearance, live in that city, is known sufficiently to all who are acquainted with it; such will not therefore be surprized, that a stranger, who went by the name of *Signor Gualdi*, and who made a considerable figure there, was admitted into the best company, though no body knew who, or what he was. He remained at *Venice* some months, and three things were remarked in his conduct. The first was, that he had a small collection of fine pictures, which he readily shewed to any body that desired it; the next, that he was perfectly versed in all arts and sciences, and spoke on every subject with such readiness and sagacity, as astonished all who heard him; and it was in the third place observed, that he never wrote or received any letter; never desired any credit, or made use of bills of exchange, but paid for everything in ready money, and lived decently, though not in splendour. This gentleman met one day at the coffee-house with a *Venetian* nobleman, who was an extraordinary good judge of pictures: he had heard of *Signor Gualdi's* collection, and in a very polite manner desired to see them, to which the other very readily consented. After the *Venetian* had viewed *Signor Gualdi's* collection, and expressed his satisfaction, by telling him, that he had never seen a finer, considering the number of pieces of which it consisted; he cast his eye by chance over the chamber door, where hung a picture of this stranger. The *Venetian* look'd upon it, and then upon him. This picture was drawn for you, Sir, says he to *Signor Gualdi*, to which the other made no answer, but by a low bow. You look, continued the *Venetian*, like a man of fifty, and yet I know this picture to be of the hand of *Titian*, who has been dead one hundred and thirty years, how is this possible? It is not easy, said *Signor Gualdi*, gravely, to know all things that are possible;

but there is certainly no crime in my being like a picture drawn by *Titian*. The *Venetian* easily perceived by his manner of speaking, that he had given the stranger offence, and therefore took his leave. He could not forbear speaking of this in the evening to some of his friends, who resolved to satisfy themselves by looking upon the picture the next day. In order to have an opportunity of doing so, they went to the coffee-house about the time that *Signor Gualdi* was wont to come thither, and not meeting with him, one of them who had often conversed with him, went to his lodgings to enquire after him, where he heard, that he had set out an hour before for *Vienna*. This affair made a great noise, and found a place in all the newspapers of that time.[1]

Whether a Rosicrucian or not, and he was almost immediately numbered amongst them by report, Signor Gualdi, possibly by an accidental resemblance to a portrait by Titian, presented an outline, still sketchy and dim, of a coming race of magicians endowed with a mysterious longevity:

...the adepts are obliged to conceal themselves for the sake of safety, and... having power not only of prolonging their lives, but also of renovating their bodies, they take care to use it with the utmost discretion, and instead of making a display of this prerogative, they manage it with the highest secrecy...the true cause of the world's being so much in doubt about this matter. Hence it comes to pass, that though an adept is possessed of greater wealth than is contained in the mines of *Peru*, yet he always lives in so moderate a manner, as to avoid all suspicion, and so as never to be discovered, unless by some unforeseen accident.[2]

We have clearly turned our backs now upon sorcerers of the type of Zyto and Faust, and are ready for the appearance of Saint-Germain.

---

[1] *Hermippus Redivivus: or the Sage's Triumph over Old Age and Death*, 2nd ed., London 1749, pp. 160ff. First ed. 1744. Translated by John Campbell from the German of Dr Cohausen. For a fuller account of Gualdi, see Hargrave Jennings, *The Rosicrucians, their Rites and Mysteries*.

[2] Op. cit. p. 162.

CHAPTER II

THE MAN OF MYSTERY (?1710–?1784)

No one knew who he was, a fact which did not astonish me in a country like England, where there are practically no secret police, but what did astonish me was that in France it was not known either.[1]

I am not aware that he has anywhere left his trail in official documents; he lives in more or less legendary documents alone.... He is a will-o'-the-wisp of the memoir writers of the eighteenth century. Whenever you think you have a chance of finding him in good authentic State papers, he gives you the slip....[2]

Napoleon III, puzzled and interested by what he had heard about the mysterious life of the Comte de Saint-Germain, instructed one of his librarians to search for and collect all that could be found about him in archives and documents of the latter part of the eighteenth century. This was done, and a great number of papers, forming an enormous dossier, was deposited in the library of the prefecture of the police. The Franco-Prussian War and the Commune supervened, and the part of the building in which the dossier was kept was burnt. Thus once again an 'accident' upheld the ancient law which decrees that the life of an adept must always be surrounded with mystery.[3]

Would that the matter had rested there; but the piety of a true believer and the painstaking researches of a sceptic have between them lifted too much of the veil. We still do not know who Saint-Germain was; but unhappily we now have a very good idea of what he was; and truth is not stranger than fiction in his case. Until the fruits of the exhaustive labours of Gustav Berthold Volz appeared in the nineteen-twenties, Count Saint-Germain remained the man of mystery whom Frederick the Great candidly acknowledged him to be in his *History of the Seven Years' War*; 'one of the most enigmatic personages of the eighteenth century', as Grillot de Givry pronounced him to be in the twentieth.[4] He still represents something

[1] I. Cooper-Oakley, *The Comte de St Germain*, London 1927 (first ed. in 1912), p. 209. From the papers of Bentinck van Rhoon, dated 18 April 1760.
[2] Andrew Lang, *Historical Mysteries*, London 1904, pp. 259, 276.
[3] M. Magre, *The Return of the Magi*, tr. Merton, London 1931, p. 233.
[4] Grillot de Givry, *Witchcraft, Magic and Alchemy*, tr. Courtenay Locke, London 1931, p. 365.

of an enigma; but, just as Funck-Brentano exploded the myth of the Man in the Iron Mask, degrading the hero from his legendary status as the twin brother of Louis XIV to that of the double-crossing Italian minister Matthioli in a black velvet mask, so too Volz has deglamourised the first of the modern magians for ever and a day. The tragic grandeur surrounding the one, the magic splendour playing round the other can never be recaptured now by those who bow to facts. The myth-makers, however (and one cannot but envy them greatly), are too deeply committed to Saint-Germain to take any cognizance of Volz.

Yet it was a theosophical myth-maker, Mrs Cooper-Oakley, who started the process of disillusionment which has ended with Volz. Unable to contact her hero personally, although certain that he was still alive, she industriously followed his traces wherever she could light on them in the past, and succeeded where Andrew Lang had failed. Volz followed in her wake; and between them they found him figuring in the French National Record Office, the French Record Office of Foreign Affairs, in the Dutch Palace Archives, the English Record Office, the Mitchell Papers, the Secret State Archives in Berlin, the Palace and State Archives in Vienna and the State Archives in Copenhagen. Therefore Magre was wrong about the ancient law, though one could wish that he had been right.

The believers in big magic and the would-be believers must bear as well as they may yet another of those disenchanting shocks which await one round every corner in a study of this kind. We ought to have guessed it, for all the clues were there, scattered broadcast in the memoirs of the time. But somehow those experiments in dyeing and tanning, occasionally referred to, seemed to be merely pastimes of a versatile genius, not the main preoccupation of his life. We thought we were following the half-obliterated traces of a wonder-working sage; we now discover that we have been dogging the footsteps of an experimental chemist, travelling Europe with his wares, a would-be company promoter with secrets to sell. Magic, mystery and romance are put to flight ignominiously by science, industry and commerce. And Saint-Germain, hitherto unlabelled and unique, is seen to be only one (if perhaps the most eminent) of that swarm of swindlers, charlatans, impostors or pure adventurers whose golden age was the second half of the eighteenth century, and who numbered such queer customers as John Law, d'Eon, Baron Neuhoff, Cagliostro, Trenck and Casanova in their midst; all of these latter being adventurers on the grand scale, all of them knowing giddy summits of glory and power, all of them coming to a sad, bad end. Was there really nothing more to Saint-Germain than that?

Volz at least has not been able to solve the mystery of his birth. Indeed, by throwing very reasonable doubts on the hero's own claim, made towards the end of his life, to be the eldest son of Prince Rakoczy of Transylvania, he has rendered it more obscure than ever. The heir apparent to a throne already lost died, it appears, in 1700. If this is true, it does away with a theory which accounted reasonably for Saint-Germain's evasiveness on the subject of his origins, especially if he were hoping to regain the crown his father had been forced to yield to the Austrian Empire after a prolonged and bitter struggle. It would also account for what appeared to be his fabulous wealth when he first became famous, for his strikingly aristocratic manners, and for the favour extended to him by many of the great ones of the earth. Moreover, there is a strong family likeness in the extant portraits of Prince Francis II of Rakoczy and his self-styled son. The two younger brothers of the heir bowed to their fate and lived openly and unmolested, and it is possible at least that the death of the heir was falsely put about. However that may be, there seem to be even less grounds for supposing that Saint-Germain was the bastard son of the King of Portugal or of the widowed Queen of Spain; and no evidence to support the statement of Casanova and others that he was in reality the violinist Catalani, beyond the fact that he was a very fine performer. Choiseul's declaration that he was a Portuguese Jew was certainly made in spite; and malice probably also inspired the tales of a paternal tax-gatherer in San Germano (Savoy) called Rotondo, and of a Jewish father Wolff who practised medicine in Alsatia. I fear that we are all too sophisticated to-day to believe in the legend of an Arabian princess mating with a jinn (or alternatively with a salamander) and producing the Count of Saint-Germain; but perhaps the theory that he was the Wandering Jew in person will be acceptable, not in itself, but for its psychological value. Blood royal, bars sinister, musical genius, base birth, supernatural origin or mysterious curse: the choice is certainly bewildering.

Hardly less so is the number of aliases adopted by the man who spoke most of the European languages fluently and many of them perfectly, but was a stranger in all the countries which he is known to have visited. 'Saint-Germain' struck just the right note of aristocratic exclusiveness in Paris. 'The Marquis of the Black Cross' sounded both dignified and enigmatic in London. 'Surmont' fitted the owner of Ubbergen in Holland like a glove. What could be more suitable in Italy than 'Count Bellamare'? (*Mare nostra!*) Although the 'Marquis of Montferrat' was even more calculated to impress the Venetians, and the title 'Chevalier Schoening' to baffle the inhabitants of Pisa. 'General Soltikov' was a sure passport to favour in Genoa during the Russo-Turkish war; and who could resist the thought-associations aroused by the reassuring cognomen 'Count Welldone'? Tzarogy finally, a transparent anagram for Rakoczy, prepared the minds of his latter-day patrons for the disclosures of his 'real' identity as the missing heir to a throne.

The actual facts of Saint-Germain's real existence so far as they are known must be given their due chronological precedence over the legends to which they gave rise. An autograph letter in his hand, preserved in the British Museum, dated 22 November 1735 proves that he was then at The Hague, but gives no other personal details. Morin, Baron von Gleichen's secretary, testified to meeting him in Holland in 1739. On 9 December 1745 Horace Walpole stated that he was said to have been in London for two years. He came into the limelight on this occasion, during the rebellion of Charles Edward, the Young Pretender, because

One who was jealous of him with a lady [in all probability this was Frederick Louis, Prince of Wales], slipt a letter into his pocket as from the young Pretender (thanking him for his services and desiring him to continue them), and immediately had him taken up by a messenger. His innocence being fully proved on his examination, he was discharged out of the custody of the messenger and asked to dinner by Lord H.[1]

Walpole commented on the incident as follows:

...The other day they seized an odd man who goes by the name of Count Saint-Germain. He has been here these two years, and will not tell who he is, or whence, but professes that he does not go by his right name. He sings, plays on the violin wonderfully, composes, is mad, and not very sensible.... The Prince of Wales has had unsatiated curiosity about him, but in vain.[2]

---

[1] Cooper-Oakley, op. cit. p. 35; from the *London Chronicle*, 13–15 May 1760. The author quotes from another paper reprinting the notice.
[2] *Letters of Horace Walpole*, ed. Toynbee, Oxford 1903, III, p. 161.

This lack of sensibility, which later in the letter led Walpole to declare that he could not be a gentleman, was deduced from the fact that he did not quit the scene of his disgrace, but seemed to take it lightly. His wealth was maliciously attributed to a marriage of convenience in Mexico from where the bridegroom had absconded to Constantinople with the jewels of his wife; and he was variously supposed to be an Italian, a Spaniard or a Pole, a priest, a fiddler, a 'vast nobleman'. Thus the censorious English gossip, giving us the first glimpse of the man of mystery, and the last for a period of twelve years. According to Saint-Germain's own account he was in India twice subsequently to 1745; and a letter written by him in 1773 describes the second of these journeys made in the company of Watson and Clive in 1755. It is a boastful and futile epistle, mentioning a son of whom no further word is ever heard, and giving no indication (unlike his conversations) of first-hand knowledge or observation. But then the three letters he has left behind him show that his almost universal gifts did not include a literary style. On the other hand, according to Lascelles Wraxall, Saint-Germain was 'notoriously' in Vienna from 1745 to 1755, much in favour with Count Zobor, Lobkowitz, and Lomberg and especially with the French Marshal de Belle-Isle who brought him to France.[1]

Appearing in Paris, probably in 1757, Saint-Germain was soon received at Court, where he cut a dazzling figure and mystified everyone by his incognito, by dropping mysterious hints, by refusing to commit himself to the possession of powers which he nevertheless seemed to be exercising before their eyes, and by his indecipherable personality. He was also such a brilliant conversationalist and raconteur, so widely travelled, so deeply read, so learned, so light-hearted, so urbane, and withal so lavish and so splendid, that he outshone even his own diamonds and sparkling precious stones. Not only did he attain to a prestige, fame and power unparalleled in that cynical, sceptical and sophisticated society, but he maintained that position for a period of three years under the eyes of the great and in the penetrating rays of the fierce light that beats upon a throne.

---

[1] *Remarkable Adventures and Unrevealed Mysteries*, London 1863, I, p. 140. Clive did not sail on the *Stretham* with Admiral Watson from England in 1755, but joined him in Bombay. Together they undertook the expedition to reduce and plunder Cheriah in 1756. If Saint-Germain were with them, he might have shared in the vast booty. There was a M. de Saint-Germain who was Governor of Chengalaput in 1752.

First insinuating himself into the good graces of Madame de Pompadour, he made the conquest of the king by virtue of his inherent power to fascinate, to entertain, to charm, persuade and convince. Louis XV, perennially in the last stages of boredom, and hard indeed to astonish or impress, was nevertheless taken out of himself when this remarkable newcomer transformed one of his flawed diamonds into a stone without blemish, and worth more than three times its original price. The man was obviously a wizard, and a most disinterested one at that. Miracles of this type, however, become stale by repetition; it was one of the secrets of Saint-Germain's success that he aimed at interesting the intellect of his patrons quite as much as arousing their emotions. He made pupils of them, one and all. Louis XV was soon whiling away his hours of ennui in a laboratory fitted up for that purpose at Trianon. Like everyone else who ever took part in Saint-Germain's secret processes, he was convinced that there was big money in them, and that they were worth backing. He assigned to the inventor or discoverer apartments in the castle of Chambord, so that he might perfect his inventions to the ultimate incalculable benefit of the French dyeing industry and of the finances of the kingdom, then in a parlous state. The scintillating star at Court, who was admitted to the *petit soupers* of the king and to the private apartments of the favourite; the brilliant scientist who was to revolutionise industry and stabilise finance; the wonderful sage who possessed the secret of perpetual rejuvenation and might perhaps impart it to a chosen few, wielded (and indeed it was a foregone conclusion that he would) no negligible influence in the political sphere. More than one member of the French Cabinet consulted him about affairs of state and even acted upon his advice. Saint-Germain was said to be responsible for the fall of the Controller General of Finance, Étienne de Silhouette, in 1759. His policy, as far as can be gathered, was anti-Austrian; and his aim was probably the dissolution of the Franco-Austrian alliance, a very natural ideal if he were indeed a Rakoczy. He certainly extolled Frederick the Great in season and out of season, blamed the French Cabinet for severing relations with him during the colonial wars between England and France; prophesied correctly that the defeat which the Prussian monarch had sustained at the hands of the Russians at Kay and Kunersdorf would speedily be made good; and in a word gave some colour to the suspicion that he was a secret agent of Prussia. It is even more probable, however, that he was merely voicing the opinions of the Marshal de Belle-Isle, whose policy was pro-Prussian. This anti-Austrian bias colouring all his remarks on public affairs cannot have endeared him to the Duke of Choiseul, the Minister of Foreign Affairs, who stood or fell by the Austrian alliance; it was probably responsible for Saint-Germain's subsequent disaster.

He had made himself prominent enough and trusted enough to be charged with a secret mission to The Hague in 1760 in connection with overtures of peace with England which were in the air at that time. Part of the French Cabinet wished for a separate peace; England under Pitt would hear of no terms which did not include her allies, foremost amongst them Prussia; the waters were deep and turbid, the conditions favourable therefore for secret diplomacy, especially for the brand invented by Louis XV, by which he used subordinate agents, such as the Chevalier d'Eon, behind the backs of his responsible ministers, without their knowledge and often with instructions to thwart them, 'undoing by night the warp and woof which his ministers wove by day'.[1]

Louis XV, weak and vacillating, his Minister of War, the Marshal de Belle-Isle, the influential Count Louis Clermont, Prince Bourbon-Condé (much in the royal confidence) and Madame de Pompadour, pulling strings in the background, were all in favour of peace negotiations or at the very least of sounding the ground. But certain members of the French Cabinet, in particular the Duke of Choiseul, were for prolonging the war. The peace-party decided (or so it would seem) to send Saint-Germain to The Hague, ostensibly to negotiate a loan for France with the Dutch Government, actually to approach General Yorke, English Ambassador at The Hague, on the subject of peace between England and France. Casanova was in Holland at the time, having also been sent there for the purpose of negotiating a loan for France, and the two men actually put up at the same hotel, 'The Prince of Orange', according to Casanova's story. The Venetian had a letter of recommendation from Choiseul to d'Affry, the French Ambassador to The Hague, already perturbed about the presence of Saint-Germain, and horrified to have to receive Casanova who had been in The Hague before, and had not left a very good reputation behind him. Making the best of a bad job,

[1] Andrew Lang, op. cit. p. 240. Cf. also Duc de Broglie, *Le Secret du Roi*, Paris 1888.

he questioned Casanova about Saint-Germain. The latter gave a bad account of him as an ambiguous and dangerous person, for they had met as rivals at the house of the Marquise d'Urfé. After seeing Saint-Germain personally, Casanova also made all haste to queer his pitch with the Amsterdam banker 'M. d'O.' (=Hope?). The financial mission was therefore a failure. The diplomatic mission was also a fiasco. Two letters from the Marshal de Belle-Isle, and one from the Count of Clermont which Saint-Germain showed to Yorke, convinced the latter that he was an unofficial agent of Louis XV, and both George II and Frederick the Great thought it, to say the least, highly likely. Delicate as the mission was, one can see how a diplomatic amateur like Saint-Germain might seem particularly suitable for it. His presence at The Hague, accounted for on other grounds, would be unlikely to arouse suspicions in the representatives of foreign powers. He had moved in high circles, had an intimate knowledge of several European courts, and had shown considerable diplomatic gifts in his conduct at Versailles. But unhappily he had other qualities too. Even those who liked him best agreed that he was a vain and boastful man; his knowledge, his powers and his pedigree were always, even if often only by implication, the subject of his discourses. He could, and generally did, display marked, indeed impenetrable reserve in order to enhance the aura of mystery by which he set such store; but he would allow hints to escape him too, and would sometimes even lift the veil in the interests of self-advertisement. The man who could make the following statement about himself was certainly the last man on earth to entrust with a real secret, the knowledge of which would add to his prestige:

I hold nature in my hands, and in the same way in which God created the world, so too I can conjure forth everything I wish from the void.[1]

Such a man would obviously be prone to overweening self-confidence; in addition to which, being full of enthusiasm for the object of his mission, and a person of great goodwill, he had the natural recklessness of the born adventurer, out to achieve speedy

[1] G. B. Volz, *Der Graf von Saint-Germain*, Dresden 1923, p. 316. This translation into German is by Oppeln-Bronikowski. The author I presume to be Dutch and the book appeared after Cooper-Oakley's memoir in 1912. The quotation is from a letter from Alvensleben, the Prussian Ambassador in Dresden, to Frederick the Great, dated 25 June 1777.

results. All these qualities combined to make him far too impetuous in his dealings with Yorke, and what was worse, induced him to take all the world and his wife into his confidence almost as soon as he had set foot in The Hague. Kauderbach, the Saxon Resident, could hardly believe his ears as he listened to Saint-Germain's references to the mission with which he had been entrusted and to his frankly expressed opinions about the weakness of the king and his mistress and the corruption and evils in France. Kauderbach came to the conclusion that Saint-Germain was too presumptuous and too incautious for the part of secret negotiator, and that he was unlikely to succeed in his mission. Meanwhile d'Affry, the accredited ambassador at The Hague, was rendered uneasy and jealous by the rumours of Saint-Germain's negotiations which were going the rounds; and although he was at first too much in awe of him to treat him otherwise than with courtesy and attention, and was clearly more than half convinced of his magical powers, still he took an early opportunity of informing Choiseul of the state of affairs. The latter acted promptly. He either intimidated Madame de Pompadour into handing over one of Saint-Germain's semi-official reports; or (as the latter believed) had it stolen, faced the king and his cabinet with the knowledge, at which all feigned surprise, and sent the following instructions to d'Affry:

Sir,

I send you a letter from M. de St-Germain to the Marquise de Pompadour which in itself will suffice to expose the absurdity of the personage; he is an adventurer of the first order, who is moreover, as far as I have seen, exceedingly foolish. I beg you immediately on receiving my letter to summon him to your house, and to tell him from me that...you are ordered to warn him that if I learn that far or near, in much or little, he chooses to meddle with Politics, I assure him that I shall obtain an order from the King that on his return to France he shall be placed for the rest of his life in an underground dungeon!...After this declaration you will request him never again to set foot in your house, and it will be well for you to make public and known to all the Foreign Ministers, as well as to the Bankers of Amsterdam, the compliment that you have been commanded to pay to this insufferable adventurer.[1]

But this was not enough. Choiseul prevailed with Louis XV to sanction harsher measures against his one-time favourite. About

[1] Cooper-Oakley, op. cit. pp. 170 ff. Choiseul to d'Affry; dated from Versailles, 19 March 1760.

three weeks after the above, d'Affry was instructed to apply to the Estates General of Holland to seize the person of Saint-Germain and have him conveyed to France, where he could be dealt with. Luckily for the unfortunate secret agent his staunch Dutch supporter, Count Bentinck van Rhoon, a person of importance in Holland, was advised in good time of this danger. He persuaded the incredulous victim of secret diplomacy that the peril was real, urged him to flee to England, and facilitated his escape to the unconcealed fury of d'Affry. But England, wise to the change of front which had made Choiseul more powerful than ever, refused to harbour him:

... as it was evident that he was not authorised, even by that part of the French Ministry in whose name he pretended to talk, as his *séjour* here could be of no use, and might be attended by disagreeable consequences, it was thought proper to seize him upon his arrival here. His examination has produced nothing very material. His conduct and language are artful, with an odd mixture which it is difficult to define.

Upon the whole it has been thought most advisable not to suffer him to remain in England, and he set out accordingly on Saturday morning last with an intention to take shelter in some part of his Prussian Majesty's Dominions, doubting whether he would be safe in Holland. At his earnest and repeated request he saw Baron Knyphausen [Prussian ambassador in London] during his confinement, but none of the King's Servants saw him.[1]

Choiseul's disproportionate measures against Saint-Germain and the violence of his language, together with d'Affry's obvious jealousy and hatred, show that he was in their eyes a man to be dreaded. Those who were most in the know certainly believed in his mission.

If the Comte de Saint-Germain had shown as much prudence as he had shown zeal, he would have, I believe, much accelerated Peace; but he relied too much on his own intentions and had not a bad enough opinion of the men with whom he had to deal.[2]

Whatever may be the rights or the wrongs of the case, the steps taken by the Count have brought matters into motion between France and England....[3]

[1] Cooper-Oakley, op. cit. pp. 125 ff. The Earl of Holderness (Secretary of State) to Mr Mitchell (English Ambassador to Prussia); dated from Whitehall, 6 May 1760.

[2] Ibid. p. 212. From the papers of Bentinck van Rhoon, 18 April 1760.

[3] Volz, op. cit. p. 188. Frederick II to Hellen, Prussian Chargé d'Affaires at The Hague; dated from Freiburg, 8 April 1760.

So much is clear: the statements made by the Count Saint-Germain have at least had the effect that the Duke of Choiseul has not been able altogether to resist the movement for peace in the Versailles Cabinet.[1]

I noticed in this connection that the Duke of Choiseul had proceeded very zealously against Saint-Germain; and this led me to judge that he was perhaps afraid lest peace between the French and English Crowns... might be brought about by his instrumentality.[2]

Moreover, Knyphausen's extreme anxiety lest Saint-Germain should seek an asylum with Frederick the Great tells the same story:

As this man whom I have known for years is dangerously impetuous, and might fascinate the king and incite him to undertake many disastrous measures, I beg Your Excellency to do your utmost to hinder his journey to Saxony[3] [at that time the headquarters of Frederick the Great].

Even Voltaire, although very sarcastically, referred to Saint-Germain's secret mission:

Your ambassadors will probably learn more in Breda than I know. The Duke of Choiseul, Count Kaunitz and Mr Pitt don't betray their secret to me. It is supposed to be known only to a certain Saint-Germain, who supped with the Fathers of the Council of Trent in the days of yore, and will probably have the honour to visit Your Majesty in about fifty years from now. The man is immortal and omniscient.[4]

Frederick replied with the witticism that 'Le Comte de Saint-Germain n'est qu'un conte pour rire'; but by that time the indiscreet emissary had been openly disavowed and had fled to England, probably greatly to the relief of Louis XV, who could hardly have wished to punish him as savagely for his failure as Choiseul would have liked him to do.

But though Saint-Germain saved his liberty and probably his life from the consequences of his own folly, of Choiseul's hostility and of royal ingratitude, he was obliged to leave the shores of 'perfidious Albion' and seek sanctuary elsewhere. It seems unlikely that he realised his own wishes and Knyphausen's fears by going to

[1] Ibid. p. 188. Hellen to Frederick II; dated from The Hague, 22 April 1760.

[2] Ibid. p. 202. Reischach, Austrian Ambassador at The Hague, to Kaunitz, Austrian Chancellor; dated from The Hague, 8 April 1760.

[3] Ibid. p. 193. Knyphausen to the Prussian Secretary of State; dated from London, 6 May 1760.

[4] Ibid. p. 215. Voltaire to Frederick II; dated 16 April 1760.

Germany; and although Casanova is often surprisingly accurate on questions of fact, it is difficult to believe that the gay Lothario saw Saint-Germain in Paris in the Bois de Boulogne with the Marquise d'Urfé in May 1761. Casanova believed that Choiseul had used him in London as a counter-spy, which tallies with Barthold's story that on hearing from the Marquise d'Urfé that Saint-Germain was in Paris, the Prime Minister replied 'I am not surprised, since he passed the night in my cabinet.'[1] But this is probably apocryphal: for when next heard of in 1762 he was the owner of the estate of Ubbergen in Holland, calling himself Count Surmont, although not yet having completed the purchase money. According to d'Affry, who nosed out these details, he had previously been wandering round the Netherlands under another name and was now completely discredited. Choiseul smugly decided to leave him unmolested to work out his own damnation, probably because the Estates General had shown very little signs of complying with the extradition order in 1760, and would be unlikely to be any more obliging now. D'Affry added scornfully that the swindler was keeping the wolf from the door by catching simpletons with the aid of his secret chemical processes.

It was all too true; although one may derive a certain comfort from the fact that his simpletons were men of standing and renown, and his processes, to put them at their lowest, outwardly dazzling. In April 1763 Kaunitz, the Austrian Chancellor, was thrown into a state of disquietude and alarm by a letter from Cobenzl, Minister Plenipotentiary in the Austrian Netherlands, full of what seemed to Kaunitz wild-cat schemes for opening factories in the town of Tournai in order to exploit Saint-Germain's marvellous and amazing secrets. These he had offered to place from pure motives of friendship unreservedly at the disposal of Cobenzl, and they would inaugurate the millennium in the Austrian Netherlands, bringing peace and prosperity to all. Never had Cobenzl met such a genius before; and if he had not seen the miracles the Count could perform produced under his very eyes, never could he have believed them to be possible. The ennobling of metals, the dyeing of silks, wools, cotton and wood in the most glorious colours imaginable, ridiculously simple to manufacture and of incredible cheapness; the tanning of

[1] F. W. Barthold, *Die geschichtlichen Persönlichkeiten in Jacob Casanova's Memoiren*, Berlin 1846, II, p. 94.

skins resulting in leather of a miraculous suppleness and quality; all this would have to be seen to be believed, and Cobenzl was willing and anxious to send any number of samples; for in his view the proposed wholesale industry should be a Government concern.

Kaunitz was in a dilemma. Whilst not wishing to antagonise Cobenzl, nor to deprive Austria of a potential source of riches, he had yet heard too much to the detriment of Saint-Germain to trust either the man or his secrets. He cautiously said as much to Cobenzl, reporting at the same time in a much more emphatic manner to the Empress Maria Theresa, who was equally sceptical. But Cobenzl was infatuated, and refused at first to hear a word against the man who had obviously bewitched him.

Although the story of his life and even his person are shrouded in mystery and obscurity, I discovered in him outstanding gifts in all the arts and sciences. He is a poet, a musician, a writer, doctor, physicist, chemist, mechanic and a thorough connoisseur of painting. In a word he possesses a culture such as I have never yet found in any other human being, and he speaks all languages almost equally well, Italian, French and English particularly so. He has travelled over nearly the whole world, and as he was very entertaining in spite of all his learning, I passed my leisure hours very agreeably with him. The only thing I can reproach him with is frequent boasting about his talents and origins.[1]

Later, when he became disillusioned on the subject of Saint-Germain's character and disinterestedness, he still believed as firmly as ever in the value of his secrets, and so did others in his confidence more competent to judge. Frau Nettine, a business woman, put up the capital to start the factories going and paid good money down for some of those secrets which their inventor had earlier promised to communicate *gratis*. Moreover, the silk manufacturers in Brussels inundated the firm with orders after seeing the samples. Kaunitz's experts were very lukewarm, not to say negative, but even they spoke well of Saint-Germain's yellow dye and of his leather samples. Expert opinion is apt to be divided; and as far as the famous secrets are concerned, Saint-Germain is entitled to the benefit of the doubt. Ethically, however, his conduct in the matter was far from irreproachable. He was in desperately low water, but

[1] Volz, op. cit. pp. 247ff. From Cobenzl to Kaunitz; dated from Brussels, 25 June 1763. Portuguese is generally mentioned by other observers as having been spoken perfectly by Saint-Germain. He was also an artist in oils, as well as a connoisseur.

deceived Cobenzl into believing that he had goods to the value of over a million gulden. One way and another he got nearly 100,000 gulden from Frau Nettine, and then made off when the game was up, without parting with his more lucrative secrets. Yet even so, Cobenzl assured Kaunitz in October 1763 that although Saint-Germain had disappeared, the factories he had established in Tournai were beginning to develop, that the owner (Frau Nettine) would almost certainly recoup herself, and probably make a profit.

The hero of this distressing story of industrial racketeering was lost to documentary evidence for eleven years. Part of this period was probably spent in Russia; for there is some evidence that he attempted, but without success, to establish a cotton factory in Moscow at that time, and that he somehow acquired a Russian mine yielding semi-precious stones which he displayed proudly in later years. It seems fairly certain that he cannot have been in Russia during the July Revolution of 1762 which cost Peter III his throne and his life, as (according to what has been discovered of his movements) he was in Holland at the time. The legend that he played a part in the revolution must therefore be discounted. On the other hand, there seems no reason to suspect the statement that he was active in some capacity in the Russo-Turkish war in the Mediterranean (1768–74). Reports of his presence in Mantua, Venice, Pisa, and Leghorn during these years are not in themselves conclusive; but the enthusiastic friendship felt for him by Count Alexei Orlov, Supreme Commander of the Russian Expedition in the Archipelago and the hero of Tschesme, has been vouched for by a trustworthy eye-witness. And Saint-Germain's famous tea, a mild laxative made with senna-pods, his panacea for all the ills which flesh is heir to, came to be called the Russian tea, because it was supplied in bulk to the Russian fleet with very happy results. Many a man has been knighted for less; and I am inclined to believe that the patent conferring the rank of a Russian general on Saint-Germain was neither a forgery (as Volz asserts on insufficient evidence) nor yet the reward of martial exploits, but for this useful contribution to the Russian war effort. He wore the uniform at Nuremberg in 1774, when he, the Margrave of Brandenburg and the Ansbach minister Gemmingen (who described the interview) went to meet Orlov in person. And not only was the latter in no way affronted by this, but on the contrary he greeted the wearer with the utmost cordiality and enthusiasm, like the bosom friend which he declared him to be. It seems certain therefore that Saint-Germain had the right to call himself General Welldone, in which name (and not in that of Soltikov) the patent was made out. Yet it is more than probable that Saint-Germain was very anxious for the Margrave to witness the meeting with Orlov in order to enhance his standing.

One can hardly blame him for this; he was getting on in years, and seemed to have found a safe haven at last. In 1774 he had gradually and quite unobtrusively attracted the favourable notice of Charles Alexander, Margrave of Brandenburg, during a residence at Schwabach in Ansbach of which the Margrave was then the Governor; and when paying his respects had offered to initiate him into the secrets which would secure the happiness and prosperity of Brandenburg. He also showed him a number of beautiful stones which were probably the product of the Russian mine, since they were found later to be deficient in weight and not to withstand the file. The interest thus aroused in the Margrave developed into a friendly patronage which, as so often with Saint-Germain's relationships, held elements of discipleship in it. Although indefatigably experimenting with dyes and skins, and as always urging those around him to do the same on the principles he laid down, and although also trying to interest his patron in the financial aspect of these experiments, he was a quiet, courteous, considerate and very retiring guest at the castle of Triersdorf where he was given rooms on the ground floor. He would emerge in the evenings to converse enchantingly and sometimes mysteriously, but would never consent to be present at the table of his host; for the diet which he seems to have adhered to religiously throughout his life did not admit of meals in public. His needs were of the simplest and his circumstances greatly reduced. The only book in his possession was a tattered copy of Guarini's *Pastor Fido*. One wonders what manner of thoughts passed through the mind of Count Tzarogy as he perused this faded classic. For this was the name under which he had introduced himself to the Margrave, prior to the confession that his real name was Prince Rakoczy, and that he was the last of that royal and unhappy line.

Unfortunately this startling announcement and the impressive manner of Orlov's greeting in Nuremberg were only too effective.

During a journey to Italy the following year (1775) the Margrave was full of the story of the recluse at Triersdorf and began to put questions about the Rakoczys; only to be told that all three sons were dead, and that this mysterious visitor was the notorious Saint-Germain, the son of the tax-collector of San Germano, an adventurer and worse, fooling the world under one alias after another. The disillusioned Margrave sent Gemmingen to confront his guest on his return, but the former could not shake him. He owned to all the aliases except Soltikov, but stuck to his story of being Rakoczy, and declared that he had adopted different names at different times to throw off the scent the enemy pursuing him as the pretender to the Transylvanian throne. He also proudly maintained that whatever name he had from time to time adopted he had never disgraced any of them, but had borne them all as a man of honour. And indeed one could hail this as the literal truth had it not been for his shabby conduct about the factories at Tournai. Even so, one is tempted to agree with Gemmingen that it would be unfair to dub him a swindler; and it is a curious circumstance of his career that, in spite of his various aliases, he never fell into the hands of the police nor was had up before a magistrate. That may have been due rather to his head than to his heart; but this at least is to his credit:

As long as he was connected with the Margrave, he never uttered a single wish, never received anything of the slightest value, never interfered in anything that did not concern him. With his extremely simple mode of life his wants were very limited. When he had money, he shared it with the poor.[1]

It is almost the picture of an Eastern sage; but his modest existence at Castle Triersdorf came to an end after the return of the Margrave from Italy, refusing to communicate with Saint-Germain except through Gemmingen and demanding his letters back. His guest surrendered all except one, which he said he had given to Orlov, probably to impress the latter; and, refusing the offer to stay quietly at Schwabach, made off into the unknown in 1776. The next three years were spent in Leipzig, Dresden, Berlin and Hamburg, but bore little fruit; not even though the undaunted adventurer sent off from Saxony to Frederick the Great, with a dignified covering letter, a list of twenty-nine items for his gracious consideration. These comprised

[1] Volz, op. cit. p. 302; quoting Gemmingen.

not only his well-known secret processes for dyeing every conceivable kind of material, bleaching, tanning, smelting, the refinery
of oils and the manufacture of cosmetics, but also some pharmaceutical
remedies for full measure. It smells sadly of quackery, and one can
quite understand that the only encouragement he received from
Frederick was the notification, through a third person, that Berlin
was a very sceptical city. Knyphausen's earlier fears appear to have
been groundless; yet Frederick's private letters show that he was not
as indifferent as he wished to appear about the movements of the
'charlatan'. There was a postscript to Saint-Germain's list: 'A further
point cannot be touched upon here for manifold reasons. I reserve
it.'[1]

Perhaps this was thrown out as a bait; but it may have been a
reminder of secret services rendered for Prussia at the Court of
Versailles, and a hint of his readiness to continue them. If this were
so, Frederick lagged not at all behind Louis in his cynical attitude
towards broken tools. Meanwhile Saint-Germain was engaging the
attention of a very different type of mentality. If he were really as
incredibly old as people said, and possessed such astounding secrets,
then he was almost certainly a member of one of the secret societies,
possibly an unknown Master. Whilst he was in Leipzig, the Grand
Master of the Prussian Masonic Lodges, Prince Frederick Augustus
of Brunswick, had him closely observed and questioned by initiates.
Dubosc, Saxon Counsellor of the Exchequer, and a banker;
Bischoffwerder, Equerry to the Saxon Prince Charles, Duke of
Courland; Fröhlich, a merchant in Görlitz; and the Saxon Minister
von Wurmb, all of them Rosicrucians as well as high initiates of
Freemasonry, approached the man of mystery and had lengthy
conversations with him; and they all gave negative reports. Dubosc's
was very pejorative; Fröhlich's was very emphatic:

I know him very well. This *Sieur Welldone* is no Mason; he is also no
magus, neither is he a Theosophist.[2]

Bischoffwerder was much more doubtful at first, but finally came to
the conclusion that he was 'not one of us'. Nevertheless, he was

---

[1] Cf. ibid. pp. 306–23 for the list and the correspondence connected
with it.
[2] Ibid. p. 328. Fröhlich to the Duke of Brunswick; dated from Görlitz,
8 March 1777.

convinced that the Count had important secrets, and that he had communicated the most important of all to him:

Although it is against all the laws of probability, (1) that the thing is actually possible, (2) that I should have been chosen as the bearer of such a rich *arcanum*, (3) that I have received it as a novice.[1]

Dubosc and Fröhlich received the impression of a needy charlatan boasting of riches and borrowing money; von Wurmb was impressed by his knowledge of dyes and the treatment of linens and woollens, and believed that there might be money in it for the local industry; he also elicited from the very indifferent sage, that he was a Freemason who had attained to the fourth grade, but had forgotten the signs and the passwords. Von Wurmb came to the conclusion that he was either dissembling or in truth not a Mason, more probably the latter, as he was a convinced materialist.

However, it was a well-known Freemason who became the last great friend and patron Saint-Germain's baffling personality procured him. This was Prince Charles of Hesse-Cassel, very unwilling at first to have anything to do with him, but finally yielding to the other's impetuous determination that they were to be friends. Uninterested at the outset in the gentle arts of dyeing, smelting, ennobling metals and purifying precious stones, he was gradually won over by Saint-Germain's earnestness and became his pupil like Louis XV, Cobenzl, the Margrave of Brandenburg, and probably many others before him. When he first came into Schleswig in 1779 Saint-Germain owned to being eighty-eight years of age, declared that he was the son of Prince Rakoczy, and that he had been brought up in the house of the last of the Medici. Prince Charles believed him implicitly, fitted him up with a factory at Eckernförde and paid a doctor called Lossau a handsome annual income to dispense his guest's medicines. Unluckily, the rooms assigned to Saint-Germain at Eckernförde were damp, the inmate contracted rheumatism, never completely recovered from it, began to fail noticeably and to become a victim of depression. In conversation with his patron, he showed himself to be an avowed materialist, whose great aim in life was to benefit humanity. He used to speak in derogatory terms of Christ; but when he realised that this distressed his friend, he promised never to touch upon that topic

[1] Volz, op. cit. p. 337. Bischoffwerder to the Duke of Brunswick; dated from Elsterwerda, 9 July 1777.

again. Perhaps it was a sense of gratitude which dictated a last message to the absent prince sent by Saint-Germain on his death-bed, through Lossau, to the effect that his eyes had been opened at the eleventh hour, and that he was dying as a true believer. But, whether in the odour of sanctity or not, it is attested that he died at Eckernförde on 27 February 1784, was buried there on 2 March, and that his death was entered in the parish register. It was a great loss and grief to the Prince of Hesse-Cassel.

He was perhaps one of the greatest sages who have ever lived. He loved humanity; he desired money only in order to give it to the poor. He even loved animals, and his heart was occupied only with the happiness of others. He believed he could make mankind happy by procuring for them new pleasures, lovelier cloths and colours; and his glorious colours cost almost nothing. I have never known a man with a clearer mind, and at the same time he was possessed of a learning, especially in history, that I have rarely found. He had been in all the countries of Europe...but France seemed to be the land which he loved best.[1]

We have the notorious adventurer Saint-Germain here. He is the completest charlatan, fool, rattle-pate, wind-bag and in a certain sense swindler that the world has seen for many a long year. Our prince esteems and honours him with all his might and heart. In doing so he is following his inborn inclination for that type of person.[2]

The history of the Count of Saint-Germain displays a cleverer and more cautious adventurer [than Cagliostro] and nothing to offend the sense of honour. Nothing dishonest, everything marvellous, never anything mean or scandalous.[3]

This Saint-Germain has told us so many other gross and palpable fairy-stories, that one can listen to him with nothing but disgust on a second occasion, unless such braggings amuse one. This man couldn't deceive a child of ten years, let alone enlightened men....I regard him as an adventurer of the first water who is at the end of his tether, and I shall be very much surprised if he doesn't end tragically.[4]

Yorke spoke of him as being a *very cheerful and very polite man*...his conversation pleased me very much, being exceedingly brilliant, varied and

[1] Ibid. p. 358; quoting Hesse-Cassel's *Memoirs*, 1816–17.
[2] Ibid. p. 361. From the Danish statesman, Count Charles Warnstedt; dated from Silesia, 24 November 1779.
[3] Ibid. p. 340. From the French savant Thiebault's *Souvenirs*, 1804. He knew Saint-Germain in Berlin.
[4] Ibid. pp. 213 ff. From Kauderbach to Count Wackerbarth-Salmour; dated from The Hague, 4 April 1760. Kauderbach had been both dazzled and puzzled by Saint-Germain at first.

full of details about various countries he had visited.... I was exceedingly pleased with his judgment of persons and places known to me; his manners were exceedingly polite and went to prove that he was a man brought up in the best society.[1]

I was neither his friend nor his admirer.... I reserve my judgment, but I confess that I still incline strongly to distrust a man, whose personality remained a perpetual riddle, who was forever making preposterous statements, continually changing his name, sometimes posing as an adept, at others as a great gentleman whom Providence had blessed more richly than most.[2]

Saint-Germain was in many respects a remarkable man, and wherever he was personally known he left a favourable impression behind, and the remembrance of many good and sometimes of many noble deeds. Many a poor father of a family, many a charitable institution, was helped by him in secret...not one bad, nor one dishonourable action was ever known of him, and so he inspired sympathy everywhere.[3]

He is a highly gifted man with a very alert mind, but completely without judgment, and he has only gained his singular reputation by the lowest and basest flattery of which a man is capable, as well as by his outstanding eloquence, especially if one lets oneself be carried away by the fervour and enthusiasm with which he can express himself.... Inordinate vanity is the mainspring driving his whole mechanism...he is stimulating and entertaining in society, as long as he is only narrating. But as soon as he tries to develop his own ideas, his whole weakness shows itself.... But woe to him who would contradict him![4]

I am well aware, Monsieur, that you are the greatest lord on earth.[5]

As for me, I, like yourself, think him somewhat of a fool.[6]

The course of Saint-Germain's real life, although presenting gaps and leaving his birth in obscurity, seems no longer essentially mysterious, however baffling his personality may be. He had some-where and somehow acquired at least a smattering of chemical

[1] Cooper-Oakley, op. cit. p. 202. From the papers of Bentinck van Rhoon; dated 16 March 1760.

[2] Volz, op. cit. p. 143. From the Danish statesman Count Bernstorff in a private letter in 1779.

[3] Cooper-Oakley, op. cit. p. 52. From Sypesteyn's *Historical Memoirs*.

[4] Volz, op. cit. pp. 310 ff. From the Prussian Ambassador in Dresden, Alvensleben, to Frederick II; dated from Dresden, 25 June 1777.

[5] Cooper-Oakley, op. cit. p. 239. From the Danish Admiral Count Danneskjold-Lawrigen to Saint-Germain; dated from Amsterdam, 27 April 1760.

[6] Ibid. p. 237. From Prince Golizyn, Russian Ambassador in London, to Kauderbach; dated from London, 1 April 1760.

knowledge and was desirous of making capital of it in a big way. More than once he was within an ace of achieving his goal, but never quite brought it off. Meanwhile he certainly caused a considerable flutter in the chancelleries of Europe, because Louis XV, and possibly others, used him as a secret diplomatic agent. His real gifts were undoubted. Very musical, a great linguist, an amateur painter who could give to the jewels with which he adorned his portraits the lustre of real stones; it must also I think be granted that he had a good deal of skill in the treatment of jewels, and probably knew how to wash diamonds and to cut them; moreover, although his industrial processes proved no gold-mine, he had obviously invented or discovered some very promising methods for dyeing, bleaching and tanning in a simple and economical way, which, however, he never perfected, and which may have had some irremediable flaw. The brilliance of his mind and personality, his scintillating conversation, his extraordinary memory, his vivid imagination, his eloquence, persuasiveness and charm are also constantly canvassed. But the greatest of all his many and various gifts was his very remarkable power over the minds of his contemporaries. The violence with which his enemies expressed themselves about him, no less than the hyperbolical language of his admirers, vouches for that. And nowhere is it more apparent that in the countless legends circulated about him during his lifetime and later. It may even be doubted whether Saint-Germain set the ball rolling in the first instance, although he took full advantage of it once it had been launched. Walpole at least (and his is the first allusion known) mentions no claim made by the 'oddity' who refused to disclose his real name. This, however, was enough to arouse the 'unsatiated curiosity' of others besides the Prince of Wales. That so striking a personality should escape identification was a challenge, since it represented a gap in contemporary knowledge which like any other void had to be filled. Saint-Germain obeyed this law of nature when he declared himself to be Rakoczy. Before that day dawned he deepened the mystery. He would describe his childhood in glowing colours, portraying himself with a large suite, wandering on splendid terraces in a glorious climate, as if (said the Baron Gleichen) he were heir to the throne of a king of Granada at the time of the Moors. To Madame de Genlis, then a girl of fourteen, in the presence of her sceptical mother, he told a moving story of wandering through the forests at the age of seven with a price upon his head, accompanied by his tutor and wearing a miniature of the mother he was never to see again in a bracelet round his wrist. To prove it he showed the miniature. This false claim to royal blood (as the child's mother took it to be) might have been nearer the truth than she thought were he indeed a Rakoczy. What is even more noteworthy is the fact that it fulfilled the conditions legend had laid down for the early lives of magi, beset and fraught with perils.

Another stock feature of all magician's lives, long and portentous journeys, was prominent enough in Saint-Germain's real existence to give birth to the fairly prevalent notion that he was the Wandering Jew. Disappearing from one country to reappear in another without any kind of explanation, he certainly covered the greater part of Europe in his early lifetime, and was supposed to have gone much farther. He himself claimed to have been in India; others declared that he told them he had been in Persia, Turkey, Japan and China; in which country, according to a not very reliable memoir writer, he had refused to give any name at all. The wonderfully vivid descriptions he gave of oriental countries in his conversations lent weight to the belief that he was familiar with them.

Although the documentary evidence of Saint-Germain's initiation into Freemasonry or any other contemporary secret society is negative, this does not necessarily prove that he was not a member; and a strong tradition exists among those more or less in the know that he was an extremely powerful and influential initiate, who founded more than one sect and was in connection with them all. Saint-Germain himself told von Wurmb (evidently making fun of the incident) that more than two hundred persons in Paris, belonging to a society presided over by the Duke of Bouillon, had desired his acquaintance because they believed him to be a Master; and it is categorically affirmed that he was chosen as a representative of the great Masonic Conference in Paris in 1785, a year after his death. As I cannot check this or any other records, I must leave the question open, merely pointing out that, with Saint-Germain's reputation, it was inevitable that many Freemasons and their kindred should take him for a fellow-member.

I must now give your Excellency news of a singular phenomenon. A man calling himself Saint-Germain who refuses to make known his origins, is lodging here in the hotel Kaiserhof. He lives in great style...and yet he never receives any letters of credit. He writes day and night, carries on a correspondence with the greatest crowned heads, but does not care to mix in society, except that of the Countess Bentinck and the French ministers. It is very difficult to get to know him. He is an amateur of the natural sciences, has studied nature; and it is thanks to the knowledge he has received, that he is now 182 years of age and looks like a young man of forty. In the strictest confidence he told a friend of mine that he possesses certain drops by means of which he achieves all his results, even the transmutation of metals. In his presence he transformed a copper coin into finest silver, poor leather into the best English variety, and semi-precious stones into diamonds. At the same time he is continually alone and by no means expansive. He has a superfluity of all sorts of gold and silver coins, which look as if they had just been minted.... And yet he gets no remittances from anyone, nor has he any introductions to the merchants. How does all this come about? Could it be that this man is one of those whom we have been seeking?[1]

Thus one Freemason to another. Seemingly without any encouragement from Saint-Germain, the legend of his adeptship grew and spread; so that when the Marquis de Luchet wrote his satirical attacks on Cagliostro and Illuminism, the first in 1785 and the second in 1789, Saint-Germain figured in both; and a good many simple souls took the mock-initiation described in the former for the naked truth:

Count Cagliostro asked him for a secret audience in order to prostrate himself before the god of the believers. Saint-Germain appointed two o'clock at night. The moment having arrived Cagliostro and his wife, clothed in white garments, clasped about the waist with girdles of rose-colour, presented themselves at the castle. The draw-bridge was lowered, a man of seven feet high, clothed in a long grey robe, led them into a dimly lighted chamber. Therein some folding doors suddenly opened, and they beheld a temple illuminated by a thousand lights, with the Count de Saint-Germain enthroned upon the altar; at his feet two acolytes swung golden thuribles, which diffused sweet and unobtrusive perfumes. The divinity bore upon his breast a diamond pentagram of almost intolerable radiance. A majestic figure, white and diaphanous, upheld on the steps of the altar a vase inscribed 'Elixir of Immortality', whilst a vast mirror was on the wall, and before it a majestic being walked to and fro. Above the mirror was written: 'Storehouse of Wandering Souls'. The most sombre silence

[1] Volz, op. cit. pp. 35 ff. From the Hamburg advocate Dresser to Baron Uffel, judge of the Court of Appeal in Celle; dated from Hamburg, 23 October 1778. Both Freemasons. The likeness to Gualdi is very noticeable in this description.

prevailed in this sacred retreat; but a voice, which seemed hardly a voice, pronounced these words: 'Who are you? Whence come you? What would you?' Then the Count and Countess prostrated themselves, and the former answered after a long pause: 'I come to invoke the God of the faithful, the Son of nature, the Sire of truth. I come to demand of him one of the fourteen thousand seven hundred secrets which are treasured in his breast. I come to proclaim myself his slave, his apostle, his martyr.'

The divinity did not respond, but after a long silence, the same voice asked: 'What does the partner of thy long wanderings intend?' 'To obey and to serve,' answered Lorenza.

Simultaneously with her words, profound darkness succeeded to the glare of light, uproar followed on tranquillity, terror on trust, fear on hope, and a sharp and menacing voice cried loudly: 'Woe to those who cannot stand the tests.'[1]

Lorenza's virtue and Cagliostro's steadfastness were then put to the proof; after which Saint-Germain was represented first as talking nonsense, then as giving cynical advice and finally as misbehaving himself with Lorenza. This libellous lampoon is nevertheless partly responsible for the persistent legends of Saint-Germain's importance in the secret societies of the age, and probably also the reason why some Freemasons so strenuously deny that he had anything to do with any of them. We are, however, assured to-day with a good deal of solemnity and complete good faith that he took part in Vienna in the foundation of the Society of Asiatic Brothers and of the Knights of Light; that he was also partly responsible for the group in France called the Philalethes, of which the Prince of Hesse, Condorcet and Cagliostro were said to be members, and which was recruited from the lodge of *Les Amis Réunis*. Eliphas Lévi, who declared him to have founded the Order of Saint-Jakin in Bohemia, also states that he seceded from it when it adopted anarchical principles, was thereupon disowned by the brethren, charged with treason, and (according to one tradition) was immured in the dungeons of the castle of Ruel. This brings in the traditional trial and persecution; and the lifelong ills he suffered as a Rakoczy at the hands of Austria, about which he was eloquent to Gemmingen, are in the nature of a contest. As for his death, it was variously reported to have taken place in the dungeons of Ruel, in the cells of the Inquisition of Rome (probably by a

---

[1] [Marquis de Luchet], *Mémoire authentique pour servir à l'histoire du Comte de Cagliostro*, 2nd ed., Strassburg 1786, pp. 4 ff. The first edition was in 1785.

confusion with Cagliostro), in mortal terror and agony of mind at Eckernförde, or never to have taken place at all.

This of course was the organic development of the belief in his longevity so sedulously circulated when he was alive. And here again, although he certainly fostered it for all he was worth, it does not seem as if Saint-Germain originated the myth of his immortality. It would appear to have arisen spontaneously in the addled wits of the octogenarian Madame de Gergy, widow of the French Ambassador in Venice. This ancient lady declared that she had seen the Count in Venice in 1710 aged about forty-five. Meeting him in Paris fifty years later looking not a day older, she supposed him to be his own son. When disabused of that notion, she naturally began to talk; and Madame de Pompadour tackled Saint-Germain on the subject. It was one of those occasions when, as often occurred, he had been describing historical events and persons with a vividness which made even the most incredulous almost believe that he must have been there at the time. Madame du Hausset, lady-in-waiting to the favourite, was present, and wrote down the ensuing conversation immediately afterwards. It went as follows:

Madame laughed and said: 'Apparently you have seen it all yourself.' 'I have a very good memory,' said he, 'and I have studied French history in detail. I sometimes amuse myself not by *making* people believe, but by *allowing* them to believe, that I have lived in the oldest times.' 'Still, you never say how old you really are, and you claim to be very old. The Countess of Gergy, who was ambassadress fifty years ago, I believe in Venice, declares that she knew you then just as you are now.' 'It is perfectly true, Madame, that I made the acquaintance of the Countess of Gergy a long time ago.' 'But according to her, you must be over a hundred years old now.' 'That is not impossible,' said he laughing, 'but, as I admit, it is even more possible that the revered lady is talking nonsense.'[1]

This is a fair sample of the mischievous manner and the mystical mannerisms with which Saint-Germain kept everyone guessing about his age:

These silly Parisians [he once said to Gleichen] believe that I am 500 years old, and I confirmed them in that belief, for I see that they get a lot

[1] Volz, op. cit. pp. 127 f.; quoting Madame du Hausset's *Memoirs*, 1824. Saint-Germain might of course have been the son of the man who wrote the letter about India in 1773, and therefore really the son of the man Madame de Gergy remembered. Considering the closeness of the dates, he might also have been (or his father might have been) the 'Sober Signor' in Venice.

of pleasure out of it. Not but what I am immeasurably older than I appear.[1]

To add fuel to the flames of a legend spreading like a forest fire, there was in Paris at the time a young wag, nicknamed Lord Gower (because he could imitate the English), who was a first-class impersonator. He was supposed to have been used as a spy attached 'to the English army during the Seven Years' War, and now served to amuse the courtiers by his lively imitations. This man was introduced into Paris society as Saint-Germain, in which character he claimed to have had conversations with Christ, to have been present at the Council of Nicaea, and so forth. And these fables, added to the dark hints the real Saint-Germain let drop from time to time, inevitably dowered him with the philosopher's stone and elixir of life, and developed into puerile anecdotes of old ladies drinking too much and becoming little girls, or babies, or even embryos in the womb.

Quite as inevitably, the belief in his longevity led to the stubborn disbelief in his death. If he ever said (which is doubtful) that his approaching dissolution was in reality a preparation for a forthcoming rejuvenation, he was talking more like an adept and a sage than a mystery-monger. According to Luchet (a very suspect source), his miraculous ascension was proclaimed at the moment of his burial. A journal published in 1785 declared that many still believed he was alive, and would soon appear amongst them. The Freemasons seem to have been of the same opinion, since they called him to the Conference in 1785. Madame de Genlis maintained that she saw him in Vienna in 1821, and the Countess d'Adhémar—but then was there ever such a person at all? According to Volz she was a fictitious personage invented by the anonymous novel-writer Étienne Léon de Lamothe-Langon, and her so-called *Souvenirs* about Marie Antoinette and the Versailles Court are an impudent fabrication. Mrs Cooper-Oakley, who made great use of them, believed them to be genuine for the excellent reason that the then Countess d'Adhémar, an American, had documents about Saint-Germain in her possession; and that Madame Blavatsky visited the family at the Château d'Adhémar in 1885. There certainly was such a family, but whether any member was ever at the Court of Versailles as a Lady of the

[1] Volz, op. cit. pp. 49 f., quoting C.-H. de Gleichen's *Souvenirs*, Paris, 1868. Appeared first in 1818.

Palace, seems less certain; and the so-called *Souvenirs*, or at least the extracts given by Mrs Cooper-Oakley, are not exactly calculated to inspire belief. Published in 1836, they are, however, documentary evidence to the lively state of the belief in Saint-Germain's bodily survival. They recounted how he approached the Countess first in 1793, uttering Cassandra-like warnings about the death of Marie Antoinette; and in answer to her question as to whether she would see him again, he replied: 'Five times more; do not wish for the sixth.'

I saw M. de St.-Germain again, and always to my unspeakable surprise: at the assassination of the Queen; at the coming of the 18th Brumaire; the day following the death of the Duke d'Enghien (1804); in the month of July, 1813; and on the eve of the murder of the Duke de Berri (1820). I await the sixth visit when God wills.[1]

In 1845 another twist was given to Saint-Germain's posthumous life by yet another set of spurious *Memoirs*, emanating from Vienna. In this publication, the sage is made to prophesy to Franz Gräffer, the author:

Towards the end of the century I shall disappear out of Europe, and betake myself to the Himalayas. I will rest; I must rest. Exactly in eighty-five years will people again set eyes on me. Farewell....[2]

Unhappily the date of the prophecy was not given; but the mention of the Himalayas was not destined to fall upon deaf ears; and, skipping other intermediate steps, it is perhaps only necessary to consider Saint-Germain's translation into one of the Mahatmas of the Great White Lodge, undertaken in the first instance by that imaginative enthusiast, Helena Petrovna Blavatsky:

The Comte de Saint-Germain was certainly the greatest Oriental Adept Europe has seen during the last centuries.[3]

Mrs Besant, in her foreword to Mrs Cooper-Oakley's book, was even more enthusiastic and explicit:

The great Occultist and Brother of the White Lodge...was the greatest force behind the intellectual reforming movement which received its death-blow in the outbreak of the French Revolution. Phoenix-like, it has

---

[1] Cooper-Oakley, op. cit. p. 54.   [2] Ibid. pp. 144 f.
[3] H. P. Blavatsky, *Theosophical Glossary*, quoted by Cooper-Oakley, op. cit. p. 1.

re-arisen, and it re-appeared in the 19th Century as the Theosophical Society, of which the great Brother is one of the recognised Leaders. Still living in the same body the perennial youth of which astonished the observers of the 18th century, He has fulfilled the prophecy made to Mme d'Adhémar that He should show Himself again a century after His farewell to her, and, in the growing spiritual movement which is seen around us, on every side, He will be one of the acknowledged Chiefs.[1]

Even more interesting is the tribute of his biographer, Mrs Cooper-Oakley, who gave to her memoir the sub-title *The Secret of Kings*, dedicated it to

THE GREAT SOUL
who in the struggles of the eighteenth
century worked
suffered and triumphed;

and summed up his existence in the following words:

Thus clearly stands out the character of one who by some is called a 'messenger' from the spiritual Hierarchy by whom the world's evolution is guided; such is the moral worth of the man whom the shallow critics of the earth call 'adventurer'.[2]

This is a striking reminder of the autonomous nature of the mythopoeic force. The conscientious biographer who had unearthed some damaging documents about Saint-Germain from the record offices, and had had the honesty to publish them, was as impervious to the hard facts she had discovered about her hero as if they had never entered her consciousness.

Saint-Germain on her own showing had been unsuccessful, to put it mildly, as a diplomatic agent. The warnings she believed he had uttered to Marie Antoinette were also unavailing; and as a counter-revolutionary worker he had totally and utterly failed. He nevertheless remained in her eyes the 'great soul who triumphed'. And in so far as Theosophy is concerned, he has triumphed indeed, since he is now worshipped in their cult as one of the Mahatmas or Masters, mythical beings whom we shall meet again, and of whose personal appearance, previous births and present functions Leadbeater has

[1] Cooper-Oakley, op. cit. pp. xii f.
[2] Ibid. p. 52. Mrs Cooper-Oakley devoted some years of her life to the search for Saint-Germain about 1900, even living for a time in a castle in Transylvania for that purpose. She never found him, but Mrs Besant said *she* met him 'first' in 19 Avenue Road in 1896.

communicated much information, for the most part clairvoyantly obtained:

The other Adept whom I had the privilege of encountering physically was the Master the Comte de St Germain, called sometimes the Prince Rakoczi. I met Him under quite ordinary circumstances (without any previous appointment, and as though by chance) walking down the Corso in Rome, dressed just as any Italian gentleman might be. He took me up into the gardens on the Pincian Hill, and we sat for more than an hour talking about the Society and its work....[1]

Though He is not especially tall, He is very upright and military in His bearing, and He has the exquisite courtesy and dignity of a grand seigneur of the eighteenth century; we feel at once that He belongs to a very old and noble family. His eyes are large and brown, and are filled with tenderness and humour, though there is in them a glint of power; and the splendour of His presence impels men to make obeisance. His face is olive-tanned; His close-cut brown hair is parted in the centre and brushed back from the forehead, and He has a short and pointed beard. Often He wears a dark uniform with facings of gold lace—often also a magnificent red military cloak—and these accentuate His soldier-like appearance. He usually resides in an ancient castle in Eastern Europe, that belonged to his family for many centuries.[2]

The Head of the Seventh Ray is the master the Comte de St Germain, known to history in the eighteenth century, whom we sometimes call the Master Rakoczi, as He is the last survivor of that royal house. He was Francis Bacon, Lord Verulam, in the seventeenth century, Robertus the Monk in the sixteenth, Hunyadi Janos in the fifteenth, Christian Rosencreutz in the fourteenth, and Roger Bacon in the thirteenth, and He is the Hungarian Adept of *The Occult World*. Further back in time He was the great Neo-platonic Proclus, and before that St Alban. He works to a large extent through ceremonial magic, and employs the services of great Angels, who obey him implicitly and love to do His will. Though He speaks all European and many Oriental languages, much of His work is in Latin, the language which is the especial vehicle for His thought, and the splendour and rhythm of it is unsurpassed by anything that we know down here. In His various rituals He wears wonderful and many-coloured robes and jewels. He has a suit of golden chain-mail, which once belonged to a Roman Emperor; over it is thrown a magnificent cloak of crimson, with on its clasp a seven-pointed star in diamond and amethyst, and sometimes He wears a glorious robe of violet. Though He is thus engaged with ceremonial, and still works some of the rituals of the Ancient Mysteries, even the names

[1] C. W. Leadbeater, *The Masters and the Path*, Madras 1925, p. 11.
[2] Ibid. p. 44.

of which have long been forgotten in the outer world, He is also much concerned with the political situation in Europe, and the growth of modern physical science.[1]

It would be a hard heart indeed which would not rejoice at this apotheosis of Saint-Germain by which he has regained, and more than regained, his pristine splendour at the Court of Versailles. For if he had not been thus rescued, his life-story, more pathetic than tragic, resembles too closely Andersen's tale of the little Christmas tree to make cheerful reading. And it is poetic justice too. For indirectly he was himself very largely responsible for the Theosophical Movement. The vitality of his personality after death led to a further life in literature; for he and no other was the title-hero of Bulwer-Lytton's novel *Zanoni*. This fell into Madame Blavatsky's hands fairly early on in her career; it affected her profoundly, and the fact that Zanoni was really Saint-Germain was probably well known in the circles in which she moved. Hence her identification of the latter with one of the Adepts, since it is in this guise that Bulwer-Lytton portrayed him.

A senile old lady (Madame de Gergy) made a queer mistake in 1760 or thereabouts. A legend was set in circulation. It inspired a work of fiction. Another old lady took the fiction for reality. From such slight and apparently unrelated causes mythologies and religions spring.

[1] C. W. Leadbeater, op. cit. pp. 286 f.

CHAPTER III

THE GRAND COPHT (?1743–1795)

Unlike Saint-Germain, Cagliostro's connection with the secret societies of the age is not a matter for guess-work. That much at least is certain in one of the most confusing tales ever told, even about magicians. The quicksands surrounding this thrice-famous figure are so treacherous that not only the would-be biographer but Cagliostro himself is threatened with being engulfed by them every time an attempt is made to approach and 'rescue' him; whether the 'rescue' takes the form of unmasking a charlatan, rehabilitating a sage or disengaging a historical figure. Facts there are in abundance, but how is one to interpret them? Lies are even more plentiful, and how is one to recognise them? The quagmire called Balsamo defeats one at every turn. Attempting to cross that obstacle in order to reach Cagliostro, one sinks deeper and deeper into the mire, and most malodorous mire it is. The first person to 'discover' the identity between the small-time crook Giuseppe Balsamo and the 'divine Cagliostro' was one of the biggest blackguards in Europe— Théveneau de Morande, a journalistic blackmailer and a paid informer. One can therefore hardly put one's trust in him. And the details he dug up about Balsamo's past were largely based on the cross-examination of Giuseppe's wife Lorenza, who was imprisoned at his instigation in Sainte-Pélagie for infidelity, and tried to prove her innocence by slandering her spouse. So that even Balsamo, in spite of his ruffianly boyhood, may not have been quite as black in after-life as he has been painted. The acceptance of the identification by the only contemporary biography which can be taken seriously is not in itself proof positive of its accuracy. For this official version of Cagliostro's career was compiled from the records of the trial of the magus by the Roman Inquisition. This elicited in the form of 'confessions' by the accused and his wife all the facts Morande had already 'discovered', which clinched the matter as far as the Inquisition was concerned; and there is no doubt that the official biographer, who was probably one of the judges, was sincerely convinced of the truth of the fairly coherent and connected biography he compiled. In fact this writer, granted his Catholic bias which made him a rabid anti-Mason, seems to have been conscientious enough; nor is his tone anything like so venomous as Carlyle's in that unpleasing essay on Cagliostro, in which he threw all decency to the winds and out-Heroded the Inquisition whilst ranting against it. Nevertheless, the Roman biographer must be regarded, if not as a tainted, then certainly as a suspect source. For the 'facts' which the wretched Cagliostro confirmed during the trial were acknowledged with the threat of torture hanging over his head, even if the rack were not displayed at every sitting, as was maintained at the time. He would clearly have confessed to almost anything if pressed hard enough, as the following pitiable scene bears witness:

The opportunity was taken here to ask how he could have believed and still believe that in his work with the 'pupils' [clairvoyant water-gazing] he had had the support of a special grace of God for the benefit of the Catholic religion. Finding himself trapped, he wriggled out with the words: 'I no longer understand myself; there is nothing more I can say; I feel remorse for my unhallowed state; my only desire is to receive help for my soul; I am steeped in a hundred thousand religious errors.' But this acknowledgment was short-lived and merely designed to give him time to think. He was attacked twice more on the same point; and he stuck to the same tale of ascribing the success of his experiments to a special grace of God. But when he was thereupon driven into a corner and convicted of wrong behaviour, he could only counter thus: 'I can only say that I must somehow be in error; I am confused and understand nothing about it all.' He was pressed to answer definitely; but he added: 'I can only repeat what I have said; tell me what you want me to say.' And when pressed still further to answer with the truth and to confess it of his own free will, he concluded with these highly significant words: 'I have never had any dealings with the devil in my experiments, and I have never undertaken any superstitious practices.' And here he broke out into violent gestures and ravings.[1]

No; neither Morande, nor the Inquisition, nor Cagliostro facing the Inquisition commands implicit belief. Yet there are too many facts connecting Giuseppe Balsamo with Alessandro Cagliostro to be lightly disregarded. Both married a Roman girl still in her teens, whose maiden name was Feliciani. But it was a common enough

[1] Taken from a German translation of the Inquisition biography; given by Guenther in his edition of various documents about Cagliostro entitled *Der Erzzauberer Cagliostro*, Munich 1919, pp. 142 f. The original Italian version was published in 1791.

surname; and would not Balsamo have changed it when he changed his own to Cagliostro if he wished to avoid detection? This coincidence might, therefore, be interpreted in Cagliostro's favour. The same argument might be used for the incriminating fact that he signed himself Joseph Cagliostro in London in 1777. Later he became Alessandro. But since he frankly owned to numerous aliases, being incognito from beginning to end, the use of Joseph at this juncture might be adduced as a proof of ignorance of Balsamo and all his works. Unhappily the long arm of coincidence, stretching back to Palermo, where Giuseppe was born, points inexorably to an uncle of that young scoundrel called Giuseppe Cagliostro; whilst another uncle stated that his nephew had often written to him over the signature Count of Cagliostro. If this uncle was telling the truth, that almost seems to settle it. Moreover, one person who had known Balsamo in London in 1772 said that he recognised him in Cagliostro in 1777, and sued him for a debt that the former had contracted. Unluckily Aylett (as this witness was called) was a most untrustworthy person, later convicted of perjury and pilloried. And even if he made the identification in good faith, the similarity between the two men is no proof of identity.. In Palermo it was taken amongst other pointers to be conclusive; and Balsamo's family, first and foremost the uncle called Braconieri, were convinced from reproductions of Cagliostro's countenance that he was none other than their rascally relative. One's legitimate doubts about the identity of the two begin to waver before this formidable array of facts. It is therefore ironical that his latest biographer, Petraccone, in his effort to give such doubts the quietus, raised them strongly again:

It is certain, as is proved by documents, that Giuseppe Balsamo married Lorenza Feliciani in Rome. It is certain that the individual arrested in Rome and tried by the Inquisition was Cagliostro. If this Cagliostro inhabited the house of the Felicianis, if his wife had always kept up a correspondence with the members of this family; and if finally these same Felicianis denounced him, what doubt can there be that Cagliostro was Balsamo?[1]

The logic is faultless, but when the documents are examined it appears that Balsamo's father-in-law gave his Christian name as Giovanni on the marriage certificate, where it is mentioned twice.

[1] E. Petraccone, *Cagliostro nella storia e nella legenda*, Milan 1922, p. 36.

Whereas the letter to Cagliostro's wife from her father is signed Giuseppe, also given as the Christian name of the same individual in the denunciation against his son-in-law. It looks therefore as if these Felicianis were the relations by marriage of Cagliostro and not of Balsamo. There is no particular reason why either family (if both existed) should not have denounced the magus under the name of Balsamo, which would certainly be used by whichever group was anxious to crush him. The resurrected doubts, however, are shaken by discovering that the Latin church entry of Balsamo's marriage calls his father-in-law Joseph and not John. There is no getting at the rock-bottom truth in this matter, although I incline myself to accept the identification. For, if one cannot feel absolute confidence in it, neither can one credit the account given of his origins by Cagliostro in his defence during the diamond necklace trial in Paris, which left his birth obscure. And if one accepts neither version of the magician's past, then the puzzling materialisation of the Cagliostros in London in 1776 leaves the door wide open into impenetrable darkness. In truth the story of this world-famous man might have been invented by the eighteenth century to illustrate the discovery that mystery and ritual are indispensable features in the contemporary fame and posthumous survival of wonder-workers of all kinds.

Cagliostro himself was consciously aware of their significance as the fabulous *Memoir* he composed in the Bastille proves. A mysterious Eastern origin, a tutelary sage, a far-flung journey, initiation into the ancient wisdom of Egypt by the anachronistic priests of the temples, association with the Knights of Malta—these are the outstanding events Cagliostro invented or embroidered for himself in imitation of the legendary pattern fixed in the first place by ritual and now once more a recognisable part of the traditional lore surrounding magicians and sages. It has been pointed out that this early life-history strongly resembles the legend of Christian Rosencreutz; but it is only a generic likeness. It has also been suggested that the tutelary genius whom Cagliostro called Althotas may possibly have been Saint-Germain, and that part of the adventures may have taken place, though on a less exalted level than described. An Althotas of some sort may very well have figured in Balsamo-Cagliostro's life. It seems unlikely that it was Saint-Germain; for the latter was never known to make common cause with any young disciples, seeking rather for followers amongst the mighty of the earth. Still this attractive theory is not completely ruled out. Cagliostro knew something about Saint-Germain, since he claimed to be that sage in 1779, when the latter was still alive in Schleswig. He must therefore by that period have disappeared from Cagliostro's ken, though they may have been acquainted earlier. But these are only speculations. It remains a fact that Cagliostro deliberately shaped the story of his life after a rediscovered model, and that he had no need to rediscover the model himself. The secret societies had done that for him.

The power of these institutions over those attracted within their orbits is nowhere more manifest than in the mind of the hero of this incredible tale. For, if Balsamo and Cagliostro were really one and the same person, then it becomes extremely significant that the low cunning of the Sicilian rogue should have given place to the lofty aspirations of the magus after he had been admitted into a Masonic Lodge in London on 12 April 1777. The metamorphosis effected (even if not all at once) was such, the extraordinary transformation of manner and address (if not of heart) were so striking, that it forms the most solid argument advanced by those who deny or at least question the identity of two such dissimilar men.[1]

Figuier is eloquent about the change:

His language, his mien, his manner, all are transformed. His conversation turns only on his travels in Egypt, to Mecca, and in other remote places, on the sciences into which he was initiated at the foot of the Pyramids, on the arcana of Nature which his ingenuity had discovered. At the same time, he talks little, more often enveloping himself in mysterious silence.[2]

If not a spiritual, then at least an intellectual regeneration seems to have occurred after his initiation into the Esperance Lodge (affiliated to the Order of the Strict Observance) at the 'King's Head' in Gerard Street, Soho. The details, satirically communicated by Morande in the *Courrier de l'Europe*, were not seriously disputed by Cagliostro in his *Lettre au Peuple Anglois*, although he pointed out that if Morande were a Mason he ought not to have divulged what he knew; and that if he were not, he should not have spoken about what he ignored. Cagliostro, however, confirmed the fact that he had been received into the Esperance Lodge and that he had passed through the four

[1] Cf. W. R. H. Trowbridge, *Cagliostro, the Splendour and Misery of a Master of Magic*, London 1910.

[2] Louis Figuier, *Histoire du Merveilleux dans les Temps Modernes*, Paris 1861, IV, p. 93.

grades of apprentice, companion, Master and Scotch Master. Morande gave the following oath:

I, Joseph Cagliostro, in presence of the great Architect of the Universe and my superiors in this respectable assembly, promise to do all that I am ordered, and bind myself under penalties known only to my superiors to obey them blindly without questioning their motives or seeking to discover the secret of the mysteries into which I shall be initiated either by word, sign, or writing.[1]

The rites and ceremonies, as caricatured by Morande, certainly do not seem to have been of that glamorous nature Luchet had such a genius for inventing. On the contrary they resemble the kind of horseplay which new boys are called upon to undergo (in novels at least) when they enter their public schools. Nevertheless the mock death and rebirth of the initiate were symbolised by an unloaded pistol which he was bidden to discharge into his own brains. There was probably a more impressive ceremony than that during the course of the assembly; but whatever the character of the rites, they clearly impressed the new initiate as to their latent possibilities; and, granted that he was Balsamo, they seem to have effected something like a conversion, to judge by his subsequent conduct. It is also highly likely that the material advantages of belonging to this benevolent institution were brought home to him when O'Reilly delivered him from the swarm of sharpers and swindlers into whose clutches he had fallen, and released him from durance vile in the King's Bench prison. For O'Reilly was the proprietor of the 'King's Head' tavern where the Esperance Lodge met and therefore almost certainly a fellow-Mason. The appallingly complicated story of Balsamo-Cagliostro's victimisation by the Scott-Fry conspiracy against him (or alternatively of his unsuccessful efforts to fleece them) shows that he was no match for the thieves among whom he had fallen, and seems to hint too that Giuseppe was not quite such a cunning crook as rumour whispered. However that may be, the cruel experience he had undergone in London's underworld may have contributed to his determination to turn over a new leaf and become Cagliostro indeed.

It was not the path of sober virtue, however, which he now began to tread, but a much more dangerous path, and infinitely more alluring. Having picked up an old manuscript entitled *Egyptian*

[1] Trowbridge, op. cit. p. 112. 'Discover', of course, means 'reveal'.

Masonry on a bookstall in London (so the story runs), he fell a victim to the mystery and glamour of the cult described, harking back as it did to the golden age of ritual, when the officiating masters of the art were gods or great prophets at least. But (to the end he was persistent about this) it was defaced by magic and superstition, a reproach he also constantly levelled at the Masonic and other secret society rites. He determined to purify the ancient doctrine from such later accretions, and to launch the system thus ennobled upon a world forgetful of the divine knowledge which it contained. No male aspirant was ever allowed to become an initiate of Egyptian Masonry unless he were an accepted Freemason first. It could therefore be regarded as a higher grade of the parent society, an inestimable advantage from the administrative point of view, since the foundations were already firmly laid and there existed as well a close connection between nearly all the secret societies of the day. Undoubtedly there was something in Cagliostro's by no means original ideas in accord with the spirit of the times; for, far from protesting against a rite which aimed at superseding theirs whilst profiting from them, the continental Lodges accepted the situation philosophically, when they did not actually acclaim it with enthusiasm, which they very often did. Cagliostro himself took the founding and spreading of the Egyptian rite very seriously, for whatever reason; he pursued this purpose with the utmost energy up and down Europe with amazing success. The doctrine itself, emanating it was claimed from Enoch and Elijah, preached the knowledge and love of God, the love of humanity, the immortality of the soul and the physical and moral regeneration of its followers. There was nothing very new or startling in any of these tenets; but Cagliostro managed to give them a sensational and personal twist:

We mentioned the Grand Copht earlier. This is the name for the founder or rather the reformer of the Egyptian Masonry; and Cagliostro did not hesitate to acknowledge that he wished to designate his own person under that appellation, and indeed everyone recognised this claim. Now in this system the Grand Copht is compared to the eternal God; he is worshipped in the most solemn manner; he has the power to command the angels; he is called upon in every distress; everything is done through his power which has been given to him by God in a special manner.[1]

---

[1] Guenther, op. cit. p. 78. Cagliostro's book was publicly burnt, together with his other papers after the trial.

Thus wrote the Inquisitorial biographer, who had Cagliostro's book on Egyptian Freemasonry before him, of which he gave an invaluable summary; this tallies with other accounts, whilst that of Elise von der Recke, written down in 1779 when Cagliostro was in Mitau, illustrated the development of the claim:

> Cagliostro is one of the agents of Elijah.... The pupils of Elijah never die unless they go over to black magic; but, when their mortal course is run, they are lifted up into heaven like their sublime master. But, until they have reached the number of twelve lives, they are occasionally purified by an apparent death from which they rise again as it were from their own ashes. The phoenix therefore is the allegorical picture of those benevolent magicians.... Should we hear after a certain time that he had died, and then that he was alive again, we might rest assured that he had with-stood the temptations of all the evil spirits and had attained to the fourth degree.... Cagliostro spoke about the love which is said to have existed be-tween the children of heaven and earth, and he let it be understood, that not only Christ, but he himself owed his existence to such a union....[1]

Another Mitau observer (unlike Elise von der Recke at that time), sceptical and hostile, commented acidly:

> The story of Frederick Gualdo in Italian, which had fallen into his hands, gave him the material for the lies about his own great age and his chemical secrets. Sometimes he declared that he was Gualdo, then again that he was Elijah, or St Germain, and even Solomon.[2]

The descriptions of the rites held by Cagliostro in his character of Grand Copht given by this writer and others (always excepting the Marquis de Luchet) suggest that, though the *mise-en-scène* was always as magnificent as possible, and sometimes dazzling, the actual ceremony was not very impressive, and generally subordinated to one of those experiments in clairvoyance made with a child of tender years, who saw angels when gazing into the water-glass and visions of what was happening elsewhere. As master of the ceremonies, the Grand Copht certainly swept most of the congregation off their feet; but dispassionate observers generally thought him supremely ridiculous with his turgid oratory and his barbarous admixture of tongues, none of which he spoke or pronounced accurately. Elise von der Recke,

---

[1] Guenther, op. cit.; Elisabeth von der Recke, *Nachricht von des berüchtigten Cagliostro Aufenthalt in Mitau im Jahre 1779...*, pp. 271, 272, 289 (footnote).

[2] Guenther, op. cit.; J. J. Ferber, *Cagliostro in Mitau*, p. 308. Gualdo is of course the 'Sober Signor' Gualdi.

when she was still under his spell, commented more than once on the strange mixture of inspiration and triviality in his speeches. That nevertheless he aroused such widespread enthusiasm, devotion and belief is a tribute to the extraordinary power which he wielded over the minds of men. And this again seems to have developed after the initiation into Freemasonry.

Giuseppe Balsamo, although possibly traduced, belonged to the type of petty trickster whose chief asset was said to be the beauty of his wife on which he shamefully traded. Even if this was an invention of the said wife, there seems little doubt that he lived a life of fraud; and (to judge by his experiences in London with the Scott-Fry group) was quite as often duped as he duped others in the effort to live by his wits. Cagliostro's frauds, for frauds there certainly were, were on a grander scale altogether. Nor were all his 'miracles' fraudulent by any means. He clearly possessed both magnetic and psychic gifts which informed his deeds and words when his *mana* was in the ascendant; but they often left him in the lurch. A large benevolence was also manifest during his period of glory, great generosity and charity too. He genuinely earned the title of Friend of Humanity by which he came to be known. Now Balsamo's hand had been against every man's, if report is to be believed, and every man's hand against his. This total reversal of conduct, this Jekyll and Hyde relationship between Cagliostro and Balsamo, hints at something like dissociation of personality, the predisposition towards which is so often found in the possessors of supernormal powers. It is possible that the tenets of Freemasonry disengaged the nobler nature of the neophyte; and even if this apparent nobility was bogus, the powers he began to exercise from then onwards had never been within the scope of Balsamo. Nor could any man, even in that age so credulous of the marvellous, have exercised the fascination over multitudes, from the highest to the lowest, which Cagliostro wielded at one time, if he had been the mere petty swindler which Balsamo is represented to be. Either the latter has been greatly maligned, or there were really two souls in the magician's breast struggling for ascendancy. This theory may help to account for the extreme incoherence of his speeches and his inability to express himself clearly in any language. When he was Cagliostro, he had no mother-tongue. Adopting this reading of the situation, the course of his life would seem to have run thus: Balsamo, Balsamo-Cagliostro,

Cagliostro, Cagliostro-Balsamo, Balsamo-Cagliostro, but never, not even at the very last, plain Giuseppe Balsamo again.

Leaving England in November 1777, he evidently travelled Europe preaching Egyptian Freemasonry, founding Lodges in Brussels, The Hague, Nuremberg, Leipzig, Milan, Danzig and Königsberg, arriving in Mitau in March 1779 with the reputation of a wonder-worker and religious teacher. Here he produced a great impression on the aristocratic and important circle round Elise von der Recke, and she herself was a fervent admirer; later she regarded him as nothing but a charlatan, publishing her account of his visit (written in 1779) eight years afterwards when he was in disgrace with sceptical, rational and pious comments. Others were suspicious at the time, and altogether it appears that, if some genuine cases of clair-voyance occurred through the mediumship of the little boy of five, there was even more fraud practised, some of it none too cleverly. Here therefore Balsamo-Cagliostro was functioning, and probably also in Russia, although nothing certain is known of this visit, beyond that it was short and was reputed to have been disastrous for the magician. It was said by hostile witnesses that the same fate met him in Warsaw, where he was rumoured to have been unmasked. But Laborde testified to a remarkable display of mantic gifts in that city, made for the benefit of an unbeliever whose past, present and future were accurately seen by the Grand Copht. His next visit was probably to Frankfort. It is suggested with a good deal of plausibility that he had an interview with Knigge here; and that the famous chief of the Illuminati supplied him with funds in order to spread the revolu-tionary doctrines which this secret society was engaged in propa-gating. Certain it is that Cagliostro made an entry of great splendour into Strassburg on 19 September 1780, accompanied by an even more dazzling reputation as a worker of miracles. During his three years' residence in this city, Cagliostro and Cagliostro only, as far as one can make out, was in evidence. Laborde (who erred on the side of enthusiasm) put the number of his cures at 15,000; and though this may be an exaggeration, it appears from all accounts, including those of his enemies, that his success as a healer was phenomenal, and that between five and six hundred persons besieged his lodgings on those days when he saw patients. Magnetism was almost certainly at the bottom of it, supported by faith-healing. Unlike Mesmer, Cagliostro used no apparatus of any kind, relying on a touch of his hands and a drop or two of his famous panacea. Nor did he ever attempt to exploit his remarkable gift financially. On the contrary he refused payment for his treatments, supplied his medicines at his own cost; and more than that, dispensed charity to the poor and needy on a munificent scale. The Friend of Humanity certainly earned that title in Strassburg; and also in Bordeaux and Lyons, where he went after the envy and consequent persecutions of the medical profession had driven him out of Strassburg. Not, however, before he had attained such an ascendancy over the mind of the brilliant and magnificent Cardinal de Rohan that the latter steadfastly believed that he had seen him with his own eyes make an enormous diamond out of nothing, a jewel worn by the cardinal and shown to the sceptical Madame d'Oberkirch; and he was further convinced that he had seen the magician fabricate five or six thousand pounds of gold, which he had also bestowed upon His Eminence. Both Monsieur and Madame d'Oberkirch distrusted the miracle-worker profoundly and despised him; but even he had to acknowledge that he was a great philanthropist; and she had to confess to his personal fascination as well as to the effect it had on society:

It would be impossible to give an idea of the passion, the madness with which people pursued this man. It would appear incredible to any one who had not seen it. He was surrounded, he was beset; happy was the person esteemed upon whom his glance fell.[1]

Engagingly truthful, Madame d'Oberkirch owned to the extraordinary impression he produced upon her.

He was not, strictly speaking, handsome, but never have I seen a more remarkable countenance. His glance was so penetrating that one would be almost tempted to call it supernatural. I could not describe the expression of his eyes, it was, so to say, a mixture of flame and ice. He attracted and repulsed, and whilst he terrified, inspired an insurmountable curiosity.... It was with difficulty that I tore myself from a fascination which I cannot yet comprehend, but whose influence I could not deny.[2]

She also testified to his prediction of the death of Maria Theresa of Austria, and the hour when it would occur. The cardinal told her of this prophecy five days before the news arrived. Dunne, in his *Experiment with Time*, has a better explanation for this mantic feat

[1] *Memoirs of the Baroness d'Oberkirch*, London 1852, I, pp. 178 ff.
[2] Ibid. pp. 163, 166.

than the obvious answer of the sceptics, that somehow Cagliostro got wind of it before the normal channels of communication brought the news to Strassburg. But whatever explanations are given for the phenomenon of Cagliostro in Strassburg, it must at least be allowed that he appeared great in the hour of his greatness, and that (what is more) he appeared good.

He had further heights to scale however. And when the 'divine Cagliostro' alighted in Paris on 30 January 1785, it was to enjoy a spell of fame and glory such as has fallen to the lot of few. As Grand Copht of Egyptian Masonry; as the proved miraculous healer; as the wizard who could make gold and precious stones; as the visionary who could foresee the future; as the prince of necromancers (so it was rumoured); and last but far from least, as the magician who possessed the secret of perpetual rejuvenation, he had all Paris at his feet, raving about the sublimity of the Grand Copht, and the incomparable beauty of his wife. Lorenza-Serafina must have been a lovely creature, and she added considerably to the glamour of the proceedings in the rue Saint-Claude, especially when initiating women into the Egyptian rites; although the description given of these by the Marquis de Luchet is too obviously spurious to be worth quoting, and too malicious in its implications for any conclusions to be drawn. It was certainly a brilliant time for her, and may have repaid those early days of squalor when she had acted as a decoy for Balsamo's dupes in such a very different manner, according to her own tale. But she had already betrayed her husband once (under great provocation it is true); she might at any moment betray him again; and she was a perpetual reminder of the Balsamo days. Nevertheless she must count as one of his major assets in Paris, her youth, her beauty and her charm supporting and enhancing the power which radiated from this Jekyll of magic in his supremely glorious hour.

> De l'Ami des Humains reconnaissez les traits:
> Tous ses jours sont marqués par de nouveaux bienfaits,
> Il prolonge la vie, il secourt l'indigence;
> Le plaisir d'être utile est seul sa récompense.

This quatrain, engraved beneath Houdon's bust of the magus, which was produced on every conceivable *objet d'art* and *bibelot*, contributed to the paroxysm of rage into which Cagliostro's features later threw Carlyle:

Fittest of visages; worthy to be worn by the Quack of Quacks! A most portentous face of scoundrelism; a fat, snub, abominable face; dew-lapped, flat-nosed, greasy, full of greediness, sensuality, oxlike obstinacy; a forehead impudent, refusing to be ashamed; and then two eyes turned up seraphically languishing, as in divine contemplation and adoration; a touch of quiz too; on the whole, perhaps the most perfect quack-face produced by the eighteenth century. There he sits, and seraphically languishes....[1]

I quote this to give some idea of the general tone of Carlyle's essay, and also because it is considerably more unflattering than any contemporary descriptions, however hostile. Baron de Gleichen, who knew and liked Cagliostro, has probably left the best pen-portrait of him:

Cagliostro was small, but he had a very fine head which could have served as a model for the face of an inspired poet. It is true that his tone, his gestures and his manners were those of a charlatan, boastful, pretentious and arrogant; but it must be remembered that he was an Italian, a physician giving consultations, self-styled Masonic grand-master, and a professor of occult sciences. Otherwise his ordinary conversation was agreeable and instructive, his actions noble and charitable, and his healing treatments never unsuccessful and sometimes admirable: he never took a penny from his patients.[2]

It was indeed the rumour of a well-nigh miraculous cure which he was said to have effected, when the life of the Prince of Soubise was despaired of by all the doctors, that sent his reputation, already very high, rocketing skywards in Paris; for, according to Gleichen, he came from Strassburg to treat him at the impassioned supplication of de Rohan. From this point of view the quatrain might truly maintain that Cagliostro prolonged life. But, since he openly claimed to possess the secret of perpetual rejuvenation, yet more was expected and rumoured about him. His book on *Egyptian Freemasonry* contained the necessary instructions for moral and physical regeneration, and the Inquisitorial biographer gave lengthy accounts of them. There was also a pamphlet circulating at the time under a satirical title giving the whole physical process, once more a labour of love which we owe to the Marquis de Luchet. As it tallies closely with the account in the biography, but names the medicines, which the

[1] Thomas Carlyle, *Miscellaneous Essays*, London 1887, II, p. 520.
[2] De Gleichen, *Souvenirs*, Paris 1868, II, p. 135.

biography does not, I propose to give what I imagine to be a copy communicated by Eliphas Lévi:

...a retreat of forty days, after the manner of a jubilee, must be made once in every fifty years, beginning during the full moon of May, in the company of one faithful person only. It must also be a fast of forty days, drinking May dew—collected from sprouting corn with a cloth of pure white linen—and eating new and tender herbs. The repast should begin with a large glass of dew and end with a biscuit or crust of bread. There should be a slight bleeding on the seventeenth day. Balm of Azoth should then be taken morning and evening, beginning with a dose of six drops and increasing by two drops daily until the end of the thirty-second day. At the dawn which follows thereafter renew the slight bleeding; then take to your bed and remain in it till the end of the fortieth day.

On the first awakening after the bleeding, take the first grain of Universal Medicine. A swoon of three hours will be followed by convulsions, sweats and much purging, necessitating a change both of bed and linen. At this stage a broth of lean beef must be taken, seasoned with rice, sage, valerian, vervain and balm. On the following day take the second grain of Universal Medicine, which is Astral Mercury combined with sulphur of Gold. On the next day have a warm bath. On the thirty-sixth day drink a glass of Egyptian wine, and on the thirty-seventh take the third and last grain of Universal Medicine. A profound sleep will follow, during which the hair, teeth, nails and skin will be renewed. The prescription for the thirty-eighth day is another warm bath, steeping aromatic herbs in the water, of the same kind as those specified for the broth. On the thirty-ninth day drink ten drops of Elixir of Acharat in two spoonsful of red wine. The work will be finished on the fortieth day, and the aged man will be renewed in youth[1]... by which he is enabled to live 5557 years, or to such time as he, of his own accord, may be desirous of going to the world of spirits.[2]

Smelling aloud of quackery as this document does, nevertheless the initiates into the Egyptian rites probably took it seriously and were enabled to do so the more readily as one can hardly imagine that anyone would have the nerve to offer himself for the treatment. Rumours were, however, afloat that the Cardinal de Rohan had undergone the process unsuccessfully. On the other hand, if this much-boasted secret proclaims the charlatan, there are good reasons for believing that Cagliostro during this period produced some remarkable results with the young male 'pupils' and the little female

[1] E. Lévi, *History of Magic*, tr. Waite, London n.d. pp. 413 ff.
[2] Waite, *Lives of Alchemistical Philosophers*, p. 311; quoting the Italian biographer, p. 87, in Guenther.

'doves' whom he mesmerised to see visions inside and outside the water-glass. In this he seems to have resembled Kelley strongly, and, like Kelley, he was also said to have evoked the phantoms of the dead. Reports of this kind were not likely to escape the notice of the Marquis de Luchet, whose anonymous *Mémoire authentique pour servir à l'histoire du Comte de Cagliostro*, published in 1785, and obviously written satirically, did a good deal to establish the Cagliostro legend. Carlyle stigmatised this book as 'a swaggering, lascivious Novelette, without talent, without truth, or worth, happily of small size'; but Figuier, Lévi and Waite all used it, and after them Sax Rohmer. The outstanding features of this mendacious 'novelette' are Saint-Germain's initiation of the Count and Countess of Cagliostro into his cult, the rites presided over by Lorenza-Serafina when introducing women into Egyptian Masonry, and the famous Banquet of the Dead or Reunion of Thirteen at which Cagliostro, six living guests and the spirits of Choiseul, Voltaire, d'Alembert, Diderot, Montesquieu and Voisenon were said to have met and held converse. Nothing very striking was said, but then nothing ever is on such occasions; and however lively the imagination of the author, it would be too much to hope that he could have struck off any Voltairean *bons mots*.

Cagliostro had undergone a real initiation into Freemasonry and it had had real effects. He was now to be involved in a real contest, ending in a temporary victory but a final defeat. Although he was obviously riding for a fall in Paris, it was yet almost accidentally that he became entangled in a gigantic fraud not of his own devising, and of which he was utterly innocent. This was the famous scandal of the diamond necklace, in which the adventuress La Motte befooled and duped the unhappy Cardinal de Rohan into the belief that Marie Antoinette (who actually disliked him) had commissioned him to purchase the necklace for her, as a signal token of her favour. The gullibility of the cardinal in this affair rather tends to diminish Cagliostro's achievement in dominating his mind to the extent which was manifest in Strassburg. And now, although he warned de Rohan against La Motte, his advice was disregarded. He obliged his eminent friend by consulting the water-glass about the queen's feelings for him; but this was the extent of his complicity. Indeed, he was in Bordeaux and Lyons whilst La Motte was elaborating her intrigue, and only returned the evening before the cardinal took delivery of the necklace and handed it over to La Motte for the queen. When he learnt the whole story from the now suspicious dupe, he advised him strongly to have La Motte arrested and go straight to the king or his ministers and recount every detail of the affair. De Rohan could not bring himself to do this. If he had, it might well have saved the whole situation. As it was, both the cardinal and Cagliostro were hauled off to the Bastille in August 1785 to stand their trial.

Cagliostro's defence, written by the very able advocate Thilorier, leaves no shadow of doubt that he was innocent, and indeed he was completely acquitted and released on 1 June 1786. The document has many interesting features. What aroused most excitement and amusement at the time was the life-story which Cagliostro invented of a legendary, even mythical past. Thilorier told the story well, in the language of contemporary fiction; making the ironical best of his client's claims, since he refused any other explanation of his origins, and declared that he did not know to that day whose child he was. But, if there was much food for laughter and even derision in this part of the defence, the opening statement is extremely eloquent and moving, and the whole presented in a masterly manner. Cagliostro took his stand and took it firmly on his public life as a healer of the sick, as the friend of the poor, and a universal benefactor. Some important letters testifying to this were included in the *Mémoire* for his defence; and they make impressive reading, all the more so as they were written in 1783, and were unsolicited testimonials produced when he was leaving Strassburg because of the hostility of the doctors.

The King [wrote the Marquis de Ségur from Paris to the Marquis de Salle in Strassburg] charges you to see to it that not only he be not *molested* in Strassburg when he judges it opportune to return; but also that he should be shown those attentions which the services he renders to the unfortunate should procure him.[1]

Another interesting feature of the defence is Cagliostro's refusal to reveal the source of his great wealth. His establishment, his lavishness, his wonderful jewels, and those of Lorenza were the talk of the town, as they had been in Strassburg; and yet, though he paid ready money for everything and was never in debt, he seemed to have no visible means of support. He referred prosecuting counsel

---

[1] *Mémoire pour le Comte de Cagliostro...*, Paris 1786, p. 22.

to his bankers; but it is doubtful whether the mystery of his riches would be divulged by them. For it seems almost certain that the secret societies were behind him. The good works he did among the poor would be in the benevolent Masonic tradition; and his devotion to their cause, his openly expressed arrogance towards the rich and the highly placed, were good subversive propaganda if he were an emissary of the Illuminati. He may also have received large subscriptions for entrance to his Egyptian Lodges; but again and again he repeated in his defence (and no one attempted to confute him) that he had never taken anything for his medical services, either in money or in kind. These were the general lines of defence which his alibi made unassailable. There were also, however, the particular charges which La Motte brought against him in the attempt to throw the guilt on him. In his answers to her accusations there are signs of that loss of nerve which incarceration in the Bastille had produced. After some of his fine and striking speeches, he would manifest such prostration and discouragement that the governor became uneasy, and fearing that he would attempt his life, appointed a 'sympathetic' officer to bear him company. There is no doubt, reading between the lines of his answers, that Cagliostro feared more than anything else any accusation of practising magic. Indeed, so wary was he, that he exploded the legend of his 'miraculous' cure of the Prince of Soubise. Arriving in Paris from Strassburg with de Rohan to see the prince, he found that the Faculty had announced an improvement in the invalid's condition.

I then told him [Rohan] that I would not visit the Prince, not wishing to usurp the glory of a cure which would not have been due to me.[1]

He also denied by implication anything marvellous in his famous water-gazing experiments, calling them innocent comedies and social entertainments, in which a certain amount of animal magnetism played a part, and repudiating utterly the suggestion that they were accompanied by ritual display. He declared that all predictions were nonsense; though answering the accusation of being a false prophet with the telling rejoinder:

Not always. If His Eminence the Cardinal de Rohan had listened to me, he would have distrusted the Countess de la Motte; and we should not be where we are now.[2]

[1] Ibid. p. 19.   [2] Ibid. p. 39.

To the charge 'base alchemist' he objected to the 'base', and left the 'alchemist' alone; refused to commit himself on the subject of the philosopher's stone, observing that whatever he might think about it, he had never spoken about it; he denied by implication at least his famous elixir of immortality by asking rhetorically that La Motte should produce any 'rich man' to whom he had ever sold it; and answered with *mentiris impudentissime* to the accusations that he claimed to be of great age and to have been present in Galilee at the marriage of Cana or that he was a Rosicrucian whose society was composed of visionaries of all ranks. Not one word did he utter from beginning to end about Egyptian Freemasonry; and to the final charge of sorcery he responded by an eloquent declaration that he forgave his unfortunate accuser, since whatever her crimes, six months in the Bastille were a sufficient expiation. In fact these evasions, subterfuges and prevarications, when considered as a whole, are tantamount to a denial of magic, and must have disappointed, when they did not actually disillusion, many of his flock.

But disillusionment on the subject of Cagliostro was in the air. He appeared very different on paper during his trial from the figure he cut in court. Here, alas! his fantastic clothes, his portentous address, his Babylonian confusion of tongues, kept on provoking outbursts of irresistible hilarity. The Grand Copht was transformed almost overnight into a figure of fun. And when, in the final scene of all, he answered the question as to who he was by the reply 'an illustrious voyager', a shout of laughter went up. What the fabulous life in the *Mémoire* had begun his own appearance completed; and the prestige that he had acquired with such miraculous ease was lost for ever with equal rapidity. So that the ovation which greeted his release and warmed his heart was probably rather a demonstration against the court than a genuine acclamation of the Grand Copht. The court retaliated; hardly had Cagliostro experienced the ecstasy of being free before he was banished from France by the incensed monarchy, trying by these means to regain something of *their* lost power and prestige. What malignant fate thereupon inspired Cagliostro to seek refuge in London, a city which had already once proved so disastrous to him?

Arriving here on 16 June 1786, he launched on 20 June that famous *Lettre au peuple françois*, in which the emotions surging in his breast were translated into admirable French by Thilorier or some other. It sold its thousands and thousands of copies, and even to-day it cannot be read unmoved:

Are all prisons like the Bastille? You have no idea of the horrors of such a place. Cynical impudence, odious falsehoods, hypocrisy, bitter irony, unbridled cruelty, injustice and death hold sway. A barbarous silence is the least of the crimes committed there.... Others have been buried there for thirty years, are reputed dead, are unhappy in not being dead; having, like Milton's damned souls, only so much light in their abyss as to perceive the impenetrable darkness that enwraps them. I said it in captivity, and I repeat it a free man: there is no crime but is amply expiated by six months in the Bastille. It is said that there is no lack of executioners and hangmen there, and I have no difficulty in believing it. I am asked if I would return to France should the ban which prohibits me from doing so be lifted. Certainly, I answer, when the Bastille shall have become a public square. May God grant it. You have all that is needed for happiness, Frenchmen.... All you want, my good friends, is one little thing: to be sure of lying in your own beds when you are irreproachable. To labour for this happy revolution is a task worthy of your *parlements*. It is only difficult to feeble souls....[1]

This is certainly revolutionary and prophetic stuff. But some copies of a variant edition have an even more mantic ending. Doubt has been cast on its authenticity, because the Inquisitorial biographer had quoted it, in order, it was thought, to show up his hero-victim in a dangerous light.[2] But Petraccone who saw both versions gives the addition in these words:

Yes, I announce it to you: a prince will reign over you who will owe his glory to the abolition of the 'lettres de cachet', to the convocation of the Estates General. He will understand that in the long run the abuse of power is deleterious to power itself. He will not rest content with being the first of his ministers, but will wish to be the first amongst Frenchmen.[3]

The first encounter between the magician and the forces ranged against him ended in an apparent victory for Cagliostro; since not only was he acquitted, but in this letter he prophesied the approaching downfall of the system which had nearly ruined him. Moreover, he had given a striking proof of the greater humanity of magicians than

[1] Cp. Petraccone, op. cit. p. 113, and Sax Rohmer, *The Romance of Sorcery*, London 1914, p. 227.

[2] Cf. Trowbridge, op. cit. p. 255. Both Sax Rohmer and Petraccone have seen the variant. I have been unable to consult either.

[3] Petraccone, op. cit. pp. 113 ff.; this variant was printed in 1787.

of those who seek riches or power by more orthodox means. It is true that Cagliostro duped many people; but he brought happiness to many more; and the protest he raised against the inhumanity of the Bastille showed him to be more civilised than the great ones of the earth who battened on the Bastille and kindred institutions. An attack of this sort would certainly provoke reprisals; and the French Government, after vainly trying to lure Cagliostro back to France, used Morande as their scourge. The editor of the *Courrier de l'Europe* was now in the pay of that country, which had suffered from him in the past. Amongst other stories current about him is the well-known tale how he had blackmailed the Duchess du Barry for the sum of 5000 guineas to prevent his publication of a scandalous biography which he had written about her. Through the good offices of Beaumarchais, sent over to England for the purpose, this sum was finally agreed upon and paid. Then, after a suitable interval, Morande published the book. This was the man to whom the French Government now entrusted the congenial task of unmasking Cagliostro. The 'illustrious voyager' of the necklace trial had owned to many aliases, besides the fanciful name of Acharat, borne in his early youth. Enquiries into his real identity must have taken place at the time, and the *dossier* of Lorenza Balsamo (which may be a forgery) was either discovered or invented then. This was the material submitted to Morande, who certainly made the most of it, supplementing it from details of Balsamo's sojourn in London in 1772 and of Balsamo-Cagliostro's visit in 1776–7. He began to launch his attack on 1 September 1786; and it can only be described as annihilating. For it certainly seemed to prove beyond the shadow of a doubt that the 'divine Cagliostro', the Friend of Humanity and the Grand Copht of Egyptian Freemasonry was none other than the unsavoury little crook called Giuseppe Balsamo. On my hypothesis of a dual personality, the identification was correct; but without that hypothesis, the problem of how Balsamo ever reached the dizzy heights of Cagliostro, performed his marvellous cures and displayed so much generosity and even nobility remains unsolved. Adopting it, one can see all the mortal harm it must have done to the unhappy magician. For not only did it prick the bubble of his reputation, it must have completely destroyed his self-esteem. He was now forced to remember Balsamo and those shady adventures of the past which he had sublimated into the mystic beginnings and mysterious wanderings of the mythical Acharat. He could never again, even in his sublimest moments (and how rare those were now to be), forget his other self. The memory of it was to break him, and his descent was headlong indeed, once he had been 'unmasked'.

One small triumph he nevertheless did achieve over the unspeakable Morande, and it bore no small likeness to the victories of legendary magicians. Morande had sneered at a story of Cagliostro's to the effect that Arabs, by feeding a sucking pig on arsenic and then turning it loose into the woods round Medina, had poisoned all the lions, tigers and leopards infesting them. He answered the gibes of Morande in the following manner in the *Public Advertiser* of 3 September 1786:

In matters of physics and chemistry, arguments prove little, and ridicule nothing at all, but experiment proves everything. Allow me therefore to propose a little experiment, which will amuse the public at your expense, or else at mine. I invite you to a collation on the ninth of November next, at nine o'clock in the morning. You will bring the wine and all the accessories. I will only provide one dish. This will be a sucking-pig fattened according to my system. Two hours before the collation I will present it to you fat and alive; you will see to its slaughter and preparation and I shall not approach it until the moment when it is served at table. You yourself shall carve it into four equal parts, choose those which most appeal to your appetite and give me what you please. Next day one of four things will have occurred: either we shall both be dead; or both alive; or else I shall be dead and you will be alive; or finally you will be dead, and I shall be alive.

Of these four alternatives I present you with three, and I wager 5000 guineas that on the day following the collation, you will be dead, and I shall be in perfect health. You must acknowledge that this is fair play.... If you accept the wager, I will immediately deposit the 5000 guineas with whatever banker you may be pleased to name; and you will do the same within a fortnight.... [1]

Morande did not venture to accept this challenge, which was a call to a magical contest, the loser to forfeit his life—a stock feature in legends. Most probably Cagliostro had a powerful emetic prepared in case Morande came to the collation. But in vain did he brand his enemy as a coward; in vain did he tear into yet smaller shreds

---

[1] Cagliostro, *Lettre au peuple anglois*, London 1786, pp. 50 ff. A very similar tale is told of a challenge made by Cagliostro to the chief physician of Catherine the Great. Cf. Figuier, op. cit. IV, pp. 9 ff. quoting from the *Gazette de Santé*.

what little reputation the journalist had left; in vain did he deny emphatically and fairly convincingly that he was Giuseppe Balsamo. It is notoriously almost impossible to prove a negative; and the weak point of his position was his pretended or real inability to say who he actually was. Another very weak spot in his armour was his wife, Serafina or Lorenza Feliciani. The very name now held sinister implications for him. If he were Balsamo, he knew that she had betrayed him once. His agony in the Bastille when he learnt that she was also a prisoner there may have been partly due to the fear that she might, in those circumstances, betray him again. On his urgent, eloquent and moving appeals she was released; but she was never to be counted on. Leaving her behind him in London when he made a getaway from that disastrous city, where the vultures were already gathering to pluck his carcase, he exposed his weak and treacherous helpmate to the solicitations of Morande, who managed to extract from her some extremely damaging admissions. It is true that she retracted these when she rejoined her husband, but the harm had been done. Cagliostro was now in any case sliding rapidly downhill to ruin. One refuge after another in Switzerland and Italy having failed him, his magical prestige and magnetic powers mere shadows of the past, he gave in finally to her ardent desire to rejoin her family and slunk nervously into Rome. Those whom the gods would destroy they first render blind. For Rome, however much Lorenza-Serafina hankered after it, was obviously the most dangerous place on earth for any kind of Mason. Had not Clement XII excommunicated Freemasonry in a Bull dated 26 April 1738; and had not Benedict XIV ratified it on 18 May 1751? What hope was there that Cagliostro would be allowed to preach and practise there? And what other means were left to him now to keep the wolf from the door? His vast fortune had melted like snow in summer: and if the secret societies had been his bankers in the past, then they must have abandoned him when he was discovered to be the rogue Balsamo. For he was certainly in dire poverty when he entered Rome. He tried to insure his life and liberty, it is said, by making a full confession to a Benedictine monk and abjuring Freemasonry. Indeed, he behaved with such circumspection at first that (owing to a letter of recommendation from the Bishop of Trent) he was favourably noticed by several cardinals. But he could no more live without Egyptian Masonry than an addict can forswear cocaine, quite apart from the state of his finances. He came to Rome towards the end of May 1789; and before the middle of September he held an opening ceremony for admission into Egyptian Freemasonry. It seems to have gone very much according to the usual plan to judge by the description given by the Abbato Lucantonio Benedetti in his journal under the date 15 September 1789, quoted, and sometimes paraphrased, by Petraccone.

'I was forced to assist at a reunion presided over by Cagliostro in the Villa Malta, near the Porta Pinciana, being unable to resist the prayers of the Marchioness M.P., who was set upon my accompanying her. I went there about two o'clock in the night; and, having entered the house after giving the countersign to a servant in livery, we were introduced into a vast hall, splendidly illuminated, on whose walls were depicted the square, perpendiculars, and horizontals and other symbols. There were also statuettes of Egyptian idols as well as Assyrian and Chinese. On one wall was written in large letters: *Sum quidquid fuit, est et erit. Nemoque mortalium mihi adhuc velum detraxit.*'...Opposite the spectators there was a kind of altar with all the apparatus of charlatanry which Cagliostro habitually used: owls, skulls, apes, serpents, crucibles, retorts, phials and amulets....'After some time, the Count of Cagliostro entered. He is of medium height, plump, haggard, with a malicious air, a suspicious look and similar in everything to the portrait that we have of him. His wife followed him; she is very like her portrait; beautiful, of just the right stature and animated looks.'

Cagliostro then made the following speech:

'It is right that I should tell you the story of my life and reveal my past to you, that I should rend asunder the thick veil which impedes your sight. Enter and listen. I see the vast desert, the gigantic palms projecting their shadows on to the sand, the Nile flowing calmly, the sphinxes, the obelisks, the pillars rising majestically. Here is the marvellous wall, the innumerable temples surging upward, the pyramids mounting to the sky, the labyrinths revealed. It is the sacred city of Memphis. Here is the King Ptolemy III, the glorious, entering triumphantly after having vanquished the Syrians and the Canaanites. I see...but I am now in other lands. Here is another city; here is the temple, the sacred temple where Jehovah and not Osiris was adored....The new gods have replaced the old. I hear voices, the prophet, the son of God, is crying aloud. Who is he? It is Christ....Ah, yes, I see Him; He is at the wedding of Cana...see, He changes water into wine....No, He was not the only one to accomplish that miracle; I will show it to you, I will reveal the secret to you; nothing is unknown to me; I am omniscient, I am immortal, antediluvian. *Ego sum qui sum.*' At this point in his chaotic, jerky discourse, Cagliostro took a jar of water, came out of his vision, and poured into the vessel a few drops of a yellow liquor from an ampoule which turned the water into a golden yellow. Several people tasted this liquid, and all found it excellent, upon which Cagliostro revealed that it was the Falerno of the Romans. After this experiment, he went on to talk of his secrets, and of his elixir of longevity, which he gave to taste to more than one of those present, in whom, he said, the effect would be immediately seen. Actually their faces became flushed and they seemed more animated. But, observed Benedetti, 'I do not believe that the specific has the same effect as a good glass of Montefiascone.' Cagliostro then undertook the experiment, in which Benedetti placed little faith, of the enlargement of precious stones, which he essayed with a ring of the Cardinal Bernis. 'After that', writes the Abbé, 'he called a young girl into the hall and made her look into a crystal vessel full of water; the girl, whom he called his pupil, said that she saw a street leading from one great city to another, a great crowd of men and women who were running and crying: *Down with the King!* Cagliostro asked her to what country they belonged, and she answered that she heard the people crying *A Versailles!* and that there was a nobleman in their midst. Cagliostro turned to us and said: Well, the pupil has foretold the future. Before long, Louis XVI will be attacked by the people of Versailles, a duke will lead the crowd, the monarchy will be overthrown, the Bastille razed to the ground and liberty will succeed to tyranny. The deuce, exclaimed His Eminence, Cardinal de Bernis; are you making this kind of prophecy about my master? I regret but these things will take place, answered the count.'...Later he spoke about his Egyptian Rite, but was very little heeded; since only two people asked to be inscribed, the Marquis Vivaldi and the Capuchin friar.[1]

This remarkable prevision of the storming of Versailles led by the Duke of Aguillon on 5 October 1789 might well hearten Cagliostro to write that moving memorial to the Estates General, begging them to allow him to return to France and to live there under their protection, exercising the civil and moral virtues. It was never answered. In the turmoil of events in Paris, the once so famous and flattered wizard was now no longer of the slightest importance. He had actually foretold the early triumphs of the revolution; to a certain extent he had helped to bring them about; he may even have taken secretly a more active part; but he was now a negligible and broken tool, and not a finger was raised to beckon him back. Meanwhile the shadows were deepening around him. In spite of his discourse, his miracles, his elixir of youth and his startling prophecy,

[1] Cf. Petraccone, op. cit. pp. 156 ff. Though the Bastille had been stormed on 14 July 1789, it was not completely destroyed till much later.

he only succeeded in enticing two very lean flies to walk into his Egyptian parlour. Worse was to come. Sickened by the insecurity of her life with the fallen magus, estranged from him very probably by harsh and even brutal treatment on his part (of which there were rumours), but more than all longing to make her peace with the Church to which she had always belonged, Lorenza-Serafina brought herself or was brought by her family to denounce him to the Inquisition, a denunciation supported by all the members of that same family and their associates and friends. Cagliostro was arrested on 27 December 1789 and conducted to the fortress of Saint Angelo. His trial lasted from 4 May 1790 to 22 June 1790, and consisted of forty-three examinations, at the end of which he was condemned to death (although not until 7 April 1791) as a heretic and a Freemason, a sentence commuted by the Pope to imprisonment for life. Lorenza, who had been interrogated by her father-confessor, and had consistently continued on her course of betrayal, was immured for life in a convent. Cagliostro, transported to the terrible dungeons of San Leo died there, it was said of apoplexy, on 26 August 1795. Such at least is the version given by the prison authorities with realistic and credible medical details, although sensationally minded writers think that he was probably murdered.

The legend that he strangled a monk whom he had asked for in order to confess himself and escaped in his clothes, subsequently being seen in America, must I think be discounted; although it may be true, as Prince Bernard of Saxe-Weimar declared, that he made the attempt unsuccessfully. Madame Blavatsky for her part had no doubt at all that he had succeeded; since he had appeared in Russia long after his supposed death, residing for some time in her father's house, where

...in the midst of winter he produced by magic power a plate full of fresh strawberries for a sick person who was craving it.[1]

The real picture, alas! is much more sombre. Cagliostro's frantic efforts, first to avoid condemnation and incarceration, and then to escape from his dungeon by confessions and recantations, make tragic reading. His desperate messages to the Pope, imploring him for an audience, so that he might reveal secrets of the utmost importance for the welfare of the Holy See; his distraught and

[1] Trowbridge, op. cit. p. 306.

incoherent missives to the outer world, which never saw them; that piteous cry: 'Me voici! à moi! me voici!' when during a terrific thunderstorm he believed the insurgent Romans were coming to rescue him; the ruling passion manifest in the 'secret' written out at last for Sempronius, the Governor of San Leo, to give to the Pope: it is all heart-rending:

> Noi Alexandro I° G.M. e Fr. dell'
> ordine egiziano per la G. dio
> ordinamo a coloro che ci appartengono
> e a quelli credenti al verbo divino
> Capo di G.
> Sempronius semper fuit
> Sempronius
> Vita di
> Smpr.
> Elion Melion
> Tetragrammaton
> La fine del vivere si
> apprende in questa sep-
> poltura per carità
> la sua
> Protesta ed abiura
> in presenza di Dio e del
> Popolo contro a
> Memoriale del Conte
> di Cagliostro a S.D.M. la
> SS. Trinità per impetrare il ...
> de' peccati,
> Supplica di Alessandro 1° alla
> Reina del cielo
> MARIA SS. NELL'
> ora della morte
> Anael
> Uriel
> Gabriel
> MICHAEL
> Rafael
> Anabriel
> Zadachiel[1]

This looks like insanity on the face of it, and it is certainly not very sensible; but it shows some continuity of thought. The seven angels

[1] Petraccone, op. cit. p. 195.

at the end (Anabriel is a miswriting or misreading for Anachiel) were very familiar to members of the Egyptian Lodges, being the seven angelic spirits at Cagliostro's command and constantly called upon. 'Elion Melion Tetragrammaton' was the Inquisitorial version of Helion, Mene and Tetragrammaton, or the sun, the moon and the secret name of God, one of Cagliostro's magic formulae. So that this apparently meaningless jumble is not quite so senseless as it seems. There is another sign that the magus did not go under completely until he died, although his mind was obviously giving beneath the strain, and had perhaps never been very securely poised. When his end approached, he twice emphatically refused the sacraments. It has been suggested to me that this was for fear of being murdered; since the Holy Office never made away with its victims until they had received the last rites of the Church. Even in that case, it would have been a sign of sanity to reject such sinister consolation. But whether helped out of the world or dying as a result of his imprisonment, the Grand Copht of Egyptian Freemasonry went the same way as Joan of Arc and countless less famous non-conformists to the creed in power. Had Cagliostro lived another two years, he most certainly would have been rescued. For when French troops invaded the Papal States in 1797, they took San Leo whither the Pope's army had withdrawn. It was the famous Polish legion under General Dombrowski who reduced that grim fortress; and the first thing the officers did on entering was to enquire eagerly for Cagliostro, whom they regarded as a martyr to liberty. But this tribute and the desire to liberate him came too late. The 'divine Cagliostro' was no more.

It seems more than likely that, if the identification with Balsamo had never been made, Cagliostro would have come down to posterity as one of the most famous healers of all time, and that his religious doctrines would also have been taken much more seriously. His was a finally unsuccessful effort to establish a new religion (or to revive an ancient one) by means of miracles. He constantly animadverted against magic, but he as constantly practised it. And his whole personality is so ambiguous that it is impossible to determine whether he used magic from religious motives, or whether his religion was a mere cloak for magic: whether he were fundamentally sincere, or fundamentally corrupt. The trail of Balsamo besmears Cagliostro and all his works. No one can ever get away from it. He has become for posterity, not the type of holy medicine-man, but the charlatan *par excellence*. Actually he is the great outstanding representative of the dual nature of all magicians. They all have their Balsamos. The white magicians conquer them and rise in legend to godhead. The black magicians are conquered by them and spend a legendary eternity in hell. Cagliostro was for ever pulled this way and that between two contending aggressive personalities, whilst his spate of miracles shows that he was a direct descendant from the medicine-man of the past. Moreover, he boasted a mysterious origin; he underwent initiation; he was caught up in a spectacular contest; he was tried, he was persecuted, he died and was said to live again. There surely is the sacrificed priest of the ancient rites. There too are the Eastern voyages; and there is the mystery-religion. But there too, wherever you look, is the blackguard Giuseppe Balsamo.

CHAPTER IV

MADAME AND THE MASTERS (1831–1891)

Cagliostro preached a doctrine of spiritual regeneration, hailing, so he said, from ancient Egypt, and came into tragic conflict with the prevailing creed. But even his martyrdom could not transform Egyptian Freemasonry into a religious movement. It died with him and vanished underground. The rehabilitation of magic, however, continued apace. Francis Barrett, in *The Magus or Celestial Intelligencer*, published in 1801, gave an impetus to the study of its ancient and modern forms and attempted to form a school of magic consisting of not more than twelve disciples. He may or may not have succeeded; but whatever effect he had on contemporary thought was thrown into the shade by the publications of the great French occultist, the Abbé Alphonse Louis Constant (*c.* 1810–75), who, under the pseudonym of Eliphas Lévi, brought the subject into a prominence that might almost be called glaring, to judge by the tribute paid to him by his English translator, A. E. Waite:

> To all schools indifferently, Eliphas Lévi has...been a source of inspiration, nor has his influence been merely of a literary character; there seems evidence to shew that his presentation of magical science has been the basis of operation in more than one school secretly or openly engaged in experiments of a practical nature;...we may regard Eliphas Lévi as a visible head and source of modern transcendentalism. He is the most brilliant, the most original, the most fascinating interpreter of occult philosophy in the West, nor is the reason far to seek, for he is essentially the modern spirit turning to the sanctuaries of initiation and carrying all its searchlights for the exploration of those recesses.[1]

It is certainly true that the dry bones of *The Magus* are made to live, and live very vividly, in the pages of Lévi, who numbered Bulwer-Lytton among his disciples. The latter was evidently involved in that strange invocation of Apollonius of Tyana which Lévi undertook in London; and occult influences are much in evidence in *A Strange Story*, *The Coming Race*, *The Haunted and the Haunters*, and in *Zanoni*. The title-hero of this last novel is certainly Saint-Germain super-

---

[1] A. E. Waite, *The Mysteries of Magic*, London 1897, pp. xii f.

imposed upon the mysterious Gualdi, the member of a hidden fraternity, nobler far than the Rosicrucians, and secretly guiding the destinies of man:

Did Zanoni belong to this mystical fraternity, who, in an earlier age, boasted of secrets of which the Philosopher's Stone was but the least; who considered themselves the heirs of all that the Chaldaeans, the Magi, the Gymnosophists, and the Platonists had taught; and who differed from all the darker Sons of Magic in the virtue of their lives, the purity of their doctrines, and their insisting, as the foundation of all wisdom, on the subjugation of the senses, and the intensity of Religious Faith?[1]

The answer to this flourishing question is, I am happy to state, in the affirmative. Zanoni did belong to that awe-inspiring brotherhood, and played the part which Saint-Germain was believed to have played in attempting to stem the Revolution. The likeness throughout is unmistakable; and it is small wonder that, surrounded as he was by the glamour of Bulwer-Lytton's romantic fervour, Zanoni should appear to the novel-reading public of that age as the *beau idéal* of the spiritual life. Among his admirers was Madame Blavatsky; whilst the works of Eliphas Lévi were her chief authority on the theory and practice of magic. The germ of the Theosophical Society lies hidden in *Zanoni*; its doctrines were very largely borrowed from Lévi. According to Emmett Coleman about 200 points were taken from his works in *Isis Unveiled*, and the same source was tapped without acknowledgement in *The Secret Doctrine*. In addition the Theosophical Society published an English translation of Lévi's *Paradoxes of the Highest Science* in 1883 from the original French manuscript, and brought out Lévi's letters to the Baron Spedalieri. An article of his on *Death* was also printed in *The Theosophist* for October 1881 with marginal comments alleged to be by Koot Hoomi, and there are numerous references to the French occultist both in Madame Blavatsky's letters to Sinnett, and in the Mahatma letters as well. I transcribe two of the most interesting from the personal point of view:

Explain to you 'a little more about Eliphas Lévi'? And what the deuce do *I* know about him? I never saw him. All I know is what I was told. He was a most learned and erudite theoretical Kabalist and occultist. But who ever told you he was a *practical* adept? Not I. He himself says in his works that he never performed ceremonial magic but once in London evoking

[1] Edward Bulwer-Lytton, *Zanoni*, Leipzig (Tauchnitz) 1842, pp. 80f.

Apollonius of Tyana...I have never heard before that he was so dirty and gluttonous. But if Mrs Gebhard says so—she knows better, for I have never met him. My aunt went to see him in Paris and she had a bad impression for he took 40 francs for one minute of conversation and explanation of the Tarrot cards.[1]

The greatest as well as most promising of such schools in Europe—the last attempt in this direction—failed most signally some 20 years ago in London. It was the secret school for the practical teachers of magick, founded under the name of a club, by a dozen of enthusiasts under the leadership of Lord Lytton's father. He had collected together for the purpose, the most ardent and enterprising as well as some of the most advanced scholars in mesmerism and 'ceremonial magick', such as Eliphas Lévi, Regazzoni, and the Kopt Zergvan-Bey. And yet in the pestilential London atmosphere, the 'Club' came to an untimely end.[2]

It is possible at least that this unsuccessful club was the outcome of Barrett's earlier attempt to gather twelve disciples round him for the study and practice of magic. However that may be, the writings of Bulwer-Lytton and Eliphas Lévi between them fired the more than combustible imagination of Helena Petrovna Blavatsky. The outlines of this strange woman's tragic career are too widely known to demand or even to bear detailed repetition. Like that of Joan of Arc, however, her life rivets the attention because the real facts of her existence follow traditional legendary lines, apart from the mythical accretions (many of them due to the statements of the magician herself) which also adhere to the age-old pattern.

Although divine descent was not claimed by or for H.P.B., the modern substitute of previous significant incarnations was an article of belief, and she categorically affirmed that she had been Paracelsus in a previous existence. She also dropped dark hints of extreme old age à la Saint-Germain and Zanoni. There was no mystery about the birth of this aristocratic Russian; but it took place on the night of 30–31 July, and thus endowed her, according to Slavonic folk-lore, with power over elemental spirits. Moreover, cholera raging at the time, she 'was ushered into the world in the midst of coffins and desolation'; and a disastrous conflagration which occurred during the christening ceremony was also susceptible of mythical inter-

---

[1] *The Letters of H. P. Blavatsky to A. P. Sinnett*, Barker, London 1925, p. 62. From H.P.B. to A.P.S.; dated from Adyar, 27 September 1883.
[2] *The Mahatma Letters to A. P. Sinnett*, Barker, London 1927, pp. 209f. From Koot Hoomi to A. O. Hume, 1881 [?].

pretation. These external accidents, however, are definitely less impressive than the family accounts of her childhood. Rarely, indeed, can there have been such an infant prodigy and such a domestic terror as Helena. Turbulent, tempestuous, indomitable, she seems to have behaved (including the performance of seemingly miraculous feats) as Heracles, Krishna and the apocryphal Christ were said to have acted in their childhood. If not in actual fact a wonder-working godling, she certainly possessed the power both to enchant and to terrify her young associates and the superstitious servants by the force of an imagination which beglamoured her own mind too. Genius of a very unusual sort was evidently present; but, although it never deserted her, it also never quite fulfilled its radiant early promise:

She never spoke in later years as she used to speak in her childhood and early girlhood [her sister wrote during H.P.B.'s lifetime]. The stream of her eloquence has dried up, and the very source of her inspiration is now seemingly lost![1]

The clouds of glory became indeed a dire and dingy fog in the last years of her life. A wild and stormy childhood and adolescence, followed by a brief and equally stormy married life, was the prelude to a period of legendary journeys, almost impossible to trace. According to her own account she visited nearly all the countries in both hemispheres in pursuit of occult knowledge during the two decades (1848–58 and 1864–73) when she was out of touch with her family; but her central claim, a period of initiation in a lamasery in Tibet, which she estimated as ten, seven or three years, and sometimes as several months, has never been satisfactorily substantiated. She certainly tried to enter Tibet on one occasion and was prevented by the British authorities. She may have been more successful subsequently. A Major Cross stated in 1927 that, during a journey through North-West Tibet, he had

traced the progress of a white woman in 1867, through the most difficult country to a lamasery far north, through the recollections of various old people who were impressed by the personality of this unusual visitor. He identified her with Madame Blavatsky.[2]

[1] A. P. Sinnett, *Incidents in the Life of Madame Blavatsky*, London 1903, p. 27.
[2] M. K. Neff, *Personal Memoirs of H. P. Blavatsky*, London 1937, p. 162, quoting from *The Canadian Theosophist*, 1927.

We shall never really know the truth about this thrice-famous initiation; but the claim is highly significant, and was obviously based on Eastern knowledge and beliefs quickening the fictitious Zanoni. Miss Anna Ballard, an American journalist, who interviewed H.P.B. in New York in July 1873, a week after her arrival, was very much struck by her triumphant announcement on the subject:

I remember perfectly well her saying with an air of exultation 'I have been to Tibet'. Why she should think that a great matter, more remarkable than any other of the travels in Egypt, India, and other countries she told me about, I could not make out, but she said it with special emphasis and animation. I now know, of course, what it means.[1]

Markedly mediumistic (it would appear), H.P.B. had already amazed her family by supernormal manifestations in Russia during the years 1858–64, and now gave further proof of those gifts in spiritualistic circles in America, and notably to Colonel Olcott, whose stories about her are remarkable indeed, whether regarded as instances of a credulity which staggers the imagination, or as evidence of extraordinary powers to produce phenomena by whatever means. Dissatisfied with spiritualism both in practice and in theory, the henceforth inseparable pair founded the Theosophical Society in 1875, removed to India in 1879, transferred their headquarters from Bombay to Adyar in 1882; whilst, chiefly owing to the phenomena produced by H.P.B., the Society began to gain adherents not only among the Indians, but also among English residents. This led through an underground conflict with a 'rival magician' (the ambiguous Madame Coulomb) and more open warfare with the priests of the old religion she had come to replace (the Madras Christian College) to the inquiry into her pretensions by the Society for Psychical Research and the final condemnation:

For our own part, we regard her neither as the mouthpiece of hidden seers, nor as a mere vulgar adventuress; we think that she has achieved a title to permanent remembrance as one of the most accomplished, ingenious, and interesting impostors in history.[2]

Although Madame Blavatsky survived this judgement by six years, and wrote *The Secret Doctrine* and *The Voice of the Silence* after it had

[1] H. Olcott, *Old Diary Leaves*, London, 1904, I, p. 24.
[2] *Proceedings of the Society for Psychical Research*, London 1885, III, p. 207.

been pronounced, she never really recovered from it, and was subject thenceforward to a ceaseless series of more or less petty persecutions which drove her nearly demented:

Has the following picture ever presented itself to your literary imagination? There is living in the forest a wild boar—an ugly creature, but doing no harm to any one as long as they leave him in peace in his forest, with his wild beast friends who love him. This boar never hurt any one in his life, but only grunted to himself as he ate the roots which were his own in the forest which sheltered him. There is let loose upon him, without rhyme or reason, a pack of ferocious hounds; men chase him from the wood, threaten to burn his native forest, and to leave him a wanderer, homeless, for anyone to kill. He flies for a while, though he is no coward by nature, before these hounds; he tries to escape *for the sake of the forest*, lest they burn it down. But lo! one after another the wild beasts who were once his friends join the hounds; they begin to chase him, yelping and trying to bite and catch him, to make an end of him. Worn out, the boar sees that his forest is already set on fire and that he cannot save it nor himself. What is there for the boar to do? Why, this; he stops; he turns his face to the furious pack of hounds and beasts, and shows *himself wholly* as he is, from top to bottom, and then falls upon his enemies in his turn, and kills as many of them as his strength serves, till he falls dead—and then he is really powerless.[1]

Spiritually at least, the tearing to pieces of the old-time saviour-god was enacted in the fate of Madame Blavatsky, although her physical death was that of an ordinary mortal. It was shortly followed by her resurrection as a spirit dictating posthumous memoirs directly to a Yost typewriter, and her appearance in an astral guise to a clairvoyant friend of the Countess Wachtmeister:

A few days after Madame Blavatsky died, H.P.B. awoke me at night, I raised myself, feeling no surprise, but only the sweet accustomed pleasure. She held my gaze with her leonine gaze. Then she grew finer, taller, her shape more masculine; slowly then her features changed, until a man of height and rugged appearance stood before me, the last vestige of her features melting into his, until the leonine gaze, the progressed radiance of her glance alone remained. The man lifted his head and said: 'Bear Witness!' He then walked from the room, laying his hand on the portrait of H.P.B. as he passed. Since then he has come to me several times, with instructions, in broad daylight while I was busily working, and once he stepped out from a large portrait of H.P.B.[2]

---

[1] V. A. Solovyov, *A Modern Priestess of Isis*, tr. W. Leaf, London 1895, pp. 176 f. H.P.B. to Solovyov.

[2] Cf. G. Baseden Butt, *Madame Blavatsky*, London 1927, p. 96.

Of the eleven stock features of tradition, H.P.B. therefore can show eight, taking reincarnation as the modern equivalent of supernatural birth. Portents and perils accompanied her infancy; long and distant journeys preceded her possibly fictitious initiation; she was involved in a magical contest, underwent a trial and persecution, and a species of resurrection after her death. There were in addition innumerable other legends told about her and by her. It was held by some that the real Helena Petrovna died in 1867 of a wound received at the battle of Mentana, and the powerful spirit, H.P.B., then took control of her body. It was also said that there were two Madame Blavatskys in Cairo in 1868. One, Natalia, died, and her secretary decamped with her manuscripts. Could this be Helena Petrovna? Happily Countess Lydia Paschkov testified to knowing them both. Then there was the legend of her virginity, industriously circulated by Madame Blavatsky herself, in spite of two short and far from sweet marriages, the second of which was unintentionally bigamous on her part, and several love-affairs to which she confessed in a letter to Aksakov from America. When various unsavoury slanders were put into circulation about her past life after the damaging report of the Society for Psychical Research, she actually obtained a medical certificate to the effect that she had never borne a child and was physically incapable of doing so. One can sympathise with this; but her insistence on her virginity would be quite incomprehensible had it been made with the forlorn hope of disarming Mrs Grundy. There was a more piteous reason behind it. It was not only and not chiefly H.P.B.'s sexual morality that was in question. It was her magical power; and virginity was traditionally supposed to be a *sine qua non* for female performers of magic. Actually, however, history shows that the most highly gifted magicians of either sex are wayward ethically, to put it mildly. As for her past life, she rather unconvincingly adopted the pose of injured innocence to Sinnett:

The whole of my life except the weeks and months I passed with the Masters, in Egypt or in Tibet, is so inextricably full of events with whose secrets and real actuality the dead and the living are concerned, and I made only responsible for their outward appearance, that to vindicate myself I would have to step on a hecatomb of the dead and cover with dirt the living. *I will not do so.*[1]

[1] *The Letters of H. P. Blavatsky to A. P. Sinnett*, p. 145; H.P.B. to A.P.S., not dated.

Peace to the poor woman's ashes in their three separate urns! Her private morality is no concern of mine, whereas the occult phenomena produced by her, or claimed to be so produced, await investigation. They are of a disillusioning nature, for the link binding her to the medicine-man of the past and of present-day primitive tribes is a woefully slender one, and her similarity with a parlour conjurer much more striking. She had no power over the elements, and but a very tenuous connection with the food supply. Some bunches of grapes, a bottle full of water, and showers of beautiful roses were her only ventures in this line. She left the healing of the sick to Olcott (who sometimes fell down on the job) and never attempted the feat of bringing the dead to life; although by sheer will-power she seems to have postponed her own imminent demise on more than one occasion. Her creative gifts took the puerile form of many and various *apports* of a trifling nature and of the duplication of a ring with precious stones. These *apports* must also be listed under the rubric of transportation. Colonel Olcott witnessed, not very convincingly, to her transformation of personality when under the influence of Mahatmas, and also saw her vanish and reappear before his eyes. She 'discovered' a lost brooch for a friend under rather suspicious circumstances; but she had no gift of prophecy; and although she took part in necromantic feats during her spiritualistic period, she was soon to deny strenuously and to persist in the denial that the spirits evoked were those of the dead. She always asserted that she had power over elemental spirits however; and it would have been the height of ingratitude to deny this; for one of the 'little fools' hemmed some towels for her on one occasion at Colonel Olcott's suggestion. It is true that they were very badly and childishly hemmed, but hardly if any worse than his mistress's normal efforts. It is clear from this list that nearly all the phenomena hitherto mentioned (I have omitted the raps and astral bells as even less impressive) are peculiarly pointless; and, apart from their entertainment value, could contribute little or nothing to the health, wealth, happiness, wisdom or spiritual progress of those who witnessed them. They were obviously performed for purposes of mere display. But the display itself served a purpose, as it is wont to do in the founding of religions. H.P.B.'s phenomenal power over the minds of men, 'hypnotising both her hearers and herself into believing the wildest inventions of her fantasy',[1] that power radiating from her enormous, uncanny pale blue eyes, was bent with all the energy of a daemonic will into making those around her accept her central occult claim, communication with the Brothers, Mahatmas or Masters. She never ascribed her most showy feats either to her own rightly directed will, or to the elemental spirits; but rather to those High Adepts in their Himalayan retreat who had commanded her by one of their number in Hyde Park on 12 August 1851 to found the Theosophical Society, and bring the light of Asia to the dark world of the West.

The White Brotherhood or White Lodge was the first article of her creed, the source of her powers, the proof of the Wisdom Religion she was preaching, the witnesses to its truth. She stood or fell by these supernatural beings who do not age, who understand all the languages of men and beasts, who foresee the future, and read the minds of men (not to mention their written or printed words in the akasic or ethereal records); who can project their astral doubles at will, leaving their real bodies thousands of leagues away, and entering those of others if need be, or making their ethereal presence externally known. H.P.B. did not herself invent these super-magicians. Not only were they to be found in the pages of *Zanoni*, but they have been an article of Eastern faith from time immemorial. Legends about them are rife in India and elsewhere; encounters with them have been claimed, instruction by them, and initiation too. Nor did she invent the feat by which they were to become so notorious in the West: the projection, precipitation or materialisation through whatever space of the so-called 'phenomenal letters'.

The *jajan* and *Kudais* [spirits venerated by the Tatars of Central Asia] frequently communicate with mortals by means of letters, and sometimes mortals in their turn write messages on paper and send them to Heaven. The latter are usually burnt in the fire, and are believed to go up through the smoke-hole in the yurt. The former generally fall down from Heaven, either through the smoke-hole or otherwise.[2]

[1] Neff, op. cit. p. 120; quoting from the *Memoirs* of H.P.B.'s cousin, Count Witte.
[2] N. K. Chadwick, 'The Spiritual Ideas and Experiences of the Tatars of Central Asia.' *Journal of the Royal Anthropological Institute*, 1936, LXVI, p. 321.

So perhaps after all the much-maligned Madame Blavatsky *was* in Tibet where she learnt this curious lore. Alas, she might also have heard of the practice considerably nearer home:

This case has a special interest for us here, because it occurred in connection with a secret society which existed some years ago at Leghorn, with branches elsewhere, and which believed itself to have constant experience of phenomena very similar to those described by the Theosophists—instantaneous intercommunication at a distance, phantasmal appearances, conveyance and precipitation of letters, disintegration and reintegration of objects, etc.[1]

We must leave it at that. But whether H. P. B. first became acquainted with the Mahatmas in Hyde Park, in Bulwer-Lytton's novel, in Egypt or in Tibet, she believed in them with that devouring intensity with which as a child she had believed in Russian folk-lore and refused to accept it as fiction. As far as such Masters are concerned, the burden of disproof is on the sceptics. There is a great deal of evidence in their favour, and since it is next to impossible to investigate it, one should keep an open mind. Madame Blavatsky's revelation of their existence to the West certainly marked an epoch in magic and religion. These majestic beings, endowed with such great occult powers, based on a deeper knowledge of nature than modern science even dreams of, were far enough removed from the common light of day to be a focus for spiritual aspirations; yet they were not so incredibly remote as to be utterly chilling to the imagination. Moreover, these guardians of true primeval wisdom were represented as watching over the destinies of the human race; and what could be more reassuring and comforting to an age which felt itself disoriented by materialism? This typically Western notion was implicit in *Zanoni*, in which the highly romanticised hero is depicted as attempting to stem the rising tides of revolution. Eastern thought has always emphasised the individual nature of the teaching and initiation granted to highly developed *chelas* or disciples. The *gurus* never seek to act upon the masses directly or indirectly. Madame Blavatsky had more sweeping and perhaps more philanthropic views, and stated that she had been chosen as the agent of the Great White

[1] *First Report of the Committee of the Society for Psychical Research appointed to investigate the evidence for marvellous phenomena offered by certain members of the Theosophical Society*, London 1884, p. ii.

Lodge to guide humanity upwards by means of Theosophy, the world religion which preached the brotherhood of man. Unhappily for mankind, it would seem that she set out to found the new era in the name of Truth by means of a series of frauds. Disastrously for herself, she also committed the unpardonable sin of being found out. It all came from the determination to force her belief in the occult Masters upon the world in a concrete form, to substantiate her claim that she was under their personal guidance. This constrained her to produce ocular proof of their existence. And since the Mahatmas Morya and Koot Hoomi existed only in her own fertile imagination, confederates had to be found.

It is ill fishing in those troubled waters of proof and counter-proof, of trickery, bribery and betrayal; of lies, blackmail, fraud, forgery, perjury, slander and abuse which were so malodorously stirred up by the investigation undertaken by Hodgson at the bidding of the Society for Psychical Research. It is one of the most painful episodes in the many distressing pages of the history of religion. And it seems as if the founder of Theosophy must be delivered up to the condemnation of posterity. For even if most of Hodgson's conclusions were wrong; if the letters to Madame Coulomb were forgeries as far as the incriminating passages are concerned; if the all too convincing explanations of Mahatmic phenomena were diabolically clever inventions of a disgruntled and vindictive employee; if the damning evidence of sliding panels and the like in the Occult Room and the Shrine were prefabricated for the investigation; if all the witnesses against H.P.B. were lying; and her own piteous self-betrayals in the letters to A. P. Sinnett were susceptible of favourable interpretations, there remains too much still to be explained away: Massey's damaging discovery of the insinuation of a Mahatma letter among his papers by fraudulent 'occult' means; Koot Hoomi's plagiarism from *The Banner of Light*, and, worse still, his attempts to explain it. But worst of all, the Mahatma letters themselves, published in 1927 and analysed by the Hare brothers in 1936. Only the extreme toughness and vitality of legend which thrives upon disproof could have survived that exposure: the evidence of the letters, so devastatingly summarised by the Hares. Indeed, the function of these critics is cathartic as well as destructive. By expressing the emotions of those who have ploughed through the epistles, they lighten the atmosphere, and give the weight of their authority to the instinctive conviction that the Mahatma letters are not the product of lofty, supra-mundane beings. We may set our minds at rest. Whatever Great White Brotherhood may exist beyond the Himalayas, the Masters Morya and Koot Hoomi at least are not among the members. The relief and satisfaction of saying this, particularly about Koot Hoomi, is a compliment (although a back-handed one) to the genius of Madame Blavatsky. Morya, much less long-winded and a more manly character than Koot Hoomi, is not nearly so maddening; for they are as distinct from each other as any other two characters in a novel in letter-form. In such a novel they would be merely boring; it is their spuriousness as human beings that makes one dislike them so much. 'When the hour comes she will be taken back to Tibet', Morya stated in a letter to Sinnett. H. E. Hare commented acidly:

Madame Blavatsky never went back to 'Bod Las'....When the time came for her to leave the East, she took her integral self to Europe, settled there, finished her work, and died among real people and good friends in a better home.[1]

He too, like other readers, compassionated the creator of these bogus personalities, and sided with her against them. Yet H.P.B. endowed Koot Hoomi with the same kind of life which Mrs Harris enjoys in *Martin Chuzzlewit*; only there it is all light-hearted fun, and here it is real deception. 'There's no sech a person' as Koot Hoomi; but he will go on living a spectral life as long as the letters are extant, and will go on doing harm. For another literary parallel suggests itself even more inevitably. The Mahatmas played the same terrible part in Madame Blavatsky's life which Frankenstein's 'Monster' did in his. And they have outlived her, producing not only such works as Leadbeater's *The Masters and the Path*, but the pitiable fiasco of Krishnamurti. She never foresaw this when she began the attempt to discredit Christianity and spiritualism by appealing to the high authority of the Mahatmas. But it may well be that Koot Hoomi and Morya are so singularly devoid of charm, because hatred of these two systems was so strong an element in the Society which she founded, one of whose aims was:

[1] H. E. and W. L. Hare, *Who Wrote the Mahatma Letters?* London 1927, p. 217.

PLATE IX

Mahatma Koot Hoomi

To oppose the materialism of science and every form of dogmatic theology, especially the Christian, which the Chiefs of the Society regard as particularly pernicious.[1]

They changed their tune later about this as about other matters, but meanwhile the Mahatma letters contain too plentiful an admixture of religious bile to be altogether edifying.

Yet had they been charity and nobility incarnate, they would still have proved her undoing. She began modestly and it would seem safely enough, possibly even sincerely, by attributing her mediumistic or psychic feats to their direct intervention. For *mana* of some sort or another she had in abundance in her hey-day. But the love of the marvellous, the fatal fascination of the occult made it inevitable that she should be driven to satisfy the desires she had aroused. This was not too difficult at first; but she was soon hard put to it by insatiable demands for more. Indomitable, reckless, fearless, fanatical and unscrupulous, she kept on. Her life during this period hardly bears thinking of. How, in the name of magic, did she find time to do everything the Mahatmas were supposed to do, and live her own life too? Here, if anywhere, is the miracle; and it has been ably used in her defence:

It must not be supposed that Madame Blavatsky, at this period, had nothing to do but invent the style and forge the script of the 'Mahatma Letters'; be the lioness of all the social gatherings, attend lectures, talk to all and everyone about Theosophy and the Society; sleep, bath, dress and eat; correspond with a hundred people all over India, write for the 'Theosophist', read, and frequently comment on, articles sent in; keep in touch with her Russian editors and run an eye over the world's reviews; be ill, organise fraudulent phenomena, such as having diplomas buried under bushes miles outside Simla; hypnotise everybody everywhere to think, say and do just what she needed for the perpetration of her frauds; handle the network of confederates she had, the person who wrote the Jhelum telegraph and the Amritsar postal employees who must have tampered with the postmark, the godlike Hindu who bamboozled the Colonel with a rose in the Golden Temple and the 'man in white' who must have stuck notes in trees; unpick a heavy old velvet and worsted cushion (and ensure that it should not be missed and asked for at any moment), unpick the inner lining, stick in a note and a brooch and sew the cushion up

[1] C. J. Ryan, *Madame Blavatsky and the Theosophical Movement*, Point Loma 1937, p. 61; quoting from *The Golden Book of the Theosophical Society* (Jinarâjadâsa), p. 26.

again, with new thread exactly the same as the old, without leaving a trace
(velvet!); have endless discussions with Hume and other sceptics; travel,
attend new Branch inaugurations, talk to new members; pass hours and
whole days in despair and rage under a hurricane of slander, explain to
friends and reply to enemies all around the country; fall desperately ill and,
barely convalescent, gather up unerringly all the threads of her huge
conspiracy....[1]

The answer of course is that, if one hardly sees how one woman
could do all this unaided, it seems more reasonable to deduce
confederates than to imagine sublime sages monkeying about with
brooches and velvet cushions. For in truth on her own showing
H.P.B.'s Masters led a dog's life. Not only were they writing endless
letters and sending streams of telegrams *à tort et à travers* by seemingly
miraculous and admittedly very exhausting means; they were also
obliged to appear 'astrally' whenever necessary and even in the
flesh. They must expound abstruse oriental philosophy to Western
invincible ignorance; answer foolish questions, give advice on ticklish
and petty matters, correct their own mistakes and mend broken
saucers at all hours of the day and night. Poor valiant H.P.B.! The
pace grew hotter, the tracks more difficult to cover, the doubts more
vocal, the attempts to allay them more hazardous, the confederate-
in-chief more dangerous, the curiosity more avid—and then the
crash came:

Ah, dear Mr Sinnett, how well it would have been had we all *never
pronounced Master's names* except in rooms with closed doors....[2]

But behold—the Occult laws—behold Karma and the result of *desecrating*
the mysteries, of desecrating holy names.[3]

...throwing their names right and left, *poured in torrents* on the public, so
to say, Their personalities, powers, and so on, until the world (the outsiders,
not only Theosophists) desecrated Their names indeed from the North to
the South Pole.... This is my chief, my greatest crime, for having brought
Their personalities to public notice, unwillingly, reluctantly, and forced
into it—by—and—[4]

She was right, so right that one has hardly the heart to point out that
in accepting the responsibility she was in fact denying the existence
of the Mahatmas, who had been very busy desecrating themselves

---

[1] Beatrice Hastings, *Defence of Madame Blavatsky*, London 1937, I, p. 23.
[2] *Letters of H.P.B. to A.P.S.* p. 158; no date.
[3] Ibid. p. 162; no date.
[4] Ryan, op. cit. p. 142; quoting *The Path*, March 1893.

by playing all those foolish parlour games, writing so much non-sense, and encouraging Sinnett to publish it. She was on firmer ground when she refused to attempt to vindicate herself in print:

> One thing in the world could do it if I ever could consent to it; and it is the *truth* and nothing but the truth—the WHOLE of it. This would, indeed, make all Europe jump from its seat and produce a revolution. But you see, I am an Occulist; a *pucka* not a *sham* one, in truth.... It is that ignorance of Occult transactions that gave such a hold to Hodgson and Massey and others. It is my *obligatory absolute silence* that now forces me to live under the shower of people's contempt.[1]

She did not, however, keep silent to Sinnett; would that she had been able to do so when one accusation after another had to be explained away to him; for the tragic twistings and turnings by which she tried to extricate herself from such predicaments reveal not only a hunted creature at bay, but also fearful moral obliquity and a most shaming ingenuity. Finally both she and Koot Hoomi had to extract what comfort they could from the fates of former magicians:

> Am I greater, or in any way better, than were St Germain, and Cagliostro, Giordono [*sic*] Bruno and Paracelsus, and so many many other martyrs whose names appear in the Encyclopedias of the 19th cent., over the meritorious titles of *charlatans* and *impostors*?[2]

> Were not St Germain, and Cagliostro, both gentlemen of the highest education and achievements—and presumably *Europeans*—not 'niggers' of my sort—regarded at the time, and still so regarded by posterity—as impostors, confederates, jugglers and what not?[3]

But these were only floating straws in the tide of calamity which now enveloped the desperately struggling Blavatsky, and which caused the Countess Wachtmeister to exclaim on opening H.P.B.'s mail: 'It is a mystery to me how all this dirt and filth seem to surround and oppress us.'[4] And the most disillusioning part of the whole business was the rank treachery of former friends and disciples, both European and Indian. The general noisomeness stirred up by Hodgson's investigations might seem to damn Theosophy for ever as a religion, did not candour remind us of the fact that this was the

---

[1] *Letters of H.P.B. to A.P.S.* pp. 142, 171; n.d.
[2] Ibid. p. 110; dated from Wurzburg, 19 August 1885.
[3] *The Mahatma Letters*, p. 306; received Simla, October 1882.
[4] *Letters of H.P.B. to A.P.S.* p. 272; from the Countess Wachtmeister to Sinnett; dated from Wurzburg, 4 January 1886.

first time in history that the claims and the conduct of a religious founder had been subjected to such searching tests, or that the miracles performed had been so closely scrutinised. Yet all of them in their day were the target of similar suspicions, betrayals and abuse.

As a religion it is not without its appeal, since it was based on some of the more striking ideas of Eastern faiths, such as the doctrine of Karma and rebirths. These notions, together with the proclamation of the universal brotherhood of man, and the stressing of spiritual as against material values, are the most valuable part of Theosophy, and were as widely and enthusiastically accepted as they deserved to be. Moreover, the Theosophical Society has many good deeds to its credit in India, such as the founding of schools and colleges, the revival of native interest in Sanskrit, and the securing of religious freedom in Ceylon. It had, of course, little or nothing to teach the East spiritually, since it merely popularised Eastern thought; and, to judge by the Indian *chelas* who gathered round H.P.B. and infamously used her in her adversity, she was a corrupting rather than an ennobling influence in some individual Indian minds. Nor did her occult teaching, approximating more and more to Buddhism, have any vitalising effect for good in the West, where it has been largely responsible for a great deal of loose and woolly thinking. Cranks and charlatans have abounded in Theosophy; it has been torn to shreds by internecine strife; and the bias away from rectitude which it received at the outset has not been corrected. It would seem to be particularly hard to be a Theosophist and retain one's intellectual integrity. The blight of the Brothers Morya and Koot Hoomi is still upon it, and in fact the blight has spread. Nor has it so far arrested the headlong descent into the Avernus of materialism which it was founded to check. And, although unlike many other religions, it has not yet brought about a war, it has been powerless to prevent the fearful catastrophes which have overtaken humanity since its foundation. In fact, the world has progressed with accelerated speed along the road to ruin in spite of the world religion, and in spite of those almost omniscient Mahatmas who are supposed to be guiding its upward course.

And what of the Old Lady (as her friends called her) who started it all? There seems no doubt that, however the Mahatma letters may have been composed, she wrote her huge doctrinal books, *Isis Unveiled* and *The Secret Doctrine*, in a genuine state of inspiration, induced by an innate passion for magic, mystery, miracles and folk-lore, especially the Eastern brand. All this was living truth to her, and impressed itself on a phenomenal memory, which seems to have retained visual images of sentences, phrases and indeed whole paragraphs and pages which had once passed before her eyes. Hence the so-called plagiarisms, of which she may well have been partially unaware. She was not reading ancient documents and manuscripts from akasic records; she was not writing down what the Masters dictated; she was seeing in her mind's eye what she had read in the past:

I am writing *Isis*, not writing, rather copying out and drawing what she personally shows to me. Upon my word, sometimes it seems to me that the ancient Goddess of Beauty in person leads me through all the countries of past centuries which I have to describe....Slowly, century after century, image after image, float out of the distance and pass before me, as if in magic panorama....Races and nations, countries and cities, which have for long disappeared in the darkness of the prehistoric past, emerge and then vanish, giving place to others....Hoary antiquity makes place for historical periods; myths are explained to me with events and people who have really existed; and every event which is at all remarkable, every newly turned page of this many-coloured book of life, impresses itself on my brain with photographic exactitude.[1]

Both Nietzsche and Rilke speak of 'dictation' when attempting to describe their states of inspiration; in both cases the inspiration seems to have been oral. Madame Blavatsky's description, equally convincing, shows that hers was of the visual kind, and helps to account for her mania for producing visual phenomena, particularly apparitions of the Masters. It was creative genius forsaking the path of imagination for that of materialisation, the cardinal error which lurks behind all magic. And H.P.B. was a magician by temperament far more clearly than a religious nature, let alone an ethical character. As such she was inevitably drawn to ceremonial magic. She possessed a diploma of the highest degree of the Rite of Memphis sent by John Yarker from London when she was in America. This links her up with Cagliostro through Freemasonry. She founded Theosophy on Masonic principles, with three stages of initiation, signs, pass-words, and so on. Later she established an esoteric circle on the lines of the

[1] Neff, op. cit. p. 279; quoting from *The Path*, January 1895; letter from H.P.B. to her sister Vera.

ancient mystery schools, which she wished to revive. Her whole
undertaking was a very interesting effort, a modern attempt to
establish a new religion on ancient lines. Whatever her predecessors
may have been, this nineteenth-century founder was far more
magician than prophet or priest; and though she magnanimously
elevated Saint-Germain to the status of Mahatma, she towers above
him, not to mention that scrubby little medieval sorcerer, Johannes
Faust. .However much doubt one may feel about her, she remains
a tremendous, if baffling, personality; and Theosophy still survives
in the era of the atomic bomb. She was certainly great; equally
certainly she was not a saint. The ghastly letters she wrote to Sinnett
after the catastrophe are those of a woman three parts demented and
piteously ignoble, a dyed-in-the-wool double-dealer. Yet even in her
decline she aroused religious awe and reverence in many, whilst to
others she appeared a common cheat. Hodgson clearly despised her
by the time he had completed his investigation; yet even he
confessed that 'she was terrible exceedingly when she expressed her
overpowering thought that perhaps her "twenty years" work might
be spoiled through Madame Coulomb'.[1] He called her with savage
irony 'a rare psychological study'; she expressed the same opinion
in a different tone of voice:

I—a psychological problem, and an enigma for future generations, a
Sphinx![2]

[1] *Proceedings of the S.P.R.* III, p. 313.
[2] Neff, op. cit. p. 243; H.P.B. to her aunt, Madame Fadeev, 1875 or 1876.

CHAPTER V

THE 'HOLY DEVIL'

It is perhaps not altogether a fluke that the next magician to astonish the world was a fellow-countryman of Madame Blavatsky's; for the kind of mysticism that accompanies the more ambitious type of magic pullulates in that enigmatic country, so much more closely akin to the East than to the West. It has harboured in the past and doubtless will continue to harbour hundreds and thousands of mystics, mages, sages, magicians and holy men of every conceivable description; and though Rasputin (1871–1916) attained to supreme notoriety, his powers could be matched and probably outshone by many a village wizard. It was without question the mystical element in his strangely compounded nature which gave him such a stranglehold over the minds of men; and this innate quality was further developed by the sect of the Khlysty or Flagellants to which he belonged. Their cardinal doctrine, salvation through sin, was bound to appeal particularly violently to a race in whom the saint and sinner, latent in all of us, live in so strangely equal an alliance. Rasputin (= the Dissolute), who helped with countless others to spread this gospel abroad, would probably never have risen to such heights in any Western country. Nevertheless he was in the main tradition of the mystery religions of the past now resurging as secret societies, and practising more or less openly ancient orgiastic rites. The frenzy he induced in himself and his worshippers, the intoxicated state of ecstasy, the scourgings, the debauches, the mixture of cruelty, love and lust are a debased, demoniacal, indeed maniacal Slavonic edition of the Dionysiac rites of Greece. This side of the magico-religious revival was predestined to attain its completest expression in Russia. Rasputin himself, fiendish and saint-like, depraved and sublime, child-like one moment, bestial the next, and well named the Holy Devil, possessed in an unexpected degree that power of living on two different spiritual planes with which Dostoyevski's novels have made us familiar, and which Euripides depicted in the *Bacchae*.

Gifted with great mesmeric powers which manifested themselves in seemingly miraculous cures and in the absolute empire he established over Nicholas II and Alexandra, Rasputin played the part in Russia which Cagliostro had played in France: precipitating a revolution whilst provoking his own doom. The tale of his assassination, however, the most appalling end of any magician in history, can only be equalled by the legend of the violent dismemberment of Faust. It probably has mythical elements in it; but that nightmare story of the magician and his killer in the basement of the house on the Moika, when cyanide failed of its effect, and bullets missed their mark, is a tribute to the belief in Rasputin's supernatural powers engendered in the author's mind:

The cyanide should have taken immediate effect; but to my utter amazement he continued to converse with me as if he were none the worse...I stood in front of him and followed each movement he made, expecting every moment to be his last...There was a nerve-racking pause. 'That's very good Madeira. Give me some more,' said Rasputin, holding out his glass...He drained it; and still the poison had no effect... We sat opposite each other in silence. He looked at me with a cunning smile. I seemed to hear him say: 'You see! It doesn't matter how you try; you can't do me any harm.' But all of a sudden his expression changed to one of fiendish hatred. Never before had he inspired me with such horror. I felt an indescribable loathing for him and was ready to throw myself upon him and throttle him. I felt that he knew why I had brought him there, and what I intended to do to him. A mute and deadly conflict seemed to be taking place between us. I was aghast. Another moment and I should have gone under. I felt that confronted by those satanic eyes, I was beginning to lose my self-control. A strange feeling of numbness took possession of me. My head reeled....I saw nothing....I do not know how long this lasted....Rasputin was still sitting in the same position. His head was bent, and he was supporting it with his hands. I could not see his eyes...Time passed....The hands of the clock pointed to half-past two. This nightmare had lasted over two hours. 'What will happen if my nerves don't hold out?' I wondered....How could his sharp eyes fail to observe that, clenched in my hand behind my back, was a revolver which in an instant would be aimed at him...'Grigori Efimovich, you had better look at the crucifix and say a prayer before it.' Rasputin looked at me in amazement and with a trace of fear. I saw a new and unfamiliar expression in his eyes, a touch of gentleness and submission. He came right up to me, looking me full in the face, and he seemed to read in my glance something which he was not expecting. I realised that the supreme moment was at hand. 'God give me strength to end it all' I thought, and I slowly brought the revolver from behind my back. Rasputin was still standing motionless before me, his head turned to the right, and his eyes on the

PLATE X

Caricature of Rasputin—'Russia's Ruling House'.
By N. Ivanov

crucifix... A streak of lightning seemed to run through my body. I fired. There was a roar as from a wild beast, and Rasputin fell heavily backwards on the bear-skin rug... The bullet had passed through the region of the heart. There could be no doubt about it; he was dead...

In the midst of our conversation I was suddenly seized by a vague feeling of alarm; I was overwhelmed by the desire to go down to the dining-room. I went downstairs and unlocked the door. Rasputin lay motionless... I stood over him for a little time longer, and was on the point of going away when my attention was arrested by a slight trembling of his left eye-lid.... I bent down over him, and attentively examined his face.... It began to twitch convulsively. The movements became more and more pronounced. Suddenly the left eye half-opened.... An instant later the right lid trembled and lifted.... And both eyes.... eyes of Rasputin—fixed themselves upon me with an expression of devilish hatred... I stood riveted to the floor as if in a nightmare. Then the incredible happened.... With a violent movement Rasputin jumped to his feet. I was horror-stricken. The room resounded with a wild roar. His fingers, convulsively knotted, flashed through the air.... Like red-hot iron they grasped my shoulder and tried to grip me by the throat. His eyes were crossed, and obtruded terribly; he was foaming at the mouth... This dying, poisoned, and shot-ridden creature, raised by the powers of darkness to avenge his destruction, inspired me with a feeling so terrifying, so ghastly, that the memory of it haunts me to this day. At that moment I understood and felt in the fullest degree the real power of Rasputin.[1]

After this, what Marie Rasputin called 'the sinister, atrocious manhunt' took place, and the magician collapsed finally after the fourth shot in the snow-covered courtyard whither he had managed to drag himself. But he was still alive when he was thrown into the Neva through a hole in the ice; for, when discovered by the police forty-eight hours later, it was obvious that the dying man had succeeded while in the water in untying the bonds which held his arms in a final effort to save himself.

[1] Cf. Prince Yusupov, *Rasputin...*, tr. Rayner, London 1927, pp. 158 ff. The omission-marks are mine, unless four are given, in which case they are the author's. There were four in the conspiracy to assassinate Rasputin; and the real facts will never be known.

CONCLUSION

It is not because the story of Rasputin's end commands implicit belief that it has been quoted fairly fully with the omission of some peculiarly gruesome details; but because it is symbolical of something indestructible in the nature of the idea animating the magus of legend. The history of the type illustrates this. The systematic poisoning undertaken by Christianity greatly enfeebled the constitution of the descendants of the magi. It was in fact a deadly poison, distilled from those flowers of evil always to be found in the garden of magic. For although it was believed throughout antiquity that to be supremely wise or great or good carried with it as a natural corollary the possession of superhuman powers, nevertheless from the very earliest times such gifts were also known to be ambiguous. The Hebrew notion of spiritual downfall and sin resulting from the commerce between mortals and angels, the Greek conception of Promethean *hybris*, the natural fear and awe attending necromantic feats illumined. magicians with a lurid light which was already threatening them with loss of caste in the days of the Roman Empire.[1] The ethics and the reality of magic have always been and will always be in question. But the Christian Church settled the matter out of hand by diabolising the whole phenomena. Forced into a position of extreme hostility towards the countless pagan creeds, which preached doctrines strongly resembling hers and claimed miracles indistinguishable from those in the Gospels as well as having similar mystery-rites, she took her stand on the striking saying: 'Habet Diabolus Christos suos.' This almost magical formula completed the transformation of the pagan deities into devils, and their priests into black magicians. This was the poison compounded of hatred and fear injected into the veins of medieval magic. It seemed to be writhing in its death-agonies in the story of Doctor Faust; and not all that Friar Bacon could do in the way of an antidote was likely to avert its doom.

[1] Lucian's mockery of Peregrinus Proteus and his exposure of Alexander the Paphlagonian in the second century A.D. are symptoms of this loss of prestige.

To make assurance doubly sure the 'dying and poisoned creature', the now discredited wizard, was further exposed to a rain of bullets in the shape of hard facts such as those which riddled the life-stories of Kelley and Dee; and, penetrating to the heart of what had once been a mystery, seemed to explode it utterly. But, in the very act of giving up the ghost, the myth of the magus was rescued by those good Samaritans, the secret societies. It found a refuge with them and went forth into the world miraculously restored. Christianity had done its subtle worst; rationalism had shot its brutal bolt; death in the icy river of ridicule now threatened to engulf the barely resuscitated magus. The laughter Cagliostro evoked during the diamond-necklace trial rang through Europe. The whole world rocked with laughter over the antics and split infinitives of Madame Blavatsky's Mahatmas. But Rasputin's assassins omitted to weight their victim's body when they cast it into the Neva, and it reappeared to confound them. It is doubtful if the weight of scepticism will ever be great enough to sink the magus-myth beyond men's sight for ever. The determination to believe in it has resulted in a fabled resurrection on the snowy slopes of the Himalayas. For the promulgators of the myth have learnt worldly wisdom from past experience. The Great White Brotherhood (which according to invariable custom is believed by many to be pitch black) has now been removed beyond mortal ken, and has achieved the kind of immortality which physical immunity bestows. The words, the deeds and above all the commands of the Secret Chiefs can be communicated to believers by the initiates; but never again will one of them be tried and tortured by the Inquisition, or be exposed to scientific investigation, or penned into a basement with murderers. They have escaped from human jurisdiction into the realms of mystery. They need no ration-books or identity-cards; they can travel without passports; they are practically indistinguishable from gods:

Let it be known that there exists, unknown to the great crowd, a very ancient order of sages, whose object is the amelioration and spiritual elevation of mankind by means of conquering error, and aiding men and women in their efforts at attaining the power of recognising the truth. The Order has existed already in the most remote and prehistoric times; and it has manifested its activity, secretly and openly in the world under different names and in various forms; it has caused social and political revolutions, and proved to be the rock of salvation in times of danger and misfortune....

Those persons who are already sufficiently spiritually developed to enter into conscious communication with the great spiritual Brotherhood (Great White Lodge) will be taught directly by the spirit of wisdom; but those who still need external advice and support will find this in the external organisation of this society.... Our place of meeting is the' Temple of the Holy Spirit' pervading the Universe (ether or astral)....[1]

The rise of the medicine-man to the status of a Persian magus; the devolution of the magus into the magician and sorcerer; the upward evolution through magician and magus to super-magus in our day, all this forms a cyclic movement continually revolving both in the history of individuals and of the type as a whole. For, by translating the magus into Himalayan heavens, we have not said farewell to the living magician, whether he be black or white. The myth of the magus has been salvaged and is now an article of widespread belief to which hundreds of sects all over the globe zealously subscribe. But the important function he was created to fulfil on earth still remains productive. It was as an intermediary between humanity and the external forces of nature, the spirits of the dead and divine or demonic agents, that the medicine-man rose to priesthood. Mankind will never be satisfied for long with beings above the skies. Flesh and blood mediators, half-gods, magi, magicians or priests arise to establish relations with them. Transform such functionaries into mysterious Secret Chiefs, and it will follow as the night follows the day that men claiming to be in contact with them will immediately spring up. This happened and is still happening in Theosophy and in many kindred creeds, brotherhoods and societies. Since the eighteenth century the earth-bound magicians have been greatly addicted to prophecy on the lines of the religious founders of the past. Zoroaster was the mouthpiece of Ormuzd; Moses was the vehicle of Jahweh; Simon Magus was the Standing One Himself. Cagliostro was the emissary of Elijah; Blavatsky was the servant of the Mahatmas; Aleister Crowley claims to be the amanuensis of Aiwaz. It may be objected that they do not speak so well nor so greatly as the magi of old, and the objection is just. But they prove at least that the magician, after a long degradation, is aspiring to the

---

[1] 'Inquire Within', *Light-bearers of Darkness*, London 1930, pp. 165 f. Quoting from the *Instructions* issued by the Fratres of the Ordo Templi Orientis, Rosicrucian Order of Freemasonry.

priesthood again; and that Mahatmas, Masters, Great White Brothers and Secret Chiefs are the heirs to a tradition perdurable indeed.

In this living tradition of magic as a perennial element in life, the real Faust plays the feeblest possible part. The 'miracles' of Joan of Arc, the 'crimes' of Gilles de Rais, even the remarkable illusions created by Zyto have a place in the history of magic to which he cannot aspire; whilst it was the occult philosophers of the sixteenth century (such as Cornelius Agrippa), and not Faust, who handed down to posterity a wealth of traditional mystical and magical lore. Kelley and Dee spent a lifetime working this material; Cagliostro, Blavatsky and Rasputin exploited it in the service of religions and used it for revelationary purposes. Yet, with the possible exception of Gilles resurrected as Perrault's Bluebeard, none of these historically important magicians has contributed so signally to legend as Solomon, Cyprian, Theophilus, Virgil, Merlin, Bacon and Faust. In this category, and at this level, the latter is overshadowed by Solomon and Merlin, but can hold his own, and sometimes more than that, with the others. The hero of the Faustbooks is a significant figure in the history of the idea. Amongst countless other braggings the real Faust had boasted by implication of an alliance with his 'brother-in-law' the devil. This set the smouldering religious imagination of the sixteenth century aflame. His obscure career and ambiguous personality aiding, he became the representative magician of the age; a black magician who achieved immortality as such in Marlowe's tragedy. Later he became the prototype of erring and questing mankind in Goethe's dramatic poem, where he gradually assumed the proportions of a symbol for humanity as a whole. This career is a miracle in itself.

It has a parallel in the legend of Saint-Germain. The real hero of this story boasted among other claims, at least by implication, of a supernatural longevity. This was in tune with the occult speculations and mysterious rumours fostered by the secret societies of his age. Though far from obscure, Saint-Germain was inscrutable and enigmatic enough to fire contemporary imagination. He became the representative magician of his day: a white magician who, after passing through literature as Zanoni, achieved immortality in the minds of the Theosophists as a glorified sage, still living and working for humanity as late as 1925; by which time, and indeed long before that, he had been multiplied into a mighty company of Masters. In the history of the myth of the magus he is therefore of greater importance than Faust, who marked the end of one period, the 'black' period, whereas Saint-Germain initiated a new 'white' period which is still pursuing its mythopoeic course. Faust had eternal damnation thrust upon him and Saint-Germain eternal transfiguration as a result in both cases of a joke made with intent to mystify. In both cases too it was the man about whom least was known who was chosen to incarnate the religious ideas associated with magic, the black art of the sixteenth century, the white art of the eighteenth. Yet to these ideas they themselves, as far as one can tell, were totally, indeed cynically, indifferent.

The Faust of poetry has a hold over men's minds which only the great myths of the world possess, and yet no one believes in his reality. Saint-Germain, worth hardly more than a footnote in history, is adored in theosophical circles as an immortal being with angels at his command and unquestioning belief at his disposal. The question as to which of the two exercises the greater influence to-day might be a ticklish one to answer. But the vitality of the magus-myth is illustrated by both: a sordid sixteenth-century trickster and an ambiguous adventurer of the eighteenth century have been transformed into mythical heroes because they were associated with magic, one of the most powerful elements in human thought which the history of ideas has to show.

SELECT BIBLIOGRAPHY

I deliberately omit from this list all those works on anthropology, witchcraft and demonology which have contributed nothing material to this study. Their name is legion.

A. WORKS OF REFERENCE

A Dictionary of Secret and other Societies, ed. Preuss, London 1924.
An Encyclopaedia of Religion and Ethics, ed. Hastings, Edinburgh 1908–21.
An Encyclopaedia of Occultism, ed. Spence, London 1924.

B. SOURCE-BOOKS

Palmer, P. M. & More, R. P. *The Sources of the Faust Tradition from Simon Magus to Lessing*. New York 1936. (Gives and translates the sources of the legends about Simon Magus, Cyprian, Theophilus and Faust. Incomplete, but extremely well done within the limits set.)

Scheible, J. *Das Kloster*. Stuttgart 1845–49, 12 volumes. (Vols. 2, 3, 5 and 11 of this invaluable collection deal with Faust and Faustiana: the Faustbooks, the puppet-plays, the black books, extracts from contemporary demonologists and critical works. Wagner, Don Juan, the Marshal of Luxemburg, Urban Grandier, Gerbert, Tritheim, Bacon, Zyto, Virgil and even Zoroaster are dealt with, although more summarily, in the same way. This collection of curious documents is ill-arranged, but contains a fund of information to which the present study is greatly indebted; indeed the section on Faust is largely based on the material in *Das Kloster*.)

Volz, G. B. *Der Graf von Saint-Germain, Das Leben eines Alchimisten*, tr. Oppeln-Bronikowski. Dresden 1923. (A complete collection of all the available documentary evidence about Saint-Germain from letters, memoirs and state archives. This work has thrown a great deal of light on the man of mystery.)

Guenther, J. v. *Der Erzzauberer Cagliostro*. Munich 1919. (A rather biased selection of documents and contemporary opinions, including Carlyle's essay on the diamond necklace trial, and Goethe's investigations in *Die italienische Reise*. It is, however, a useful book, as it gives not only Elisabeth von der Recke's observations of Cagliostro, but also a German translation of the biography prepared by one of the judges of the Inquisition. This is now exceedingly rare.)

SELECT BIBLIOGRAPHY

C. GENERAL

1. *Texts*

The Bible.
The Apocrypha.
The Apocryphal New Testament, tr. and ed. James. Oxford 1926.
The Book of Enoch, tr. and ed. Charles. Oxford 1912.
The Talmud, tr. Polano. London n.d. (Extracts.)
Josephus, F. *The Antiquities of the Jews,* tr. Whiston, ed. Margoliouth. London 1906.
[Philo.] *Biblical Antiquities,* tr. James. London 1917.
The Koran, tr. Palmer. Oxford n.d. (World's Classics.)
The Sacred Books of the East, ed. Max Müller. Oxford.
The Arabian Nights Entertainments. 2 vols. London 1807.

2. *Works*

Adams, W. H. D. *Witch, Warlock and Magician.* London 1889.
Anon. *Secret Societies in the Middle Ages.* London 1848.
Barrett, F. *The Magus or Celestial Intelligencer.* London 1801.
Cauzons, Th. de. *La Magie et la Sorcellerie en France.* 3 vols. Paris n.d.
Chadwick, H. M. and N. K. *The Growth of Literature.* Vol. 1. Cambridge 1923.
Chadwick, N. K. 'Shamanism among the Tatars of Central Asia, The Spiritual Ideas and Experiences of the Tatars of Central Asia.' *Journal of the Royal Anthropological Institute.* London 1936.
Cornford, F. M. *The Origin of Attic Comedy.* Cambridge 1934.
Figuier, L. *Histoire du Merveilleux dans les Temps Modernes.* 4 vols. Paris 1860–61.
Floegel, K. F. *Geschichte der Hofnarren.* Liegnitz and Leipzig 1789.
Frazer, J. G. *Folk-Lore in the Old Testament.* London 1923.
— *The Golden Bough.* London 1934. (Abridged edition.)
Garçon, M. and Vinchon, J. *The Devil,* tr. Haden Guest. London 1929.
Gibbon, E. *The Decline and Fall of the Roman Empire,* ed. Bury. London 1897.
Givry, Grillot de. *Witchcraft, Magic and Alchemy,* tr. Courtenay Locke. London 1931.
Glanville, J. *Sadducismus Triumphatus.* London 1681.
Gleadow, R. *Magic and Divination.* London 1941.
Godwin, W. *Lives of the Necromancers.* London 1876.
Graf, A. *The Story of the Devil,* tr. Stone. London 1931.
Guthrie, W. K. C. *Orpheus and Greek Religion.* London 1935.
Harrison, J. E. *Prolegomena to the Study of Greek Religion.* Cambridge 1908.
— *Themis.* Cambridge 1927.
— *Ancient Art and Ritual.* London 1918. (Home University Library.)
Hocart, A. M. *Kingship.* London 1941. (Thinker's Library.)
— *The Progress of Man.* London 1933.
'Inquire Within.' *Light-bearers of Darkness.* London 1930.
— *The Trail of the Serpent.* London 1936.
James, W. *The Varieties of Religious Experience.* London 1902.

Jennings, H. *The Rosicrucians, their Rites and Mysteries.* 7th ed. London n.d.

Knoop, D. and Jones, J. P. *An Introduction to Freemasonry.* Manchester 1937.

— *A Short History of Freemasonry to 1730.* Manchester 1940.

Lang, A. *Historical Mysteries.* London 1904.

— *Myth, Ritual and Religion.* London 1887.

Langton, E. *Satan, a Portrait.* London 1945.

Lecky, W. E. H. *History of the Rise and Influence of the Spirit of Rationalism in Europe.* London 1865.

Lehmann, A. *Aberglaube und Zauberei,* tr. Petersen. Stuttgart 1898.

Lévi, E. *History of Magic,* tr. Waite. London n.d.

— *Transcendental Magic,* tr. Waite. London n.d.

Liebstoeckel, K. *The Secret Sciences in the Light of our Time,* tr. Kennedy. London 1939.

Long, M. F. *Recovering the Ancient Magic.* London 1936.

Lowie, R. H. *Primitive Religion.* London 1936.

Magre, M. *The Return of the Magi,* tr. Merton. London 1931.

Marrett, R. R. *Anthropology.* London 1921. (Home University Library.)

Mead, G. R. S. *Fragments of a Faith Forgotten.* London 1900.

Michelet, J. *La Sorcière.* Brussels 1863.

Murray, M. *The Witch-Cult in Western Europe.* Oxford 1921.

— *The God of the Witches.* London n.d.

Myres, J. L. *The Dawn of History.* London 1937. (Home University Library.)

Naudé, G. *Apologie pour tous les grands hommes qui ont esté faussement soupçonnez de magie.* Paris 1625.

Papus. *Traité élémentaire de magie pratique.* Paris 1893.

Peuckert, W. E. *Pansophie.* Stuttgart 1936.

Raglan, Lord. *The Hero.* London 1936.

— *Jocasta's Crime.* London 1940. (Thinker's Library.)

Reade, Winwood. *The Martyrdom of Man.* London n.d. (Thinker's Library.)

Robertson, J. M. *Christianity and Mythology.* London 1900.

— *Pagan Christs.* London 1911.

Robertson-Smith. *The Religion of the Semites.* London 1894.

Rohmer, Sax. *The Romance of Sorcery.* London 1914.

Seabrook, W. *Witchcraft. Its Power in the World Today.* London 1941.

Scott, C. *An Outline of Modern Occultism.* London 1935.

Scott, W. *Demonology and Witchcraft.* London 1831.

Spence, L. *The Outlines of Mythology.* London 1944.

Summers, M. *The History of Witchcraft and Demonology.* London 1926. (Contains a most admirable bibliography.)

— *The Geography of Witchcraft.* London 1927.

— *Witchcraft and Black Magic.* London 1946.

Thompson, R. C. *Semitic Magic.* London 1908.

Thorndike, L. *A History of Magic and Experimental Science during the first thirteen centuries of our Era.* London 1923.

Tylor, E. B. *Primitive Culture.* London 1871.

Vivian, H. *Secret Societies Old and New.* London 1927.

Waite, A. E. *Lives of Alchemystical Philosophers.* London 1888.

Waite, A. E. *Devil Worship in France.* London 1896.
— *The Mysteries of Magic.* London 1897.
— *The Brotherhood of the Rosy Cross.* London 1924.
Weston, J. L. *From Ritual to Romance.* Cambridge 1920.
Williams, C. *Witchcraft.* London 1941.
Wittemans, F. R. *A New and Authentic History of the Rosicrucians,* tr. Durvad. London 1938.
Wraxall, L. *Remarkable Adventures and Unrevealed Mysteries.* 2 vols. London 1863.
Wright, T. *Narratives of Sorcery and Magic.* 2 vols. London 1851.

D. SEPARATE WORKS AND STUDIES

following the order of the chapters

Part I

Schuré, E. *Krishna and Orpheus,* tr. Rothwell. London 1919.
Herodotus. *Works,* tr. Macaulay. New York 1905.
Plutarch. *Über Isis und Osiris,* tr. Parthey. Berlin 1850.
Bidez, J. and Cumont, F. *Les mages hellénisés.* Paris 1938.
Crawford, F. Marion. *Zoroaster.* London 1901.
Dhalla, M. N. *History of Zoroastrianism.* New York 1938.
Firdausí. *Sháhnáma,* tr. Warner. London 1910.
Gorwalla, D. M. *The Light of Iran or the Coming of Zarathustra.* 1935.
Williams Jackson, A. V. *Zoroaster, the Prophet of Ancient Iran.* New York 1899.
Wilson, J. *The Pársí Religion.* Bombay 1843.
   The Assumption of Moses, tr. Charles. London 1897.
Fleg, E. *The Life of Moses,* tr. Haden Guest. London 1929.
Freud, S. *Der Mann Moses und die monotheistische Religion.* Amsterdam 1939.
   The Key of Solomon, ed. Mathers. London 1889.
   The Testament of Solomon, ed. McCown. Leipzig 1922.
Fleg, E. *The Life of Solomon,* tr. Garvin. London 1929.
Hammer-Purgstall, J. von. *Rosenöl.* Stuttgart and Tübingen 1813.
Salzberger, G. *Die Salomo-Sage in der semitischen Literatur.* Berlin 1907.
Seymour, St John D. *Tales of King Solomon.* London 1934.
Weil, G. *Biblical Legends of the Mussulmans.* London 1946.
Wünsche, A. *Der Talmud.* Zürich 1879.
Euripides. *The Bacchae,* tr. Murray, Way, Lucas, ed. Dodds. Oxford 1944.
Norwood, G. *The Riddle of the Bacchae.* Manchester 1908.
Verrall, A. E. *The Bacchants of Euripides.* Cambridge 1910.
Iamblichus. *Life of Pythagoras,* tr. Taylor (1818). London 1926.
Lévy, I. *Recherches sur les sources de la légende de Pythagore.* Paris 1926.
— *La légende de Pythagore de Grèce en Palestine.* Paris 1927.
Philostratus. *Life of Apollonius of Tyana,* tr. Conybeare. London 1917. (Loeb Classics.)
Renan, E. *La vie de Jésus.* Paris 1891.
Strauss, D. F. *Das Leben Jesu.* Stuttgart 1836.
Irving, W. *The Life of Mahomet.* London 1944. (Everyman's Library.)

Part II

Bowen, C. *Virgil in English Verse.* London 1887.

Comparetti, D. *Vergil in the Middle Ages,* tr. Benecke. London 1908.

— *Virgilius,* ed. Thoms, in *Early English Prose Romances.* London 1858. Vol. II.

Geoffrey of Monmouth. *British History,* ed. Giles, in *Six Old English Chronicles.* London 1848. (Bohn's Antiquarian Library.)

— *Vita Merlini,* ed. Parry, *University of Illinois Studies in Language and Literature.* Illinois 1925.

Heywood, T. *The Life of Merlin....* London 1813.

Malory, T. *Le Morte Darthur.* London 1906. (Everyman's Library.)

Nennius. *History of the Britons,* ed. Giles, in *Six Old English Chronicles.* London 1848. (Bohn's Antiquarian Library.)

Merlin, or the Early History of King Arthur, ed. Whetley and Meade, E.E.T.S. 2 vols. London 1899.

Reid, M. J. C. *The Arthurian Legend.* Edinburgh 1938.

Rowley, W. *The Birth of Merlin....* London 1662.

San Marte. *Die Sagen von Merlin....* Halle 1843.

Skene, W. F. *Four Ancient Books of Wales.* Edinburgh 1868.

Spenser, E. *The Faerie Queene.* London 1872.

Villemarqué, H. de la. *Myrddhin ou l'enchanteur Merlin.* Paris 1862.

Dubravius. *Historia Bohemia.* Basel 1575. In Scheible, *Das Kloster,* Vol. II.

Malého. *Chronicle,* 1845. In Scheible, *Das Kloster,* Vol. II.

Michelet, J. *Jeanne D'Arc,* ed. Rudler. Paris 1925.

Shaw, G. B. *Saint Joan.* London 1924.

Huysmans, J.-K. *Œuvres Complètes.* Paris 1928–34. Vol. XII.

Wilson, T. *Blue-Beard, Gilles de Retz, 1404–1440.* New York and London 1899. (Gives the documents of the trial.)

Laver, J. *Nostradamus....* London 1942.

Gundolf, F. *Paracelsus.* London 1927.

Faust (See Source-books.)

Kiesewetter, C. *Faust in der Geschichte und Tradition.* Leipzig 1893.

Frier Bacon. *His discovery of the Miracles of Art, Nature and Magick.* Faithfully translated out of Dr *Dee's* own Copy, by T. M. and never before in English. London 1629. (There was an earlier translation in 1597, but I have not seen it.)

Roger Bacon. *The Cure of Old Age and Preservation of Youth.* London 1683.

Friar Bacon's *Prophesie: A Satire on the Degeneracy of the Times.* A.D. *1604.* *The Famous Historie of Fryer Bacon,* ed. Thoms, *Early English Prose Romances.* London 1858. Vol. I.

Little, A. G. 'Roger Bacon.' *Proceedings of the British Academy.* London 1928.

Sandys, J. E. 'Roger Bacon.' *Proceedings of the British Academy.* London 1914.

Ward, A. W. Ed. *Old English Drama.* 3rd ed. Oxford 1892.

Winthrop, W. *Roger Bacon.* London n.d. (recent).

Wood, A. *Antiquities.*

Dee, J. *The Private Diary of Dr John Dee*, ed. Halliwell for the Camden Society. London 1842.
— *A True and Faithful Relation of what passed for Many Years between Dr John Dee and Some Spirits...*, ed. Casaubon. London 1659.
Fell-Smith, C. *John Dee.* London 1909.
Hort, G. M. *Dr John Dee*, in *Three Famous Occultists*. London [1939].

Part III

Saint-Germain. (*See* Source-books.)
Cooper-Oakley, I. *The Comte de St Germain. The Secret of Kings*. 2nd ed. London 1927.
Genlis, Mme de. *Mémoires inédits....* Paris 1825. Vol. I.
Maynial, E. *Casanova et son temps.* Paris 1910.
Cagliostro. (*See* Source-books.)
Cagliostro, A. di. *Lettre au peuple françois.* London 1786.
— *Lettre au peuple anglois.* London 1786.
Mémoire pour le Comte de Cagliostro.... Paris 1786. (Diamond necklace trial.)
Mémoire pour le Comte de Cagliostro.... Paris 1786. (Suit against Chesnon, etc.)
The Life of Count Cagliostro. London 1787.
Vie de Joseph Balsamo. Paris 1791. (Translation of the Italian Apostolic biography. Given in German by Guenther.)
Carlyle, T. *Miscellaneous Essays.* London 1887. Vol. II.
Casanova, G. *Mémoires.* Brussels 1871.
Funck-Brentano, F. *L'affaire du collier.* Paris 1901.
Gleichen, C.-H. de. *Souvenirs.* Paris 1868.
Harrison, M. *Count Cagliostro....* London 1942.
Haven, Marc. *Le maître inconnu: Cagliostro.* Paris 1912.
King, F. *Cagliostro....* London 1929.
Laborde, L.-B. de. *Lettres sur la Suisse en 1781.* Geneva 1784.
[Luchet, Marquis de.] *Essai sur la secte des Illuminés.* Paris 1789.
— *Mémoire authentique pour servir à l'histoire du Comte de Cagliostro.* 2nd ed. Strassburg 1786.
Morande, Th. de. Articles in the *Courier de l'Europe.* London 1786–87. Nos. 15–22.
Oberkirch, H. L. d'. *Mémoires....* Paris 1853.
Petraccone, E. *Cagliostro nella storia e nella legende.* Milan 1936.
Trowbridge, W. R. H. *Cagliostro, The Splendour and Misery of a Master of Magic.* London 1910.
Blavatsky, H. P. *The Letters of H. P. Blavatsky to A. P. Sinnett*, ed. Barker. London 1925.
— *The Mahatma Letters to A. P. Sinnett*, ed. Barker. London 1923.
— *Some unpublished Letters of Helena Petrovna Blavatsky*, ed. Corson. London n.d.
H.P.B. In Memory of Helena Petrovna Blavatsky by some of her Pupils. London 1931.

SELECT BIBLIOGRAPHY

Society for Psychical Research. *First Report of the Committee for the S.P.R. appointed to investigate the evidence for marvellous phenomena offered by certain members of the Theosophical Society.* London 17 December 1884.
— *Proceedings of the S.P.R.* London 1885. Vol. III.
— *Journal of the S.P.R.* London 1884–85. Vol. I, 2nd ed.
Baseden Butt, G. *Madame Blavatsky.* London 1927.
Coulomb, E. *Some Account of my Intercourse with Madame Blavatsky from 1872 to 1884.* London 1885.
Ephesian [Bechofer Roberts, C. E.]. *The Mysterious Madame.* London 1931.
Hare, H. E. and W. L. *Who Wrote the Mahatma Letters?* London 1936.
Kingsland, W. *The Real H. P. Blavatsky.* London 1928.
— *Was she a Charlatan?* London n.d.
Neff, M. K. *Personal Memories of H. P. Blavatsky.* London 1937.
Olcott, H. *Old Diary Leaves.* London 1904.
Sinnett, A. P. *The Occult World.* London 1881.
— *Incidents in the Life of Madame Blavatsky.* London 1903.
Solovyov, V. A. *A Modern Priestess of Isis,* tr. Leaf. London 1895.
Ryan, C. J. *Madame Blavatsky and the Theosophical Movement.* Point Loma 1937.
Wood, E. E. *Is this Theosophy?* London 1936.
Fülop-Miller, R. *Rasputin, the Holy Devil,* tr. Flint and Tait. London 1928.
Yusupov, Prince. *Rasputin...,* tr. Rayner. London 1927.
Rasputin, M. *The Real Rasputin,* tr. Chambers. London 1929.

INDEX

[Figures in black type indicate principal references]